Getting Into Business

Getting Into Business

Wylie A. Walthall College of Alameda

Canfield Press 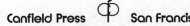 San Francisco
A Department of Harper & Row, Publishers, Inc.
New York Evanston London

Getting Into Business

Book and Cover Design by Joe di Chiarro

Library of Congress Cataloging in Publication Data

Walthall, Wylie A
    Getting into business.

    Includes index.
    1. Business.   2. Management.   I. Title.
HF5500.W24   658.1′1   74-22434
ISBN 0-06-389125-5

77   10   9   8   7   6   5   4

To the "Big Three"

Nancy
Lauren
Jason

Contents

Figures and Tables   xi

Memorandum to the Instructor   xiii

Memorandum to the Student   xv

Acknowledgments   xvii

PART I   THE AMERICAN BUSINESS SYSTEM   1

1 BUSINESS AND SOCIETY: A QUICK OVERVIEW   3

Productivity Is the Name of the Game   4
Instant Economics   7
Capitalism and Other Isms   8
Issue The Case for Competition   11
Business and the Economy   12
Summary   16
Issue Are Businessmen Bad Guys?   17
Appendix Grit and Bear It: Basic Business Arithmetic   27

2 BUSINESS AND GOVERNMENT   31

Government Assistance to Business   32
Government Regulation of Business   33
Issue Whatever Happened to Free Enterprise?   34
Taxation   37
Issue The Problem of Business Giantism   38
Summary   43
Issue Taxes: Who Pays How Much?   44

PART II   ORGANIZATION OF THE FIRM   57

3 FORMS OF BUSINESS OWNERSHIP   59

The Proprietorship   60
The Partnership   62

The Corporation 66
Issue The Social Responsibility of Business 67
Summary 71
Issue A Glimpse Into the Future: Is the Corporation Doomed? 72

4 MANAGEMENT AND ORGANIZATION 83

What Is Management? 84
Issue Perspectives on Management 91
Principles of Management 92
Types of Internal Organization 95
Issue The End of the Organization Man? 99
Committees 100
Summary 100

PART III THE TOOLS OF MANAGEMENT 115

5 ACCOUNTING AND BUDGETING 117

Accounting: Who Needs It? 118
Accounting Statements 118
Financial Analysis 122
Issue The Billion-Dollar Rip-Off: Employee Theft 123
Budgeting 126
Issue Business Forecasting: What Does the Future Hold? 127
Summary 131
Issue Risk, Insurance, and the Businessman 132

6 STATISTICS AND DATA PROCESSING 143

Sources of Statistical Information 144
Statistical Analysis 145
Presentation of Statistical Data 147
Interpretation of Statistics 148
Data Processing 148
Issue Is "Big Brother" Watching You? 152
Computers in Business 153
Summary 155
Issue The Thinking Machines Are Coming! 156
Appendix Recognizing a Computer Application 157

PART IV BUSINESS OPERATIONS 167

7 FINANCE 169

Financial Management 170
Issue How's Your Dun & Bradstreet Rating? 174
Marketing Corporate Securities 178
The Securities Markets 182
Summary 187
Appendix Bonds: Premiums, Discounts, and Yields 189

8 PERSONNEL 203

Human Relations   204
Issue Job Enrichment: The End of Worker Boredom?   206
Personnel Management   210
Issue The Other Side of the Coin: Are Managers Treating
       Employees Like Spoiled Brats?   211
Labor Relations   215
Issue What's Your Job Psychology?   216
Summary   222
Issue Union Shootout: UFW vs. The Teamsters   224

9 MARKETING 237

The Key Role of Marketing   238
Marketing Management   238
Consumers: The Target Market   240
Product   242
Place   243
Issue Franchising: The Magic Formula for Success?   247
Promotion   248
Price   252
Issue Advertising: Consumer Friend or Foe?   253
The Marketing Mix   254
Summary   255

10 PRODUCTION 269

Production: A Bird's-Eye View   270
Issue Automation: Is Your Job Next?   271
Production Processes   272
Manufacturing Systems   273
Production Management   274
Purchasing and Inventory Control   279
Summary   281

Index   295

Figures
and
Tables

FIGURES

1-1 United States GNP, 1930-1974   5
1-2 United States per Capita GNP, 1920-1970   6
1-3 The Range of Economic Systems   12
1-4 How the Economy Operates   13
1-5 The Business Cycle   13
2-1 Federal, State, and Local Spending, 1930-1974   32
2-2 Sources and Uses of Tax Dollars   41
3-1 An Advertisement for a Limited Partnership   64
3-2 Corporate Structure   68
4-1 Why Business Firms Fail   85
4-2 Top, Middle, and Operating Management   85
4-3 The Functions of Management   89
4-4 The Management-by-Objectives Process   90
4-5 Spans of Control in Two Firms   94
4-6 Line Organization   95
4-7 Functional Organization   96
4-8 Line and Staff Organization   97
4-9 Who the Staff Man Is and What He Does   98
5-1 Hailwood Department Store, Inc., *Balance Sheet,*
    December 31, 1974   120
5-2 Hailwood Department Store, Inc., *Income Statement,*
    For the Year Ended December 31, 1974   122
5-3 Income Statements for Zoe's Candy Company,
    for the Years 1972-1974   126
5-4 Cash Budget for Tom Henderson, July 1-June 30   128
5-5 Projected Income Statement for Zoe's Candy Company,
    January-December, 1975   129
5-6 Break-Even Chart for the Carter Widget Company   130
6-1 Line Chart: Consumer Price Index, 1967-1974 (1967 = 100)   148
6-2 Pie Diagram   149
6-3 Bar Chart   149
6-4 The Components of a Computer   151
6-5 The Information Feedback Principle   154
7-1 An Invoice   171

7-2 A Promissory Note   172
7-3 A Corporate Bond   177
7-4 Tax Treatment of Interest and Dividends   180
7-5 How to Read Newspaper Stock Quotations   186
8-1 Maslow's Hierarchy of Needs   205
8-2 Management Recruiting   211
8-3 An Employment Application Form   213
8-4 Union Membership, 1930–1972   218
9-1 Marketing Strategy: The Consumer Target and the Four P's   240
9-2 Channels of Distribution   243
9-3 How Wholesalers Help   248
9-4 Spending on Advertising by Medium, 1960 and 1972   251
10-1 Process Layout   276
10-2 Line Layout   276
10-3 A Requisition Form   280
10-4 Inventory Chart for Part 10A   281

TABLES

1-1 Economic Indicators   15
2-1 Progressive, Proportional, and Regressive Taxes (Hypothetical Data)   39
2-2 The Regressive Effect of a General Sales Tax   40
3-1 Forms of Business Ownership in the United States   60
5-1 Selected Business Ratios, Median Figures for 1971   125
6-1 Hours of Overtime in Department 10 for May   145
6-2 Sales of District C and Conn Paper Products, 1970–1974   147
6-3 Sales Indexes for District C and Conn Paper Products, 1970–1974 (1970 = 100)   147
7-1 Summary of Corporate Securities   179
8-1 McGregor's Theory X and Theory Y   209

Memorandum to the Instructor

To: The Instructor
From: The Author
Subject: The Why, What, and How of *Getting Into Business*

This textbook was written because I couldn't find one like it on the market. After nearly a decade of teaching the introductory course in business, I became convinced that a fresh approach was needed. Many of the traditional textbooks tend to be encyclopedic; in my opinion, they are too long and too detailed for an introductory course. As a result, students often become engulfed in a mountain of minutiae and lose sight of key concepts. In short, too many students become turned off.

Getting Into Business attempts to introduce the American business system to college students taking their first course in business. The title is not intended to imply that the book is a manual for starting a small business. Rather, it suggests the major goal of the book: getting the student interested and involved in the exciting world of business. I have tried to make the book concise, uncluttered, lively, and easy to read by emphasizing major principles and concepts rather than detailed explanations. The extensive end-of-chapter exercises provide a means of stimulating student interest and involvement. In short, the book is intended to be *used* rather than merely carried around like a piece of superfluous baggage.

Organization is straightforward, employing the traditional or functional approach. Each chapter includes short issues which focus on contemporary business problems and practices. The issues serve to introduce the student to the role and challenges of modern business in our increasingly complex society.

The questions at the end of each chapter assist the student in reviewing major concepts and building his business vocabulary. The problems and short cases serve to sharpen analytical skills and encourage the application of principles and techniques described in the chapter. The Student Feedback System has proved to be a highly effective instructional tool. It encourages the student to relate topics covered in the text to his own experiences in the business world and it identifies areas which need clarification and/or elaboration. The Student Feedback System helps the instructor to make the most effective use of class time by focusing on problem areas and building on student interests and experiences.

After two years of testing *Getting Into Business* in my classes and in courses offered at other colleges, I am convinced it is a valuable instructional tool. Student response has been overwhelmingly positive. Most important of all, students actually *use* the textbook!

Memorandum to the Student

To: The Student
From: The Author
Subject: Why This Book Is Worth What You Paid for It
and What You Should Do With It

This book is about American business. As the title says, it's intended to help you understand how the business system works, to introduce you to the major areas of business, and to assist you in selecting a career in business. The perspective of the book is that of the manager, who plays the key role in every business firm from General Motors to the corner ice cream store. *Getting Into Business* aims at giving you a taste of the management decision-making process; that is, how managers make decisions.

That, in a nutshell, is what the book is all about. You should also know what it is *not* about: this is not a "how to" manual for starting a business of your own, nor does it provide a sure-fire formula for getting rich in business. (On the other hand, a knowledge of the business world won't stop you from earning a fortune.)

Each chapter is organized the same way. The first paragraph or so tells you what the chapter is all about. Then comes the main body of the chapter, followed by a summary of the key points. You may want to read the summary first to find out what's important. At the end of each chapter you'll find some questions, exercises, and a few case studies. Most of these will be assigned and they are important. Why? The entire book is based on the assumption that the best way to learn is to do. This idea is summed up by an old Chinese proverb:

> I hear, and I forget;
> I see, and I remember;
> I do, and I understand!

You can think of this textbook as a useful tool for opening up the exciting and fascinating world of business. A little hard work and practice with this tool should yield a substantial profit on your investment.

Good luck!

Acknowledgments

It is impossible to mention all the individuals who made a contribution to this book. I am indebted to my colleagues for reviewing the manuscript and offering numerous comments and suggestions. Special thanks go to Richard Bidleman, Robert Darland, Jerry Katapotis, John Olson, Alex Pappas, Ida Pound, and Ron West. I am also grateful for the valuable suggestions offered by my students, especially Brian Roth, James Simons, and Waltraud Spinnato.

John Elliott of San Joaquin Delta College, Joseph Werner of Green River Community College, and Robert Litro of Mattatuck Community College reviewed the manuscript, and I am grateful for their many helpful recommendations. Not all the suggested changes have been included in the textbook, and I bear full responsibility for all errors and omissions.

The help, cooperation, and support I have received from the staff at Canfield Press have been outstanding. Special credit goes to Gerald Papke and Pearl C. Vapnek.

Finally, I would like to thank Geraldine Bobb and Donna Cheng, who typed the manuscript under less than ideal circumstances.

W. A. W.

Part

1

The American Business System

Chapter 1

Business and Society: A Quick Overview

You are part of the system—the American business system.

Many students have jobs with business firms. Everyone is a consumer. We all buy a variety of goods and services each week. More than likely you will choose a career in business. Either as a consumer or as a businessman, you should know something about how our business system operates.

This chapter and the next are intended to give you a look at "The Big Picture"—some of the key principles that influence the operation of business in our society.

KEY QUESTIONS

1. Why is the United States the richest nation on earth?

2. What is productivity and why is it important?

3. How can productivity be increased?

4. What is economics all about, anyway?

5. What are the key features of capitalism, socialism, and communism?

6. How does the United States economy operate?

7. What role does government play in our economy?

PRODUCTIVITY IS THE NAME OF THE GAME

You've heard it said many times: The United States is the richest nation on earth. Does this mean that every American citizen is wealthy? Of course not. We all know that many Americans live in poverty. When we refer to the United States as rich, we actually mean two things. First, every year our country produces more goods and services than any other nation. Second, the average income per American is the highest in the world.

Gross National Product (GNP) is the dollar measure of goods and services produced by a country during a year. In other words, if we added up the final selling price of all the automobiles, T-shirts, movie tickets, Frisbees, machine tools, and the millions of other goods and services produced in the United States during the year, the sum would be Gross National Product. Figure 1–1 shows GNP for the years 1930–1974. Note that GNP topped one trillion three hundred billion dollars ($1,300,000,000,000) in 1974.

Gross National Product does not tell the whole story. A nation's output must be divided among its citizens. A better measure of a society's standard of living is *output per capita*—the average amount of goods and services produced per individual. Obviously, the larger a nation's population, the more pieces the economic pie (GNP) must be divided into. We can get an estimate of a country's standard of living by using a simple formula:

$$\text{Standard of Living} = \frac{\text{GNP}}{\text{Population}}$$

Therefore, for example, if a nation has a population of 200 million people and a GNP of $1 trillion, then the average output per capita would be $5,000 worth of goods and services:

$$\$1,000,000,000,000 \div 200,000,000 = \$5,000$$

Two factors complicate our calculations: (1) No nation divides its output equally. Some families in the United States have very high incomes while others are relatively poor. (2) Not all of gross national product is distributed to individuals. For example, some is used by business firms to invest in new plant and equipment. And, of course, government taxes take a share.

Figure 1–2 shows per capita GNP over the past half century. It is interesting to compare the United States figure for 1970 to those of some other countries:

Canada	$2,300
France	2,000
Soviet Union	1,500
Japan	1,300
Mexico	550
India	75

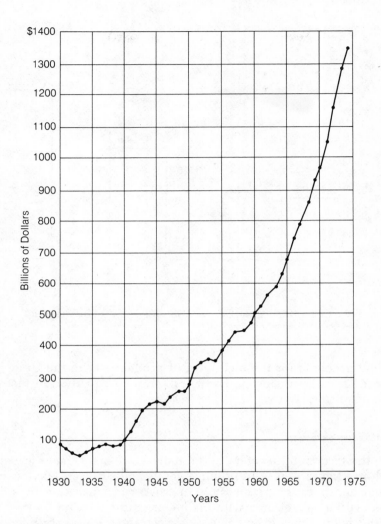

Figure 1–1 United States GNP, 1930–1974
Source: United States Department of Commerce, *Survey of Current Business*. (Note: Data for 1974 are estimates.)

Why does the United States have the highest GNP and the largest per capita output? The answer can be summed up in one word: *productivity*. Productivity is the measure of output per worker—that is, how much a worker produces during a particular period of time (for example, an hour, a week, or a year). In the United States, average worker productivity is the highest in the world, and productivity is the basic determinant of standard of living. Increased productivity means more goods and services are available for the citizens of a nation. It can also mean that workers may enjoy more leisure time without having to sacrifice their standard of living.

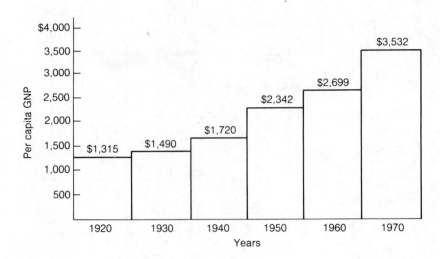

Figure 1–2 United States per Capita GNP, 1920–1970 (1958 Dollars)
Source: United States Department of Commerce.

What accounts for the high level of productivity in the United States? There is no single answer—rather, a combination of factors influence productivity.

Capital Investment

Here the term *capital* refers to the tools, equipment, factories, and machines that are used to produce goods and services. Obviously, capital improves the productivity of workers. A man can dig a ditch faster with a shovel than with his hands, and his output is increased many times if he has a motorized ditch digger. In the United States, the capital investment per worker exceeds $30,000, and in some industries such as oil refining and airlines, the total may top $100,000. Greater capital investment permits each worker to produce more, thereby increasing his value to his employer. Increased productivity means higher wages.

Technology

Technology refers to the application of scientific discoveries to develop new and improved products and more efficient methods of production. The growing use of computers by business firms is an example of technology, as is the use of radar ovens, which enable convenience-food sellers to prepare hamburgers in a few seconds. Obviously, technology influences productivity.

Education, Health, and Training of the Work Force

There are 90 million workers in the United States, roughly 40 percent of the population. On an average these workers enjoy better health and education than do workers in most other parts of the world. Many companies spend millions of dollars a year on training programs to help their employees increase knowledge and skills and thereby boost productivity. Why are you attending college?

good question!

Management

Another factor that influences productivity is management. A business firm may adopt the latest technology, own hundreds of millions of dollars in plant and equipment, employ highly skilled workers, and still fail if it has poor management. American businessmen have pioneered in the development of improved organizational and management techniques. Many countries send their managers to the United States to receive training in American management practices. A few years ago, the Soviet Union established a series of management schools patterned after the Harvard and Stanford Business Schools.

Summing Up

To sum up, productivity is the name of the game because it is the key determinant of a nation's standard of living, both present and future. Do you want to be rich? It's easy. Simply develop a high degree of productivity in the production of some good or service that people want. Then you'll have it made.

INSTANT ECONOMICS

Economics is the study of how a society or nation produces the goods and services it wants and how they are distributed. The basic problem in economics is that every society has unlimited wants for goods and services, but only limited resources to produce these goods and services. Economic resources are called the *factors of productions*. They are: land, labor, capital, and the entrepreneur.

  Land means all natural resources including iron ore, timber, petroleum deposits and crop land. *Labor* refers to manpower, the physical and mental output necessary to produce goods and services. *Capital* has already been defined as machinery, tools and equipment—any man-made resource used to produce goods and services. Finally, the *entrepreneur* organizes the other three factors of production in such a way as to produce those goods and services that people will buy. In a broad sense, the entrepreneur is a manager because he is responsible for combining land, labor, and capital in the most efficient way. He is also a risk-taker since he pits his money and talent against the possibility of making a loss rather than a profit.

Given the fact of unlimited human wants and limited resources, every nation must decide what combination of goods and services it will produce. It must ration or economize its scarce resources among alternative uses. In economics, scarcity is the name of the game and economizing is the way it's played. Our business system plays a critically important role in attempting to solve the basic economic problem of scarcity.

CAPITALISM AND OTHER ISMS

Every society must select an economic system—some arrangement of institutions (business firms, farms) and people (workers and managers)—to produce and distribute the products it wants.

Capitalism

Capitalism is an economic system where the means of production (economic resources) are owned and operated by private individuals (or business firms) to make a profit. Pure capitalism is often referred to as *laissez-faire* capitalism. This French term means "hands off," or more precisely, noninterference by the government in the affairs of business. In other words, the economic system should *not* be subjected to government planning, control, or regulation. Capitalism is based on four key principles: (1) right of private property, (2) economic freedom, (3) competition, and (4) the profit motive.

Right of Private Property   The United States Constitution guarantees the right of individuals to own, operate, and dispose of property. This guarantee is based partly on the belief that property owned by individuals receives better care. For example, people tend to take better care of a home they own than of one they rent. Moreover, the right to own property serves as an incentive for an individual to work hard in order to expand his wealth by acquiring more property. Critics of private property argue that it permits property owners (rich landlords and business firms) to exploit those who have no property and that it leads to a highly unequal distribution of income in our society. This criticism is one of the principles of socialism, a system where much property is owned publicly (by the government).

Even under pure capitalism, the right of private property is subject to some restrictions. Property owners must pay taxes, and they are subject to *eminent domain* (the right of the government to take private property for public use on paying just compensation). For example, if the state decides to build a freeway through your living room, you must sell your home to the government.

Economic Freedom   The principle of economic freedom is often referred to as *freedom of choice* or *freedom of enterprise*. It means that businessmen are free to engage in the business of their choice, workers may seek out jobs that suit them, and consumers can select those goods and services on which they wish to spend their incomes.

Economic freedom is rarely complete. Some business activities are illegal—for example, the sale of pot. Moreover, many types of businesses require very large sums of money to start, which effectively bars most people. It has been estimated that a minimum of $1 billion would be required to establish a major automobile manufacturing firm. In addition, certain union practices and government licensing laws restrict economic freedom. Some craft unions limit membership to drive up wages. A high school dropout cannot become a doctor. Despite such restrictions, economic freedom is far more extensive under capitalism than under alternative economic systems.

Competition   Under capitalism, business firms compete against each other for the consumer's dollars. Workers compete for desirable jobs and promotions. Competition is the foundation of capitalism and it provides numerous benefits for society. Businessmen recognize that they can attract customers and increase sales with low prices. There is also a built-in incentive for business firms to reduce waste and inefficiency—to cut unnecessary costs. Many firms compete by offering customers more and better services. For example, a retail store may offer air conditioning, attractive decor, numerous clerks, free delivery, gift wrapping, and liberal credit.

Competition also encourages firms to improve existing products and develop new ones in an attempt to capture a larger share of the market. Some firms are unable to compete effectively and they tend to fail. From society's standpoint this failure is desirable, because scarce resources are allocated to those firms that are most efficient in fulfilling consumer wants.

Economists distinguish between perfect and imperfect competition. Perfect (or pure) competition refers to an industry with a large number of firms (perhaps tens of thousands) each selling an identical product, with no single firm large enough to influence product price. Very few industries in the United States can be described as perfectly competitive. For example, there are only three companies which produce aluminum in this country, and only four major automobile manufacturers. Most industries are imperfectly competitive. This means that business firms have some control in setting prices for their products. But it would be a mistake to think that competition does not exist in these industries. For example, in what ways does General Motors compete with Ford?

The Profit Motive   Profit is the difference between the income from sales and the expenses of doing business:

$$\text{Profit} = \text{Sales} - \text{Expenses}$$

Profit serves as the prime mover in a capitalistic economy. Businessmen (or entrepreneurs) will strive to produce the goods and services that consumers want in order to increase sales and earn profits. Therefore, the consumer, by spending his dollars, largely determines what goods and services the business system will produce. The pursuit of profit also spurs businessmen to develop new products and technology and to invest in capital goods. Profit is a major source of funds for business expansion. The successful (profitable) firm will reinvest part of its earnings by acquiring more plant and equipment, and thus be able to increase productivity and boost wages. In short, profit may be viewed as a report card on the past, as incentive to meet consumer wants, and as a source of funds for capital investment and technological improvement.

Competition is not always present in an industry. Some firms earn profit not through efficiency or successfully developing improved products but by maintaining a monopoly position. Monopoly is the absence of competition. More on this in the next chapter.

Socialism

An alternative to capitalism is socialism. Unfortunately, the term *socialism* is confusing because it has been defined in so many different ways. To some, any degree of government involvement in the economic system is socialism, while others consider only the Soviet or Chinese economies as socialist. We shall use the term *democratic socialism* to refer to those economic systems where major industries—such as steel, coal, transportation, and utilities—are owned and operated by the government. However, private ownership of property still exists in democratic socialism and many business firms are privately owned and operated for profit. Examples of democratic socialist economic systems would include Sweden, Great Britain, and France.

The proponents of democratic socialism claim this system provides more stable employment because during periods of unemployment and recession government-owned industries can hire laid-off workers. In addition, heavy taxation of large incomes coupled with

---

ISSUE   THE CASE FOR COMPETITION

Private enterprise seeks profit. But, to obtain profit, it must serve consumers, for this is the only way to profit that competition will allow.

Human wants are many and growing; the productive resources through which they can be satisfied—land, labor, capital, materials, and power—are scarce. The central problem of economics is to determine how these resources shall be allocated; to decide what goods shall be produced. The goods produced by private enterprise, in a market economy, will be those that the consumer demands. Each time he spends a dollar he casts a vote for the production of the thing he buys. His dollar votes, recorded in his purchase, express the character of his demands. Where his demand for a commodity declines, its price will fall. Where demand increases, price will rise. When producers, in their turn, compete against each other to obtain resources, those with products where demand is weak will find themselves outbid by those with products where demand is strong. Resources will be diverted from the one field to the other, away from producing goods that are wanted less and toward producing goods that are wanted more. Competition is thus the regulator that compels producers to follow the guidance of consumer choice.

Competition operates to enhance quality and reduce price. The producer who wishes to enlarge his profits must increase his sales. To do so, he must offer the consumer more goods for less money. As he adds to quality and subtracts from price, his rivals are compelled to do the same. Competition also makes for efficiency. It leads some producers to eliminate wastes and cut costs so they may undersell others. It compels others to adopt similar measures in order that they may survive. Competition is congenial to material progress. It keeps the door open to new blood and new ideas. The resulting gains in efficiency open the way to still lower prices. Goods are turned out in increasing volume, and the general plane of living is raised.

The existence of competition is not always assured. Many firms may agree among themselves that they will not compete. Two or more firms may combine to make a single unit. One or a few firms may come to dominate an industry, through the employment of unfair methods or through the enjoyment of special advantages. If the consumer is to reap the benefits of competition, government must make sure that competition is maintained.

Reference
Adapted with permission from Clair Wilcox, *Public Policies Toward Business* (Rev. ed.; Homewood, Ill.: Richard D. Irwin, 1960), pp. 11–12.

---

extensive social welfare programs (such as free medical care) are used to make family incomes more equal.

Critics of socialism maintain that the system severely limits economic freedom and that it reduces the incentive to achieve. They argue that government-owned industries become bogged down in red tape and political interference, which leads to inefficiency and higher prices for goods and services.

Communism

Communism is another confusing term. In his famous book *Das Kapital*, Karl Marx, the father of communism, described a future utopian economic system with a classless society and no government at all. However, most people use the term *communism* to refer to the present economies of the Soviet Union and China. In these nations, the state owns and controls virtually all the factories, farms, and other means of production. Moreover, a vast economic plan is developed by the government, which guides all economic activity. Individual economic freedom is subordinated to the government's economic objectives. In addition, political freedom, as we know it in this country, does not exist under communism.

Mixed Economy

Is the United States economy capitalistic? Yes and no. There is some government ownership of enterprises such as the Postal Service, Tennessee Valley Authority (TVA), and many local utility companies. Moreover, pure competition is difficult to find in this country. Finally, the government exercises considerable control over individuals and private business firms through taxation, regulation, and a host of social welfare programs (for example, social security and unemployment insurance). For these reasons it would be inaccurate to describe our economic system as laissez-faire or pure capitalism. Rather we have a *mixed economy*—a mixture of pure capitalism and democratic socialism, although the United States economy is closer to capitalism than it is to socialism.

Another way of viewing our economic system in comparison to other nations can be found in Figure 1–3.

The American business system is largely capitalistic, with extensive economic freedom, substantial competition, and emphasis on the profit motive. Most property is owned by private individuals. However, the economic role of government has expanded during the past century.

BUSINESS AND THE ECONOMY

The role of American business is to produce goods and services for society. Figure 1–4 presents a simplified illustration of how a free

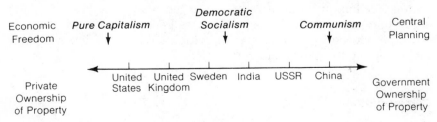

Figure 1–3 The Range of Economic Systems

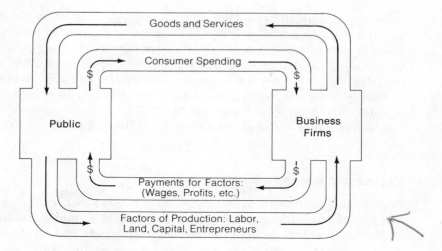

Figure 1-4 How the Economy Operates

enterprise economy operates. The upper loops show the sale of goods and services produced by business firms in response to consumer spending. The lower loops represent the purchase of economic resources (the factors of production) by business firms from private owners. One way to view the economy is in terms of a continuous flow of dollar payments between business firms and the public. This illustration omits government, which plays a significant role in our mixed economy.

Business Cycles

The long-term growth in United States GNP has been interrupted by periodic up and down movements in economic activity. These recurring periods of expansion and contraction are called *business cycles*. Figure 1-5 shows the stages of the business cycle which occur over a number of years.

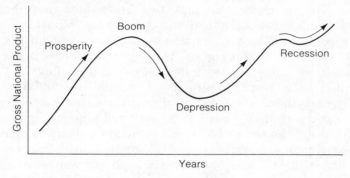

Figure 1-5 The Business Cycle

During periods of expansion the nation enjoys economic prosperity with increased production, employment, and business profits. However, prosperous times may be accompanied by rising prices (inflation). Depressions bring sharp drops in output, large-scale unemployment, and a decline in profits. During the Great Depression of the 1930s the output of goods and services fell by one-third and one-quarter of the labor force lost their jobs. A recession is a "mini-depression"—a small and short-lived decline in economic activity.

Keynes and the "New Economics"

Prior to the depression of the 1930s, most economists, businessmen, and politicians were convinced that government should maintain a "hands off" attitude toward the economy. However, the length and severity of the Great Depression caused many people to call for government action to bring about a recovery. British economist John Maynard Keynes proposed that the federal government should intervene directly to fight depressions and halt inflationary booms. During periods of depression, he advocated increased government spending to expand the demand for goods and services and thereby to stimulate production and employment. Keynes also suggested that tax cuts could be used to stimulate consumer and business spending during depressions. The opposite strategy could be used to halt inflationary booms. According to Keynes, the economy could be "cooled off" through tax increases and a reduction in government spending.

Keynes' theories form the basis of modern fiscal policy, sometimes called *the new economics. Fiscal policy* is the use of government spending and taxing powers to smooth out the business cycle by taking direct action against depressions and inflationary booms.

After World War II, Congress passed the Employment Act of 1946, which made the federal government responsible for using its powers to achieve full employment, stable prices, and a growing economy. The government attempts to achieve these goals through the use of both fiscal policy and monetary policy. *Monetary policy* refers to control of the nation's money supply, which consists of both cash and checking accounts. The supply of money in the economy influences prices, interest rates, output, and employment. Monetary policy is the responsibility of the Federal Reserve Board, a federal agency that exercises control over the nation's banks.

Although the United States has not suffered a major depression since the 1930s, the use of fiscal and monetary policies to achieve full employment, steady prices, and economic growth has not been a complete success. There have been several postwar recessions, and inflation has been a persistent problem. In 1971, President Nixon initiated a series of wage and price controls intended to halt inflation. Despite the various control programs—known as *Phases I, II, III,* and *IV*—prices have risen at an accelerated pace. The problem of inflation has been complicated by the energy crisis.

How's Business?

Economists have developed elaborate theories to explain why and how business cycles occur, but the experts have not enjoyed great success in predicting the timing of changes in the level of business activity. Since most business decisions involve future operations, businessmen are vitally interested in what will happen to the economy in the coming weeks, months, and years. Many larger firms employ economists to make economic forecasts on which to base business plans.

Some of the most widely used tools for analyzing current economic conditions and prospects are the *economic indicators* developed by the National Bureau of Economic Research.[1] The economic indicators are selected time series that fall into three broad groups:

1. *Lead Indicators* tend to change direction prior to changes in the level of general business activity.
2. *Coincident Indicators* make moves that approximately coincide with changes in the business cycles.
3. *Lag Indicators* change direction after changes in general business activity.

Examples of typical lead, coincident, and lag indicators are shown in Table 1–1.

The lead indicators are most useful in making economic forecasts since they often signal changes in business activity several months

Table 1–1   Economic Indicators

Lead	Coincident	Lag
1. Common Stock Prices	1. Gross National Product	1. Business Spending for Plant and Equipment
2. Corporate Profits After Taxes	2. Industrial Production	2. Business Loans
3. Average Work Week in Manufacturing	3. Sales of Retail Stores	3. Bank Interest Rates on Short-Term Business Loans
4. Changes in Consumer Installment Debt	4. Unemployment Rate	

[1]The economic indicators and other forecasting tools are described in more detail in Leonard S. Silk and M. Louise Curley, *A Primer on Business Forecasting* (New York: Random House, 1970). The United States Department of Commerce publishes a monthly report entitled *Business Conditions Digest,* which contains tables and charts of the various economic indicators.

in advance. Each month the United States Department of Commerce publishes a *Composite Index of Twelve Leading Indicators,* which is carefully studied by both economists and businessmen for clues about the future level of business activity.

SUMMARY

A nation's total output of goods and services during a year is measured by Gross National Product (GNP). The standard of living of a nation may be estimated by dividing population into GNP to find output per capita.

Productivity can be roughly defined as output per worker during some period of time. Productivity is the basic determinant of a nation's standard of living. There are several ways to raise productivity, including increased capital investment, improved technology, more effective management, and expanded education and training for the labor force.

Economics is the study of how goods and services get produced and distributed. Because every nation is faced with unlimited material wants and limited resources, these resources (land, labor, capital, and the entrepreneur) must be rationed. Scarcity means a society must decide what goods and services it wants to produce with its scarce resources.

Every nation must choose some economic system to produce goods and services. Under laissez-faire capitalism, property is owned by private individuals or companies. Workers, consumers and business firms enjoy extensive economic freedom. Competition among businessmen results in low prices, improved services, and technological progress. Profit serves as the major incentive for firms to produce those goods and services wanted by consumers.

Democratic socialism provides for government ownership of key industries, heavy taxation of large incomes, and extensive social welfare programs. Under communism, nearly all property is government-owned and the economy is operated according to a central plan.

The United States economy is a mixture of pure capitalism and democratic socialism.

Business cycles are recurring up and down movements in business activity. Ever since the 1930s, the federal government has attempted to use its taxing and spending powers to prevent depressions and inflationary booms. Fiscal policy is based on theories developed by British economist John Maynard Keynes. Regulation of the nation's money supply by the Federal Reserve Board is monetary policy. Both fiscal and monetary policies attempt to ensure full employment, steady prices, and a rising standard of living.

The economic indicators are a useful tool for analyzing current economic conditions and making forecasts of future business activity.

ISSUE   ARE BUSINESSMEN BAD GUYS?

Today, criticizing American business seems to be "in", particularly among college students. If you listen to the critics, the sins of businessmen are many and growing. Even a partial list of the charges levied against business firms leaves the impression that the vast majority of managers are evil schemers out to deceive and cheat the public. Here are some of the accusations often made against American business:

—Large corporations exert undue influence over government through lobbying and political contributions thereby gaining favorable treatment from lawmakers and public officials.

—Business firms fail to pay their fair share of taxes by taking advantage of loopholes in the law.

—Business spends billions of dollars in wasteful advertising to manipulate people into buying products they really don't want.

—Many companies deliberately design products with built-in obsolescence that fall apart or fail within a short time after purchase.

—Businessmen are guilty of racism and sex discrimination.

—Giant corporations create monopoly power so they can charge exorbitant prices and earn excessive profits.

—Many firms produce dangerous products that injure or kill thousands of consumers.

—Business is responsible for environmental pollution.

Even this partial list of sins is impressive. But does it really prove that all—or even most—businessmen are sinners? The truth is, every society has its share of problems, and it is always easier to single out some group on which to blame these problems. No doubt there are some crooked and unethical men and women in the business world, but should the reputation of an entire group be tarnished for the sins of a few? Just because Jimmy Hoffa, former head of the Teamsters' Union, was sent to jail for jury tampering, does this mean that all union leaders are crooked? Does the conviction of a government official for corruption prove that most politicians are immoral?

Ask yourself some other questions. If there are a large number of dishonest businessmen, how do they stay in business? Would you buy from a firm you considered unfair? Would you work for such a firm?

In the following chapters, we will examine some of the charges listed above. After you have studied and thought about American business, then make up your own mind: Are businessmen bad guys?

Reference
George Melloan, "Business Morality and Its Vocal Critics," *Wall Street Journal,*
    August 26, 1971, p. 11.

Student _____

REVIEWING MAJOR CONCEPTS

1. List and briefly explain four methods for increasing productivity. Can you think of a way to boost productivity that is not described in the chapter?

2. Why do many large corporations spend millions of dollars each year on research?

3. In what ways does the American economic system differ from pure capitalism?

4. Safeway owns and operates thousands of supermarkets. This giant chain cuts costs by purchasing food in large quantities and passes the savings on to consumers in the form of lower prices. How can a small food store compete against Safeway?

5. International Business Machines (IBM), the giant computer maker, spends millions of dollars on training programs for its employees. Why?

6. True or false? Most American business firms operate under perfect (or pure) competition. Explain your answer.

7. Briefly explain John Maynard Keynes' "new economics".

8. Why are businessmen concerned about the future?

9. How do lead, lag, and coincident indicators differ? Which type would be most valuable for forecasting? Why?

Student _____

SOLVING PROBLEMS AND CASES

1. Given the information below, which nation, Zunder or Morcon, is economically better off? Explain your answer.

	Zunder	Morcon
Gross National Product	$100,000,000	$60,000,000
Population	100,000	30,000

2. *Case:* Ivan Danovich

   Ivan Danovich is the factory manager of the Kiev Nail Plant in the Soviet Union. Each year his plant is given a production quota of nails as a part of the economic plan for the USSR. In addition, the plant is assigned workers, machinery, and steel based on the government's estimate of the resources needed to meet the quota. If the plant exceeds the quota, Comrade Danovich and his workers will earn a bonus. This year, the factory quota is 200,000,000 nails.

   a. If you were Comrade Danovich would you produce large or small nails? Why? Would your answer be different if the quota were 7,500 tons of nails?

   b. Does Comrade Danovich have any incentive to reduce production costs by finding more efficient ways of manufacturing nails?

   c. Is Comrade Danovich responsible for selling the nails produced by the Kiev Nail Plant? Why or why not?

    d. Would it be accurate to call Comrade Danovich an entrepreneur? Why or why not?

    e. Who decides what goods and services will be produced in the Soviet Union?

3. India has a population of 500 million people and a Gross National Product of about $50 billion. Both GNP and population have been growing at a rate of roughly 2 percent a year over the past decade.

    a. What is India's output per capita?

    b. What steps would you suggest that India take to improve the standard of living of its people?

4. After graduating from college, you join the Peace Corps and are sent to a small ''neutralist'' nation in Southeast Asia. The people in the village where you live have asked you to explain the capitalist profit system since several local communists have denounced profits as ''capitalist exploitation of the workers''. Outline your arguments supporting the role of profits under capitalism.

APPENDIX GRIT AND BEAR IT: BASIC BUSINESS ARITHMETIC

Let's face it, a knowledge of mathematics is essential in business. Modern business managers are relying more and more on the analysis of numerical data to make good decisions. For this reason, most business schools require students to study mathematics through calculus.

This appendix is intended to provide a quick review of basic business arithmetic. It includes examples of addition, subtraction, multiplication, and division of whole numbers, fractions, and decimals. The ability to perform these operations represents the minimum level of arithmetical skill for students considering a career in business.

If you are already proficient in basic arithmetic, then skip this appendix. If not, let's try to refresh your memory.

Example 1 You are employed in the billing department of a fuel company. During March, your firm delivered to Harris & Company the following amounts of coal: 1½ tons, 1¾ tons, 2⅓ tons, and 3 1/6 tons. If the price per ton is $121.75, how much does Harris & Company owe?

Solution: Step 1. Express the amounts in fractions with a common denominator (in this case, 12).
Step 2. Find the total tons of coal sold.
Step 3. Multiply the number of tons by the price per ton. (Note: to make the multiplication easier, you can change the fractional ton into a decimal by dividing the denominator into the numerator.)

Illustration:

(1) 1 1/2 = 1 6/12
   1 3/4 = 1 9/12
   2 1/3 = 2 4/12
   3 1/6 = 3 2/12

(2)   7 21/12 = 8 9/12 = 8 3/4

$$(3)\ 3/4\ \text{tons} = 4\ \overline{\smash{)}\ 3.00}\ \ \ ^{.75\ \text{tons}}$$

               28
               20
               20

  $121.75 price per ton
  × 8.75 tons

    6.0875
   85.225
  974.00

$1,065.3125 = $1,065.31

Example 2 You are the new loan officer for the Rockwell Bank. Janice Sung is ready to repay a 9-month loan which is due today. The loan is for $8,100 plus interest at 12% per year. Ms. Sung wants to know how much to repay. You know the equation for computing simple interest is PRT, where P is the principal (the amount of the loan), R is the interest rate, and T is the time expressed as a fraction of a year.

Solution: Step 1. Arrange the numbers according to the equation. Note that 12% is 12/100 and 9 months is 9/12 of a year.
Step 2. Cancel where possible and multiply.
Step 3. Add the interest to the principal to find the amount owed by Ms. Sung.

Illustration:
$$P \times R \times T = \text{Interest}$$

$$(1)\&(2) \quad \$8100 \times \frac{12}{100} \times \frac{9}{12} = \frac{729}{1} = \$729$$

(3) $8,100 Principal
 + 729 Interest

 $8,829 Amount owed by Ms. Sung

Example 3 Power's Yamaha, a motorcycle dealership, charges its customers a 15% restocking fee on returned parts. Harry Maddox returned an unused camshaft for which he had paid $22.65. What is the amount of Harry's refund?

Solution: Step 1. Multiply $22.65 by 15%. (Note: The decimal for 15% is .15, found by moving the decimal point two places to the left and dropping the % sign.
Step 2. Subtract the fee (Step 1) from $22.65 to obtain the net refund.

Illustration:
(1) $ $22.65
   ×.15

   1.1325
   2.265

  $3.3975 = $3.40 (rounded off)

(2) $22.65 Purchase Price
  −3.40 Fee

 $19.25 Refund

Shortcut:
$22.65 × .85 = $19.25
(Since 100% − 15% = 85%, which is the net percent of the refund
on the $22.65.)

Example 4 The Homita Paint Company has received a bulk
shipment of red paint in a 500-gallon drum. If the company plans
to resell the paint in 2 1/2-gallon cans, how many cans are
needed?

Solution: Step 1. Express 2 1/2 gallons in the equivalent form of
5/2 gallons.
        Step 2. Divide 5/2 into 500 gallons by inverting the frac-
tion and multiplying.

Illustration:
(1) 2 1/2 = 5/2 (2 1/2 = 2 + 1/2 = 4/2 + 1/2 = 5/2)
(2) 500 ÷ 5/2 = 500 × 2/5 = 1000/5 = 200 cans

Example 5 As a management trainee for an investment advisory
company, you have been asked to compute the yield on several
stocks and bonds. You know the yield is the percentage return on
a security found by dividing the interest or dividend payment by
the current price of the security. Compute the yield for:

a. A bond selling for $800 that pays interest of $48 a year.
b. Common stock of XYZ Company paying $1.76 per share in divi-
dends and selling for $22 per share.
c. A preferred stock with a dividend of $9 per share selling for
$104.

Solution:
In each case, find the yield by using the following equation:

$$\text{Yield} = \frac{\text{Return (Interest or Dividend)}}{\text{Current Price of Bond or Stock}}$$

Illustration:

(a) $\dfrac{\$48}{\$800} = 6\%$

(b) $\dfrac{\$1.76}{\$22} = 8\%$

(c) $\dfrac{\$9}{\$104} = 8.65\%$

$$\begin{array}{r} .06 \\ 800\overline{)48.00} \\ 48.00 \\ \hline \end{array}$$

$$\begin{array}{r} 08 \\ 22\overline{)1.76} \\ 1.76 \\ \hline \end{array}$$

$$\begin{array}{r} .08653 \\ 104\overline{)9.000} \\ 832 \\ \hline 680 \\ 624 \\ \hline 560 \\ 520 \\ \hline 400 \\ 312 \\ \hline \end{array}$$

Now test yourself by solving the following problems.

1. What is the yield on a stock selling for $72 and paying a dividend of $4 per share?

2. A $600, 4-month loan with a 9% per year interest rate is due. What is the amount of the interest?

3. A customer buys 2 1/4 yards of red cloth at $4.00 per yard and 3 3/8 yards of blue cloth at $4.80 a yard. How much does the customer owe if the sales tax on the purchase is 5%?

Chapter 2 Business and Government

Pure (laissez-faire) capitalism has never existed in the United States, and it probably never will. From our earliest history government has always exerted some influence on business.

Over the past few decades the economic role of government has accelerated rapidly. One way to gauge this growing influence is to look at spending by local, state and federal governments. Figure 2–1 illustrates the rise of governmental expenditures over the last forty-five years. In 1930, government purchases of goods and services accounted for about 8 percent of GNP; today, the figure is nearly 30 percent.

This chapter is intended to help you explore three areas of government involvement in our economic system: (1) government assistance to business, (2) government regulation of business, and (3) taxation.

KEY QUESTIONS

1. In what ways does government assist business firms?

2. What are the objectives of government regulation of business, and what methods of regulation are used?

3. Why does government levy taxes?

4. What are the major taxes used by federal, state, and local governments and how are revenues spent?

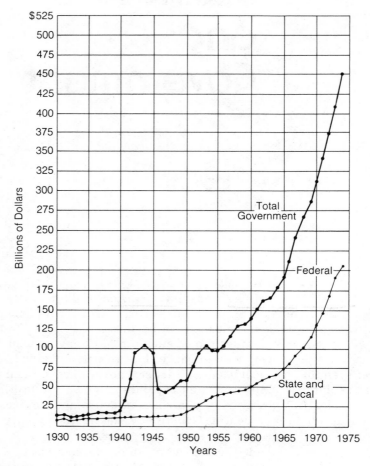

Figure 2–1 Federal, State, and Local Spending, 1930–1974
Source: *Economic Report of the President* and Federal Reserve Bank of St. Louis, *Federal Budget Trends.* (Note: Data for 1974 are estimates.)

GOVERNMENT ASSISTANCE TO BUSINESS

Government has always acted to promote or assist American business firms. This assistance has often been indirect: by providing a system of laws and courts; by educating the work force; and by coining money to serve as a medium of exchange in business transactions.

For nearly two hundred years the United States government has levied tariffs—taxes on imported goods—first to raise revenue and then to protect American business firms. Tariffs increase the price of goods produced in other nations and shipped to the United States, thereby protecting domestic firms from foreign competition. It is often argued that tariffs are necessary to protect our high standard of living from the competition of low-wage labor overseas. But high wages in this country reflect the high productivity of our work force. In other words, the relatively low wages received by workers in India are a result of low productivity. Tariffs result in higher prices to American consumers, a reduction in competition, and special protection for some American business firms. To sum up, when tariffs are imposed, you pay more.

Often government makes direct payments to business firms or industries in the form of subsidies and outright grants. The farm price support program involves payments to farmers amounting to billions of dollars each year. American shipbuilders also receive government subsidies. During the nineteenth century, millions of acres of public land were given to the railroads to encourage construction of rail lines across the country. In 1971, Lockheed Corporation, a major defense contractor, was granted $250 million in government-guaranteed loans to save the firm from bankruptcy.

Government also provides a host of services to American business. Many federal, state, and local agencies collect and publish statistical data that are helpful to businessmen in planning future operations. The Department of Commerce provides valuable information on a variety of economic activities including gross national product, consumer prices, and employment.

The Small Business Administration, with offices throughout the country, offers management training, assistance, and loans to small businessmen. If you plan to start a business, don't overlook this source of valuable information and possible financing.

Government has actively promoted business in the United States through a variety of services, grants, and assistance programs. Moreover, government purchases of goods and services is the primary source of sales for many firms. Where, for example, would General Motors be today without the billions of dollars of government spending on streets and highways?

GOVERNMENT REGULATION OF BUSINESS

> People of the same trade seldom meet together, even for merriment and diversion, but the conversation ends in a conspiracy against the public, or in some contrivance to raise prices.
>
> *Adam Smith*

During the early nineteenth century, government exercised very little control over American business. Most companies were small, rarely employing more than a few dozen workers, and competition was vigorous. However, after the Civil War a host of new inventions, including the steam engine and advances in metallurgy,

---

ISSUE WHATEVER HAPPENED TO FREE ENTERPRISE?

Most Americans think of their country as the capital of capitalism and the home of free enterprise. Private ownership of property and competition are indeed more extensive in the United States than in any other nation. However, in recent years, the role of government in this country has been growing at an accelerated pace. President Nixon's New Economic Policy, with its controls over wages and prices, represented a dramatic setback for the free enterprise system. Amtrak, the government-backed railroad corporation, and the subsidies to the aerospace industry are other examples of the expanding influence of government on the American economy. Perhaps the most significant point is that it has been businessmen themselves who have most often urged the government to step in.

Does this mean that free enterprise is dead? Is our nation marching down the road to democratic socialism? The answer to these questions is a qualified no. There is little enthusiasm in Washington or elsewhere for the federal government to take over ownership of major industries. However, the influence of the government on the business world may be expected to increase in the areas of regulation and control. Recent legislation in the area of consumer protection is but one example. Moreover, many prominent business leaders back federal efforts to establish a guaranteed annual income, to develop a national health program, and to attack environmental pollution. Most businessmen want clear, national standards for pollution control to prevent "cheating" at the local level and to ensure equal competition among firms.

The free enterprise system will survive for the foreseeable future. At the same time, however, government will expand its role as a goal-setter and rule-maker for business. In addition, government will increasingly enlist the help of business in solving the complex social and economic problems facing our nation.

References

"The Future of Free Enterprise," *Time,* February 14, 1972, pp. 50–51.

Ralph Nader, "A Citizen's Guide to the American Economy," in Ralph Nader, ed., *The Consumer and Corporate Accountability* (New York: Harcourt Brace Jovanovich, 1973), pp. 4–18.

---

brought about the substitution of machinery for manpower. The need to purchase expensive machinery led to the widespread adoption of the corporate form of business organization which permitted businessmen to raise money through the sales of stock to the public. Many corporations grew rapidly in size, often employing thousands of workers.

By the 1880s some industries were dominated by huge monopolies called *trusts*. The Standard Oil Company, under the direction of John D. Rockefeller, controlled 90 percent of the American oil industry, while the United States Steel Corporation accounted for more than two-thirds of all steel production. Competition was eliminated either by deliberately driving smaller firms into bankruptcy or by agreements among competing firms to fix prices at high levels and divide up the market. One of the foundations of capitalism—competition—was being destroyed.

Small businessmen, farmers, and the public urged government to take action against the huge monopolies and their unfair business practices. Between 1890 and 1914 a series of federal laws were passed that outlawed monopolies and unfair methods of competition. Theodore Roosevelt, elected President in 1900, proclaimed that "there must be an increase in the supervision exercised by government over business enterprise." The federal government launched an attack on the monopolies by bringing many corporations to trial for violations of the antitrust laws.

Purposes of Government Regulation of Business

There are three major reasons why government intervenes in the affairs of business: (1) to preserve competition, (2) to protect the public welfare, and (3) to regulate "natural monopolies."

Monopoly may be defined as the absence of competition. Without competition there is no incentive for businessmen to charge low prices, reduce costs, or develop new and improved products. In other words, you end up paying more for less. The growth of unregulated monopolies is a threat to the capitalist economic system; indeed, capitalism cannot exist without competition. For these reasons, the government, representing the public, steps in to maintain competition and prevent monopoly.

There have always been a few dishonest businessmen who have attempted to deceive and cheat the public. For many years, the guiding principle for consumers was *caveat emptor*—"let the buyer beware." If a man bought a faulty or overpriced product, it was considered his own fault.

At the turn of the century, Upton Sinclair wrote a novel called *The Jungle,* describing the filthy conditions in the Chicago meatpacking industry, which often sold diseased meat to the public. The uproar caused by this book resulted in the 1906 passage of the Pure Food and Drug Act, which was aimed at preventing the sale of unsafe food and drugs and forcing manufacturers to accurately label their products. Since then several laws have been passed to protect the public, including the Water Quality Act, the Air Quality Act, and the Toy Safety Act.

Sometimes competition is unworkable. There are some industries in which competition would lead to higher prices and poorer service. Examples include most utilities, such as telephone, natural gas, and electricity companies. These firms perform essential public services and require a large investment in capital equipment.

Would you be better off if three telephone companies served your community? This competition would mean three times as many telephone lines as well as the difficulty of trying to call someone served by another company. The increased costs of operating three systems would raise the price of telephone service.

Because of the undesirable effects of competition, most utility companies are considered "natural monopolies." The government grants one firm the exclusive right to provide service to a particular area (a city, county, or state). In return the government regulates the rates (prices) charged by the utility and sets minimum standards for service.

Methods of Government Regulation

Government attempts to preserve competition, protect the public welfare, and control natural monopolies by: (1) enforcing antitrust laws, (2) establishing regulatory agencies, and (3) occasionally by direct public ownership.

At the end of the nineteenth century the growing power of monopolies, coupled with unfair methods of competition, led to the passage of the antitrust laws. Three major acts provide the legal basis for the federal government's continuing efforts to prevent monopoly and unfair business practices.

The *Sherman Act,* passed in 1890, contains two key provisions: (1) monopolies are outlawed and (2) it is illegal for any person to conspire to monopolize or restrain trade. Violators can be fined up to $50,000, sent to prison for a year, or both. In addition, convicted individuals or firms can be sued for triple damages by injured parties.

The provisions of the Sherman Act were so broad in scope that the courts had difficulty interpreting their meaning. In 1914 Congress passed the *Clayton Act,* which declares certain business practices to be unfair and illegal when they lead to reduced competition. These unfair practices include:

1. *Price discrimination* among competing buyers of the same quantity of a product.
2. *Exclusive contracts* where a firm promises to buy only from one supplier.
3. *Tying contracts* where, for example, a computer manufacturer sells his equipment only on the condition that the buyer also purchase all supplies (cards, tape, etc.) from the manufacturer.
4. *Interlocking Directorates* that involve one person serving as a director of two or more competing corporations.
5. *Corporate purchases of stock* in competing firms.

The third major antitrust law is the *Federal Trade Commission Act,* also passed in 1914. Under this legislation unfair methods of competition were declared illegal and the Federal Trade Commission (FTC) was created to investigate violations of the antitrust laws. Later the FTC was also given the power to investigate cases of false and misleading advertising.

The Federal Trade Commission and the Justice Department have brought lawsuits against hundreds of business firms for violating the provisions of the Sherman, Clayton, and FTC Acts. Some of these suits have dragged through the courts for years. In an attempt to avoid the delays of court actions, federal and state governments have established dozens of regulatory agencies which exercise control over various industries. The Interstate Commerce Commission (ICC) regulates railroads and trucking firms which operate across state lines. The Federal Reserve Board (FRB) supervises the commercial banking system while the Securities and Exchange Commission (SEC) oversees the securities industry. At the state level, the California Public Utilities Commission, for example, establishes the rates charged by natural monopolies and ensures that consumers receive adequate services. These agencies offer the advantages of rapid action as well as flexibility. If a business firm disagrees with the decision of an agency, it can appeal to the courts.

In a relatively few cases government in the United States owns and operates business enterprises. At the federal level examples include the United States Postal Service, retail stores on military posts, the United States Government Printing Office, and certain hydroelectric power facilities such as the Hoover Dam. Many cities operate water, electric, and natural gas distribution systems, while a few states maintain monopoly ownership of retail liquor stores.

TAXATION

The wisdom of man never yet contrived a system of taxation that would operate with perfect equality.

Andrew Jackson

Local, state, and federal government levy taxes on both individuals and business firms. Most people believe the purpose of taxation is to raise revenue for financing government-produced goods and services. This is only partly true. Taxation is also used to control the level of economic activity and to regulate the production and sale of certain products.

You will recall that the Employment Act of 1946 made the federal government responsible for ensuring full employment, keeping prices stable, and promoting economic growth (a rising standard of living). Taxes are used to control the income and spending of both individuals and business firms, and the level of government spending influences employment, prices, and growth.

Some products and activities are taxed, not to raise revenue, but to control their use. Taxes on narcotics and gambling require detailed record keeping, which provides information to detect illegal activities. Somewhat different reasoning is used to justify high taxes on cigarettes and liquor. Since these products are considered sinful or unhealthy, they are heavily taxed. Following this reasoning, perhaps we should tax war or even deep breathing in smoggy cities.

ISSUE   THE PROBLEM OF BUSINESS GIANTISM

Although there are more than eleven million business firms in the United States, most people think of American business in terms of a few giant corporations such as Ford, General Electric, IBM, and Safeway. The fact is, many industries in this country are dominated by a handful of huge corporations. Moreover, in the past two decades, there have been a growing number of corporate mergers that have often resulted in the creation of gigantic supercorporations. A few examples will serve to underline the scope of industrial concentration in the United States: (1) Over two-thirds of all manufacturing assets are owned by the 200 largest manufacturing corporations. (2) The "Big Three" automobile manufacturers produce 83 percent of all cars sold in this country and 97 percent of all domestic models. (3) In the steel industry, four firms account for 55 percent of all production. (4) Similar concentration exists in dozens of other industries including aluminum, computers, and oil refining.

Is bigness necessarily bad? After all, doesn't corporate growth reflect efficiency and good management? What worries many observers is that concentrated economic power leads to anticompetive behavior in the form of higher prices, rising costs, reduced innovation, and unfair competitive methods. Moreover, economic power gives rise to political power which enables some corporations to exercise influence over local, state, and federal government.

What, if anything, should be done?

1. *Leave well enough alone.* Many businessmen are quick to point out that our system has produced the highest standard of living in the world. They further argue that bigness is necessary to gain efficiency, and only large corporations can afford to support the research necessary to develop modern technology. Moreover, there is still "reasonable" competition among firms even in concentrated industries. "Why abandon a winning system?" they ask.

2. *Government ownership and control* is the only logical answer to economic concentration, according to some critics of the United States economic system. The evils of big business, particularly the exploitation of consumers and workers, they say, can only be halted if the government nationalizes the major industries and exercises strict control over the remainder of the business system. Capitalism is doomed, they continue, and the sooner we recognize this fact and take action, the better off the country will be.

3. *The antitrust alternative* calls for restoring competition through vigorous enforcement of the antitrust laws. In their best-selling book, *America, Inc.,* Morton Mintz and Jerry Cohen argue that government ownership will not work: "The root of evil is concentrated economic power. It cannot be trusted to either public or private hands." Moreover, many economists believe the giant corporations have grown far beyond the point of efficiency so that the disadvantages of size have offset the advantages. The only effective solution to the problem of industrial concentration is to break up giant corporations into several competing firms. A staff report by the Federal Trade Commission estimates that "if highly concentrated industries were deconcentrated to the point where the four largest control forty percent or less of an industry's sales, prices would fall by twenty-five percent or more."

Which course of action do you favor?

References

Walter Adams, ed., *The Structure of American Industry.* 4th ed. (New York: Macmillan, 1971.

Morton Mintz and Jerry S. Cohen, *America, Inc.* (New York: Dial Press, 1971), p. 376.

Mark J. Green, "The High Cost of Monopoly," *The Progressive,* March 1972, pp. 15–19.

Principles of Taxation

Two major principles are used to measure the fairness of taxes.

The *benefits principle* maintains that people should pay taxes according to the amount of government goods and services each receives. For example, if you consume $500 worth of public services a year, you should pay that amount in taxes. Applying the benefits principle raises two problems. How can an individual measure the dollar benefits he receives from public education, national defense, or police protection? Moreover, if the benefits principle were applied for everyone, what would happen to welfare programs and free public education? Nevertheless, some taxes do conform to the benefits principle; for example, gasoline tax revenues are used to build and maintain streets and highways.

The *ability-to-pay principle* holds that each person should pay taxes according to his financial ability as measured by wealth or income. In other words, the rich should pay more taxes than the poor. Can you think of a tax based on this principle?

Tax Rates

Taxes are often judged on whether they are progressive, proportional, or regressive. These terms refer to the relationship between the *tax base* and the *tax rate*. The tax base is what is being taxed—for example, income, property, or spending. The tax rate is the percent of the tax base which is paid in taxes.

Progressive Tax A progressive tax is one whose rate increases as the tax base increases. The illustration in Table 2-1 shows the tax rate rising from 5 percent to 50 percent as income increases from $100 to $100,000. High incomes are taxed at a larger *percent* than are low incomes. The federal individual income tax, with rates beginning at 14 percent and rising to 70 percent, is an example of a progressive tax.

Table 2-1 Progressive, Proportional, and Regressive Taxes (Hypothetical Data)

Tax Base (Income)	Progressive Tax Rate	Progressive Tax Amount	Proportional Tax Rate	Proportional Tax Amount	Regressive Tax Rate	Regressive Tax Amount
$ 100	5%	$ 5	20%	$ 20	30%	$ 30
1,000	10	100	20	200	20	200
10,000	25	2,500	20	2,000	10	1,000
100,000	50	50,000	20	20,000	5	5,000

Proportional Tax   A proportional tax is one whose rate remains constant as the tax base increases. Table 2–1 shows a fixed tax rate of 20 percent regardless of income. A property tax where all real estate is taxed at 10 percent may be considered proportional when property value is used as the base.

Regressive Tax   A regressive tax is the opposite of a progressive one; the tax rate declines as the tax base rises.

Soak The poor

Some taxes which appear to be proportional are actually regressive in effect. A general sales tax of 5 percent is proportional when spending is used as the tax base; but if income is the tax base, the tax is regressive. Table 2–2 demonstrates this point.

The poor family must spend all its income, and its sales tax payments are $100 (5% of $2,000). However, the rich family saves half its income, and therefore the sales tax represents only 2 1/2 percent of family income. To sum up, using income as a tax base, the poor family is taxed at twice the rate of the wealthy family. Some states exempt food, rent, and prescription drugs from the sales tax to reduce its regressive effect.

Major Taxes

What are the major sources of revenue and the main expenditures of federal, state and local governments? Figure 2–2 provides a summary of how each level of government raises tax revenue as well as how these funds are spent.

Individual Income Tax   Over two-fifths of all federal tax revenue comes from the individual income tax. The tax rates begin at 14 percent of taxable income and rise to 70 percent. Remember that the tax is not levied on total income, but on taxable income. This formula illustrates how the tax is computed:

Total Income − (Exemptions and Deductions) =
Taxable Income × Tax Rate = Tax Owed

The federal government allows taxpayers to reduce total income by $750 for each dependent. For example, a family consisting of a husband and wife and two children can deduct $3,000 (4 × $750) in exemptions. Deductions fall into two main categories: (1) business

Table 2–2   The Regressive Effect of a General Sales Tax

	Poor Family	Rich Family
Annual Income	$2,000	$100,000
Spending	2,000	50,000
5% Sales Tax	100	2,500
Tax Paid as a Percent of Income	5%	2½%

deductions, which are the expenses of doing business such as wages, advertising, supplies, etc.; and (2) individual deductions, which include charitable contributions, interest paid, state and local taxes, large medical expenses, etc.

After subtracting all exemptions and deductions from income, you have taxable income. Now, using a tax table, you find the appropriate rate and compute what you owe. Of course, most workers have a part of their pay checks withheld each pay period to cover their income tax.

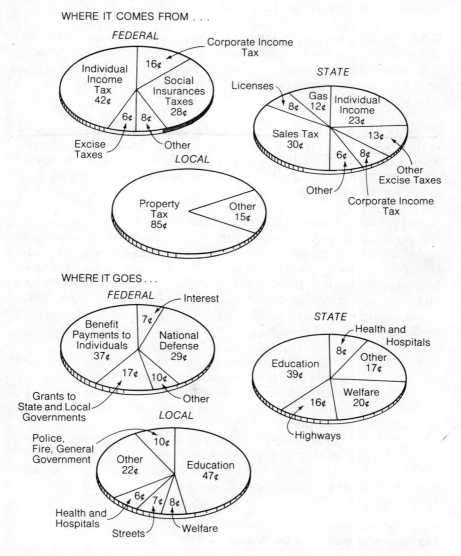

Figure 2–2 Sources and Uses of Tax Dollars

Source: *Economic Report of the President, 1974;* United States Department of Commerce, *State Tax Collections in 1973;* United States Department of Commerce, *State Government Finances in 1972;* United States Department of Commerce, *Statistical Abstract of the United States, 1973.*

In addition to the federal government, many states also levy a tax on income.

Corporation Income Tax   The earnings (or profits) of corporations are taxed by the federal government and some state governments. The federal corporation income tax, which accounts for nearly one-sixth of federal revenues, has two tax rates: (1) the first $25,000 of earnings is taxed at 22 percent, and (2) all earnings over $25,000 is taxed at 48 percent. This means that large corporations pay nearly half their earnings in taxes.

Sales Taxes   The vast majority of state governments levy a tax on the sale of goods (and sometimes services) to the consumer. This is the major source of revenue for most states. (Remember that a general sales tax is regressive in effect if income is used as the tax base.)

Property Taxes   The major source of support for local government is the property tax. It is levied on the value of land and buildings owned by individuals and business firms. In some localities personal property (such as furniture) and business inventories are also subject to the property tax.

Social Security Taxes   Payroll taxes, paid by both employers and employees, provide for unemployment insurance; old age, survivors, and disability insurance plus medicare; and workmen's compensation. Federal social security taxes account for over 25 percent of all federal tax revenues. In 1974, the rate was 5.85 percent for *both* the employer and employee on the first $13,200 of taxable wages. This tax is highly regressive, taking a larger proportion of the low-income worker's earnings than it does from upper-income individuals.

Other Taxes   Both state and federal governments levy *excise taxes* on selected products and services including gasoline, tires, cigarettes, liquor, and telephone service. Although these taxes are paid by the manufacturer or retailer they are normally passed on to the consumer in higher prices.

Death taxes are levied by federal and state governments against the wealth left by deceased persons. As Benjamin Franklin said, "only two things in life are certain—death and taxes—and I resent they don't come in that order." Sometimes they do come in that order, Ben.

Taxation and Business Decisions

Many business decisions are influenced by tax considerations. For example, in deciding on the location of a new plant, management should consider local taxes. The accounting system used by a company must conform to standards established by the Internal Revenue Service. If a corporation wants to raise money by selling securities, it must take into account that bond interest may be deducted as an expense, thereby reducing corporate income taxes, while dividends on stock are not deductible. Even a firm's choice of legal ownership form—proprietorship, partnership or corporation—is influenced by different tax treatment.

SUMMARY

The role of government in the American economy has expanded rapidly over the past century. This expansion is partly a result of the growing demand for government-produced goods and services—highways, education, parks, national defense, space exploration, and police protection, to name a few. A growing population and inflation (rising prices) have also caused government spending to increase.

Government has always assisted American business through grants and subsidies, tariffs, loans, highway and airport construction, as well as a variety of services.

At the end of the nineteenth century, the federal government began to take steps to fight monopoly and halt unfair business practices in order to preserve competition and protect the public welfare. The major antitrust laws—the Sherman Act, the Clayton Act, and the Federal Trade Commission Act—serve as the legal framework for government intervention. In addition, a series of regulatory agencies have been established to oversee certain industries. In a few cases, government has assumed ownership and operation of some businesses such as the Postal Service, federal power projects, and some local utilities.

Taxation is used to regulate the level of economic activity, to raise funds for public goods and services, and to control the production of certain products. Most taxes are based on either the ability-to-pay or the benefits principle. A tax may be progressive, proportional, or regressive depending on the relationship between the tax base and the tax rates.

The major progressive tax in the United States is the federal individual income tax whose rates range from 14 percent to 70 percent of taxable income. The corporation income tax is levied on corporate profits. Local governments derive the vast majority of their revenue from the property tax, while state governments rely primarily on sales and excise taxes.

Businessmen must give careful consideration to the tax consequences of most business decisions.

ISSUE   TAXES: WHO PAYS HOW MUCH?

Have you ever heard anyone complain he pays too little in taxes? Of course not! Each of us is convinced we are paying more than our fair share of the tax burden. The poor man feels cheated by regressive taxes that take a larger share of his earnings than of his higher income neighbor's. The rich man complains that the federal income tax has sharply progressive rates that go up to 70 percent. The middle income earner feels caught in the middle, hit by both progressive and regressive taxes.

Some people maintain that business firms should be subjected to heavier taxation, but this overlooks the fact it is people, not business, who ultimately pay all taxes. Taxes paid by business are passed on to consumers in higher prices or to owners in lower profits.

The biggest single tax for most people is the federal individual income tax, with rates ranging from 14 to 70 percent. However, due to deductions and exemptions, the effective rates are much lower. The following table, based on a study conducted by the Brookings Institution, shows what percentage of income is paid by the average family in each income bracket.

Effective Rates for the Federal Individual Income Tax

Income Per Year	Average Effective Tax Rate
Under $5000	1.4%
$ 5,000– 10,000	5.3
10,000– 15,000	8.7
15,000– 20,000	10.7
20,000– 25,000	12.1
25,000– 50,000	14.5
50,000– 100,000	23.5
100,000– 500,000	29.5
500,000–1,000,000	30.4
Over $1,000,000	32.1

The federal income tax is generally progressive. But what about all the other taxes you pay to federal, state, and local governments? Accurately measuring the tax burden is a difficult job because it is necessary to consider not only the taxes paid but also the benefits received from government transfer payments such as social security benefits, welfare, unemployment insurance, and

---

ISSUE TAXES: WHO PAYS HOW MUCH? (*CONTINUED*)

so on. The following table is based on a comprehensive study conducted by Roger Herriot and Herman Miller of the United States Census Bureau using data for the year 1968. It shows total taxes paid as a percent of income after making adjustments for transfer payments.

Total Taxes as a Percentage of Income

Income Per Year	Taxes Paid
Under $2,000	25.6%
$ 2,000– 4,000	24.7
4,000– 6,000	27.9
6,000– 8,000	30.1
8,000–10,000	29.9
10,000–15,000	30.9
15,000–25,000	31.1
25,000–50,000	33.6
Over $50,000	46.6
Average for All Groups	31.6

For the vast majority of Americans earning $25,000 a year or less the tax system is clearly proportional, not progressive. Does this mean our tax system is fair? The answer to this question depends on what you consider a just and equitable distribution of income. In the final analysis, what you consider fair comes down to your personal value system, which is likely to be very different from your neighbor's.

One thing you may be sure of: no tax system is likely to make many people happy. As Edmund Burke said in 1774, "To tax and to please, no more than to love and be wise, is not given to man."

References

Henry Aaron and Martin McGuire, *Public Goods Income Distribution,* Bulletin Number 202 (Washington, D.C.: The Brookings Institution, 1971).

Herman P. Miller, *Rich Man, Poor Man* (New York: Crowell, 1971).

Joseph A. Pechman, *Distribution of Federal and State Income Taxes by Income Groups,* Bulletin Number 234 (Washington, D.C.: The Brookings Institution, 1972).

Student _____

REVIEWING MAJOR CONCEPTS

1. Briefly describe the major provisions of the following antitrust laws:

   a. Sherman Act.

   b. Clayton Act.

   c. Federal Trade Commission Act.

2. Why has government spending grown so rapidly over the past forty years?

3. "If government would only stop interfering with business and return to free enterprise we would all be better off." Do you agree or disagree? Explain your answer.

4. In the space provided, designate whether each of the following taxes is progressive, proportional, or regressive.

   a. Federal Corporation Income Tax _____

   b. General Sales Tax_____

   c. Property Tax _____

   d. Individual Income Tax _____

   e. Social Security Taxes _____

5. List four ways in which the federal government assists business.

6. Some people feel that huge corporations should be broken up into smaller companies to increase competition. For example, it has been suggested that General Motors might be divided into five or six independent automobile firms. Would you support this plan? Why or why not?

Student _____

SOLVING PROBLEMS AND CASES

1. The table below represents the current federal income tax rate schedule for married couples. Use the table to answer the following questions:

Married Couples Filing Joint Returns

Taxable Income		Amount of Tax	
Over—	But Not Over—		Of Excess Over—
0	$ 1,000	14%	—
$ 1,000	2,000	$ 140 + 15	$ 1,000
2,000	3,000	290 + 16	2,000
3,000	4,000	450 + 17	3,000
4,000	8,000	620 + 19	4,000
8,000	12,000	1,380 + 22	8,000
12,000	16,000	2,260 + 25	12,000
16,000	20,000	3,260 + 28	16,000
20,000	24,000	4,380 + 32	20,000
24,000	28,000	5,660 + 36	24,000
28,000	32,000	7,100 + 39	28,000
32,000	36,000	8,660 + 42	32,000
36,000	40,000	10,340 + 45	36,000
40,000	44,000	12,140 + 48	40,000
44,000	52,000	14,060 + 50	44,000
52,000	64,000	18,060 + 53	52,000
64,000	76,000	24,420 + 55	64,000
76,000	88,000	31,020 + 58	76,000
88,000	100,000	37,980 + 60	88,000
100,000	120,000	45,180 + 62	100,000
120,000	140,000	57,580 + 64	120,000
140,000	160,000	70,380 + 66	140,000
160,000	180,000	83,580 + 68	160,000
180,000	200,000	97,180 + 69	180,000
200,000	_____	110,980 + 70	200,000

a. Mr. and Mrs. Watt have one child. Their total income in 1973 was $6,500 and their deductions amount to $1,250. How much tax do they owe? What is their average tax rate? (Hint: divide the tax owed by taxable income and express the answer as a percent).

b. In 1973, Mr. and Mrs. Kant earned total income of $13,000. They claim 12 dependents including themselves and have deductions of $3,000. What is their tax?

c. Mr. and Mrs. Starr are a childless couple who both work in motion pictures. Their 1973 total income was $351,500, and their deductions amounted to $50,000. Compute their income tax and average tax rate.

Student _____

2. *Case:* Poe Products

Frank Truly has been employed for over a year as a salesman for Poe Products, a large manufacturer of farm equipment. Although he likes his job and is well paid, Frank is concerned about several events which have occurred during the past months.

Last October he attended an industry convention where he overheard executives from several companies discussing plans for establishing standard prices for various types of farm equipment.

The following January, Poe Products brought out a revolutionary new grape harvester that made competing products obsolete. Frank's sales manager suggested that customers be informed that the new harvester would be available only if the farmer promised to buy all his equipment from Poe. If a customer agreed to this plan, he would be given a special 10 percent price discount on the harvester.

In May, Frank was surprised to read an advertisement for a Poe tractor that made claims that he knew were untrue.

Just last week, Frank learned that one of the directors of Poe Products is also a director for a major competitor.

Frank has asked for your assistance. He wants to know if Poe Products is engaged in any illegal activities and, if so, which laws are being violated. In addition, he would like your advice on what, if anything, he should do.

Part II

Organization of the Firm

Chapter 3

Forms of Business Ownership

The first two chapters have provided a broad overview of the economic and political environment of American business. Now we turn our attention to the business firm itself. This and the next chapter are concerned with how businesses are organized and managed.

Suppose you are planning to start a business. One of the first decisions you must make is the best form of ownership for your firm. Should you select the proprietorship, partnership, or corporation? There is no right answer to this question. Business firms differ in many ways: in the type of products and services they produce and sell; in size; in their need for funds; in the personal characteristics of the owner(s). The most appropriate form of ownership is determined by weighing the advantages and disadvantages of each type of organization against the requirements of the particular firm.

This chapter describes the major features of the proprietorship, partnership, and corporation.

KEY QUESTIONS

1. What are the main advantages and disadvantages of each form of ownership?

2. What is a limited partnership?

3. How may partnership profits and losses be shared?

4. How are corporations organized?

5. Who controls the corporation?

Table 3-1 Forms of Business Ownership in the United States

	Proprietorships	Partnerships	Corporations	Total
Number of Firms	9,400,000	936,000	1,665,000	12,001,000
Percent of Total Firms	78%	8%	14%	100%
Percent Volume of Sales	11%	5%	84%	100%

Source: *Statistical Abstract of the United States,* 1973.

Table 3-1 compares the three major types of ownership in terms of number of firms and combined sales. What is the most important form of business ownership?

THE PROPRIETORSHIP

The proprietorship, sometimes called the *single* or *sole proprietorship,* is a firm owned and controlled by one individual who receives all the profit and takes all of the risks. It is by far the most popular type of organization in the United States, accounting for over three-quarters of all firms. Proprietorships are particularly common in the fields of retailing and personal services. Most neighborhood stores and shops are solely owned. In addition, nearly three million farms are operated as proprietorships.

Advantages of the Proprietorship

The popularity of the proprietorship stems from its three key advantages: (1) ease of formation; (2) freedom and speed of action; and (3) maximum incentive.

Ease of Formation   Recently, a college student living in a rural community was unable to find a summer job. He decided to go into business for himself, operating a roadside stand selling fresh fruit and vegetables. He acquired permission from a farmer to set up a stand next to a highway, painted some advertising signs, and purchased a supply of fresh produce. He was in business! By the end of the summer the student had earned a profit of $1,800.

The proprietor needs no state charter. Since there is little or no red tape, organizational expenses are low. He may have to spend a few dollars for a business license, but that is about it in terms of legal formalities.

Freedom and Speed of Action   Since the proprietor is his own boss, he need not be concerned about consulting with stockholders or partners. As a result, he can make rapid decisions and can thus

make the most of opportunities. For example, the owner of a grocery store can take advantage of a special price on several crates of
peaches offered by a farmer who is anxious to make an immediate
sale. The single proprietorship enjoys flexibility usually unmatched
by the partnership and corporation.

Maximum Incentive Why do many proprietors work ten to four-
teen hours a day, six or seven days a week? For one reason, they
directly reap the benefits of their efforts. The store owner who
stays open in the evening for the convenience of his customers recognizes that the additional income he earns need not be shared
with others. There is also the personal satisfaction involved in
working for yourself. If the business is a success, the proprietor can
take all the credit.

Disadvantages of the Proprietorship

Partly offsetting the advantages of proprietorship are four disadvantages: (1) unlimited liability; (2) limited life; (3) limited funds for expansion; and (4) lack of specialized management.

Unlimited Liability Perhaps the major disadvantage of the single
proprietorship is that the owner is liable to an unlimited extent for
the debts of his business. If the firm fails, its creditors can claim
not only the business assets of the proprietorship but the personal
assets of the owner as well. Suppose, for example, Todd's Shoes, a
retail store, goes bankrupt with $2,000 in assets and $8,000 in liabilities (or debts). If Mr. Todd has a personal savings account, his creditors may lay claim to it to cover the $6,000 in unpaid debts. Thus
the unlimited liability feature of the proprietorship makes the
owner highly vulnerable in case of poor business decisions or plain
bad luck.

Limited Life In the eyes of the law, the proprietorship and its
owner are considered one and the same. Therefore, if the proprietor
dies, is imprisoned, or is otherwise incapacitated, this terminates the
proprietorship. If the proprietor's heirs attempt to operate the business after his death, legally a new firm has been created.

Limited Funds for Expansion It is difficult for a proprietor to raise
money to expand his business. Normally, he is limited to his savings and what he can borrow. Although a proprietorship may have
a good credit rating (due to the unlimited liability of the owner),
banks and other financial institutions are hesitant to extend long-
term loans for expansion due to the firm's limited life. After all, the
proprietorship is truly a one-man business, and if the owner dies, so

does the firm. This is one reason that few proprietorships ever grow into large companies.

Lack of Specialized Management As the sole owner and manager, the proprietor is required to be skilled in a variety of management jobs. For example, the owner of Todd's Shoes must be his own purchasing agent, advertising manager, financial manager, sales manager and so on. It is very unlikely that he will be expert at all these jobs. Nor is it easy for a proprietor to hire good management assistance. Ambitious and talented employees may prefer to seek jobs with a partnership or corporation, where the opportunities for advancement are greater.

THE PARTNERSHIP

In terms of both volume of sales and number of firms the partnership is the least popular form of business ownership. While it is true that the partnership possesses some significant weaknesses, in some circumstances it is the best choice for a firm.

A partnership may be defined as an association of two or more persons as co-owners of a business. There is no limit on the number of partners, although nearly three-quarters of all partnerships have only two owners. Partnerships are common in personal service industries such as law, medicine, real estate, and insurance as well as in retailing.

Advantages of the Partnership

In comparison to the proprietorship, the partnership enjoys three significant advantages: (1) more funds for expansion; (2) improved credit rating; and (3) increased specialization of management.

More Funds for Expansion It is not unusual for a proprietorship to convert to a partnership in order to raise needed funds. A business firm may be highly successful and still run short of finances. One way to overcome this problem is by inviting an investor to become a partner in the firm. Of course, the existing owner must give up a share of his ownership, but this may be offset by greater profits through expansion of the business.

Improved Credit Rating As a rule, the partnership enjoys the best credit rating of the three forms of business ownership. This is because each general partner has unlimited liability for the debts of the business. Suppliers are much more willing to provide credit when two or more owners are liable to an unlimited extent.

Increased Specialization of Management   A law firm in a large
western city has five partners, each of whom is a specialist in a different area of the law—contracts, taxes, personal liability, criminal
and corporate law. Through the advantages of specialization, the
firm can offer its clients a wider range of expert assistance than
any single attorney. In operating a retail store, two partners may divide responsibilities according to their interests or talents. For example, one owner may handle sales and advertising while the other
takes charge of purchasing, accounting, and finance. The partners
will consult on general management decisions, in the hope that two
heads are better than one.

Disadvantages of the Partnership

Why are partnerships relatively unpopular? There are four main
reasons: (1) unlimited liability; (2) divided authority; (3) limited life;
and (4) frozen investment.

Unlimited Liability   All general partners are liable to an unlimited
extent for the debts of the partnership. Suppose, for example, that
a firm with three owners fails after going deeply into debt. If two
of the partners have no personal assets, the firm's creditors can collect all debts from the third partner. The partnership is a highly
risky form of ownership, particularly for a partner with substantial
personal wealth.

Divided Authority   It is often said that choosing a good partner is
more difficult than choosing a wife. Each partner is held responsible for the decisions of all partners. A poor decision by one owner
is binding on the firm. With authority spread among two or more
owners, it is easy for disputes to arise, and unresolved disputes may
lead to termination of the business. Moreover, a dishonest or stupid
partner can not only destroy a business, he can financially ruin the
co-owners as well.

Limited Life   Under the law, the death, imprisonment, or incapac-
itation of any partner terminates the partnership. If the firm is reor-
ganized to include a new partner, legally a new firm has been
created. Can you imagine the problems this causes in a large partnership with dozens of partners?

Frozen Investment   It is often difficult for an owner to withdraw
from a partnership. If he wishes to sell his share of the business,
the buyer must meet with the approval of the other partners.

The Partnership Agreement

An agreement to form a partnership may be oral or written. A word to the wise: if you ever decide to enter a partnership, insist on a written agreement. This simple precaution may save you a great deal of disagreement, grief, and financial loss.

A partnership agreement simply states the rules under which the business will operate. It normally includes: (1) the name of the firm; (2) the amount invested by each partner; (3) how profits and losses are to be divided; (4) the duties and responsibilities of each partner; (5) the length of life of the partnership; (6) any provisions for payment of salaries or interest on investment; and (7) the method by which a partner may withdraw from the partnership.

The Limited Partnership

The unlimited liability feature of the general partnership often discourages investors from becoming co-owners. A limited partnership

Figure 3–1   An Advertisement for a Limited Partnership

may be used to overcome this disadvantage. This type of firm consists of at least one general partner with unlimited liability and any
number of limited partners whose liability is restricted to their investment in the business. However, limited partners may not take
an active role in the management of the firm. Most states require
that a limited partnership have a formal written agreement on file
with the county clerk. This requirement provides public notice to
creditors that some of the firm's partners have limited liability.

The limited partnership is frequently used to finance ventures
such as Broadway shows, oil-drilling expeditions, and real-estate
speculations where the risks are great, but the potential profits are
large.

Division of Profits and Losses in the Partnership

One of the first decisions that must be made by the partners in a
new firm is how profits and losses are to be shared. Any formula
should take into consideration the amount invested in the business
by each owner, the skill and experience of the partners, and the
time devoted to the business. If there is no agreement covering
profits and losses, they are shared equally.

The most common method of dividing profits and losses is according to the amount invested by each partner. Suppose, for example, that Partner A invests $8,000 and Partner B invests $12,000. If
the profit at the end of the first year is $10,000, it will be divided
in the following way:

Partner	Investment	% Invested	×	Profit	=	Share of Profit
A	$ 8,000	$\frac{8{,}000}{20{,}000} = 40\%$	×	$10,000	=	$ 4,000
B	12,000	$\frac{12{,}000}{20{,}000} = 60\%$	×	10,000	=	6,000
Totals	$20,000					$10,000

Another method of splitting profits takes into account the time
devoted to the business as well as each partner's investment.
Partner X invests $30,000 and Partner Y contributes $10,000. However, since Partner Y works twice as many hours as Partner X, the
partnership agreement provides that Y will be paid an annual salary (out of profits) of $6,000 while X will receive a salary of $3,000.
In addition, each partner will be paid interest at 10 percent on his
investment and any profits in excess of salary and interest will be
divided equally. During the first year of operation the firm earned
$25,000 in profit. What is each partner's share?

Partner	Salary	+	10% Interest on Investment	+	Equal Division	=	Share of Profits
X	$3,000	+	$3,000	+	$ 6,000	=	$12,000
Y	6,000	+	1,000	+	6,000	=	13,000
Totals	$9,000	+	$4,000	+	$12,000	=	$25,000

It should be clear from these examples that there are many methods for dividing profits and losses in a partnership.

THE CORPORATION

Now we turn to the most complicated, and in many ways the most important, form of ownership. Corporations account for over 80 percent of the business transacted in the United States despite the fact that they represent only about one-eighth of the total firms. Many corporations are as small as most proprietorships and partnerships, but the 500 largest corporations produce two-thirds of our nation's goods and services.

What is the corporation? The most famous definition was written in 1819 by Chief Justice John Marshall: "A corporation is an artificial being, invisible, intangible, and existing only in contemplation of the law." This definition means that the corporation is a legal entity (or legal person) created by the law and granted certain rights by the state. Since the corporation is considered a legal entity, it exists apart from its owners. In the eyes of the law, the proprietorship and proprietor are one in the same as are the partners and the partnership. But the corporation has an identity all its own; it can own property, make contracts, sue and be sued. None of these rights directly involves its owners.

A corporation is created by applying to a state government for a charter. This can be a fairly lengthy and expensive process that includes filing the articles of incorporation. This document provides detailed information about the incorporators, the purpose of the corporation, its by-laws (rules of governance), and the firm's financial structure. The company must conform to state requirements and pay certain fees before a charter is granted.

The Structure of the Corporation

The owners of a corporation are called stockholders. They elect a board of directors to protect the owners' interests and oversee the operation of the business. In many small corporations, the major stockholders are also directors. The board selects the major corporate officers who are responsible for the day-to-day operation of the firm. Often the president and other key officers are also directors.

ISSUE THE SOCIAL RESPONSIBILITY OF BUSINESS

Those who do not take responsibility for their power, ultimately shall lose it.
Keith Davis and Robert Blomstrom, *Business and Its Environment*

Up to a few years ago it was an easy task to define business responsibility. Nearly everyone agreed the role of business was to produce the goods and services society wanted as efficiently as possible. This point of view is best summed up by Milton Friedman, a widely respected conservative economist, who states: "In a (free) economy, there is one and only one social responsibility of business—to use its resources and engage in activities designed to increase profits so long as it stays within the rules of the game, which is to say, engages in open and free competition, without deception or fraud."

In the past decade, however, this doctrine has come under increasing attack both from within and without the business community. The critics insist that business must look beyond profits and give more consideration to those individuals and groups who are affected by the firm's actions—employees, owners, consumers, and community neighbors.

Ralph Nader and his supporters have taken the concept of business responsibility one step further. They believe business has an obligation to help achieve broad social goals such as curing urban ills, cleaning up the environment, hiring and training the hard-core unemployed, and fighting racial and sex discrimination. They claim that business has the power, money, and expertise to lead the fight against our nation's social problems.

Somewhat surprisingly, the banner of corporate responsibility is gaining followers from a growing number of corporation managers. Hundreds of firms are voluntarily spending millions of dollars on programs ranging from pollution control to community development. However, these programs are not popular with everyone. Some observers believe the new emphasis on "good deeds" will reduce incentive to innovate and cut costs thus turning managers into bureaucrats. They argue that by devoting resources to social programs business's major contribution—increasing productivity—will be undermined.

In 1971, a team led by Nader issued a report criticizing the giant chemical company E. I. DuPont de Nemours for not making an adequate commitment to social welfare programs. DuPont pointed out that the average price of its products had declined 24 percent since 1960, thereby creating a "social dividend" for its customers. Did DuPont behave in a socially responsible manner?

Critics of business social activism point out that many of the corporations most actively engaged in social programs exercise significant monopoly power in the market place. Milton Friedman goes so far as to state that "no businessman has money to spend on social responsibility unless he has monopoly power. Any businessman engaged in social responsibility ought to be immediately slapped with an antitrust suit."

Whatever the appropriate social responsibility of business may be, the fact remains that the trend toward broader responsibilities is more than a passing fad. Every sign points toward business assuming a more active role in social programs. Before deciding whether this trend is desirable or not, ask yourself: What will you gain and lose from the expanded social responsibility of business?

References

Milton Friedman, "The Social Responsibility of Business Is to Increase Its Profits," *The New York Times Magazine,* September 13, 1970, pp. 32–33.

Charles E. Gilliland, Jr., ed., *Readings In Business Responsibility* (Braintree, Mass.: D. M. Mark Publishing Co., 1969).

Joseph W. McGuire, "The Future Social Role of Business Organization," *Review of Social Economy,* 28 (March, 1970): 9–14.

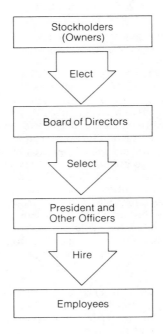

Figure 3–2 Corporate Structure

Advantages of the Corporation

As you might suspect, the corporate form of organization offers owners several significant advantages over both the proprietorship and partnership. These include: (1) limited liability; (2) ease of transferring ownership; (3) continuous life; (4) ease of raising funds for expansion; and (5) specialized management.

Limited Liability The key advantage of the corporation is that stockholders are limited in liability to the extent of their investment. In other words, their personal wealth is safe from the claims of creditors if the corporation fails. The limited liability feature stems from the fact that a corporation is considered a legal entity, separate from its owners.

Ease of Transferring Ownership Stockholders of a corporation can transfer their ownership simply by selling their shares of stock. The stock of large corporations is usually traded on organized stock exchanges, where millions of shares are bought and sold daily. Neither the other stockholders nor the corporation itself can prevent an owner from disposing of his shares.

Continuous Life The corporation, like Superman, is immortal. The death, insanity, or imprisonment of a stockholder, director, or officer does not terminate the corporation.

Ease of Raising Funds for Expansion Almost without exception, the giant business firms in the United States are corporations. This popularity is derived from the ability of corporations to raise money for expansion by selling corporate securities (stocks and bonds) to the public. Investors find stock attractive because of the corporation's limited liability and continuous life as well as the ease of transferring ownership.

Specialized Management Large corporations are divided into departments or divisions, each of which is headed by a manager. These professional managers are often experts in a particular area of business—for example, production, marketing, finance, or purchasing. Management by specialists can lead to improved decision-making and greater efficiency.

Disadvantages of the Corporation

The drawbacks of the corporate form of organization are fourfold: (1) double taxation; (2) expense and difficulty of organization; (3) employee apathy; and (4) government regulation.

Double Taxation In Chapter 2 we pointed out that the profits earned by corporations are subject to taxation by the federal government. Moreover, any dividends (distribution of profits) are taxed as personal income to stockholders under the individual income tax.[1] It should be noted that neither the profits of the proprietorship nor the partnership are subject to special taxes. Instead, profits are considered income earned by the proprietor or partner and are subject only to the individual income tax.

The special tax on corporate profits is a result of its legal status. Since the corporation is considered a legal entity, its earnings are taxable, and dividends paid from after-tax profits are also subject to taxation as income to stockholders.

Expense and Difficulty of Organization The process of applying for and receiving a corporate charter from the state may require several months and cost hundreds or even thousands of dollars. Normally the assistance of a corporate attorney is required to com-

---

[1]Under current tax law, the first $100 in dividends is tax-free.

plete the articles of incorporation. In addition, there are incorporation fees to be paid to the state.

Employee Apathy A few years ago, a large corporation experienced a major increase in employee theft. Several employees were caught pilfering and were questioned about their motives. In nearly every case, the same response was given: "I wasn't hurting anyone."

This incident illustrates a key problem faced by many giant corporations. Employees may come to feel they are working for a huge impersonal machine with no concern for their welfare. In the corporation, there is no owner–manager to personify the firm. Employees rarely see top management, and they wouldn't know a stockholder if they bumped into one.

Government Regulation To a far greater extent than the proprietorship or partnership, the corporation is the target of regulation by state and federal government. Corporations must register in all states where they conduct business. The Securities and Exchange Commission requires detailed financial reports from large corporations. Indeed, the variety and number of reports required by various governmental agencies can represent a major expense of doing business.

Who Controls the Corporation?

In theory at least, the corporation is the most democratic of institutions. It would appear that stockholders can exercise substantial control over the firm's activities by electing directors. This is true in many small and medium-size corporations. However, in the case of most giant corporations, with hundreds of thousands of stockholders, the owners have little influence over how the firm is run. If a stockholder is disappointed with the performance of the company or its management, he is much more likely to sell his shares than to engage in an expensive fight to replace the directors.

Does this mean that control of the corporation is in the hands of the board of directors? After all, the directors have the right to declare dividends, select the corporate officers, and approve or reject major management decisions. In fact, the boards of directors of many large corporations serve as little more than rubber stamps for recommendations presented by the president and other top executives. Increasingly, the control of giant corporations is passing into the hands of professional managers many of whom may not even own a share of stock.

The separation of ownership and control in today's huge corporations raises a puzzling question: For whose benefit should the corporations be run? The stockholders? The management? The employees? The consumer? Society as a whole? Or all of these?

SUMMARY

There are three major forms of business ownership: the proprietorship, the partnership, and the corporation. Each has both advantages and disadvantages that must be carefully weighed in deciding which type to choose for a particular business firm.

The proprietorship is a one-owner business. It is easy to start, permits rapid decision making, and provides maximum incentive for the proprietor. The disadvantages include unlimited liability of the proprietor, limited life, the difficulty of raising funds, and the lack of specialized management. Despite these limitations, the proprietorship is by far the most popular form of ownership with over 9 million currently operating in the United States.

A partnership is a business jointly owned by two or more partners. It normally enjoys greater access to financing and more specialization of management than the proprietorship. The partnership's disadvantages are the unlimited liability of all general partners, limited life, and divided authority.

Although the partnership agreement may be written or oral, it is strongly recommended that a written document be executed to avoid misunderstandings.

The limited partnership may be used to overcome the unlimited liability feature of the general partnership. In this form of ownership there must be at least one general partner with unlimited liability, and any number of limited partners whose liability is limited to their investment.

The sharing of profits and losses among partners is often based on the amount invested in the business, the skill and experience of the partners, and the amount of time each owner devotes to the business.

The corporation is a legal entity created by the law and existing apart from its owners. Corporations account for over four-fifths of all business transacted in the United States. The stockholders (owners) of the corporation elect a board of directors which in turn selects corporation officers to run the firm. Stockholders enjoy limited liability as well as relative ease in transferring ownership. The corporation has an unlimited life and funds may be raised by selling corporate securities to the public. Moreover, there are ample opportunities for specialization of management in large corporations. Disadvantages of the corporation include double taxation, the expense and time required to obtain a charter, employee apathy, and extensive government regulation.

The control of many corporations is largely in the hands of professional managers with relatively little influence exerted by either stockholders or directors. This situation is often referred to as *separation of ownership and control*.

ISSUE A GLIMPSE INTO THE FUTURE: IS THE CORPORATION DOOMED?

Americans are fascinated by the future. The accelerated pace of change in our society has given prominence to a new profession—the futurists. These crystal-ball gazers try to decipher what the future holds for us. Unlike traditional business forecasters who are primarily concerned with relatively short-run predictions of economic changes, the futurists aim at revealing the future course of society as a whole.

One of the most respected futurists is Harvard sociologist Daniel Bell. In a recent book entitled *The Coming of Post-Industrial Society,* Professor Bell maintains that major social, economic, and technological forces are at work which will massively reshape United States society by the year 2000. Among Bell's major predictions are:

1. The United States has already changed from a manufacturing economy to a service economy as growing numbers of workers are employed in government, finance, communications and education. This trend will continue, and by the end of the century only a small fraction of the work force will be employed in factories.

2. The United States is rapidly becoming a knowledge society. Bell predicts that by the year 2000, the basis for power and status will be knowledge, not property or wealth. Industries that depend on scientific knowledge such as chemicals, optics, electronics and computers will be leaders in the coming decades, while "nineteenth-century industries" (for example, steel, automobiles, and electricity) will decline in importance.

3. As scientific knowledge increasingly becomes the basis for economic expansion and innovation, the research-based university will replace the corporation as the principal economic institution in our society. Bell believes that major influence will shift away from entrepreneurs and managers to scientists, engineers, and economists.

4. Finally, Bell sees increasing government control over the economy through central planning. Corporations will give up much of their freedom of choice, and the free-enterprise system will play a declining role in allocating resources.

Will the future bring a paradise on earth? Bell doesn't think so. He foresees increased conflict and tension resulting from centralization of economic and political power and the inevitable growth of bureaucracy.

How do Bell's predictions affect your career planning?

Reference
Daniel Bell, *The Coming of Post-Industrial Society* (New York: Basic Books, 1973).

Student _____

STUDENT FEEDBACK SYSTEM

Directions: Your questions and ideas are important! Here's a chance to get more information and relate your experiences to the materials in the chapter. Answer the following questions and turn in this page to the instructor. Use the reverse side of the page if you need additional space.

1. What topics, problems, and terms found in this chapter require more explanation by the instructor?

2. Do the concepts presented in this chapter agree with your experiences in the business world? Briefly explain why or why not, using examples.

3. Does this chapter suggest any career opportunities to you?

Student _____

REVIEWING MAJOR CONCEPTS

1. Explain what is meant by "double taxation" of corporate profits.

2. Suppose there are three firms of about equal size and financial condition—a proprietorship, a partnership, and a corporation. Which one would
   probably have the best credit rating? Why?

3. Why is the partnership a relatively unpopular form of business ownership?

4. How does a limited partnership differ from a general partnership?

5. Can you think of any ways that a corporation might overcome worker apathy?

6. Why are most business firms proprietorships?

7. Who controls General Motors? For whose benefit is the firm being operated?

Student _____

SOLVING PROBLEMS AND CASES

1. On January 1, 1975, Ms. Hope, Mr. Carp, and Mr. Snider formed a partnership. Ms. Hope invested $21,000, Mr. Carp, $9,000, and Mr. Snider, $6,000. Profits for the first year were $48,000.

   a. If the partnership agreement did not mention how profits were to be divided, how much would each partner receive?

   b. Suppose the partners had agreed to divide profits according to the amount invested by each. How much would each partner receive?

   c. If the partners had agreed to pay a salary of $12,000 to Mr. Snider only, plus interest of 8 percent on the amount invested by each partner, and split any remainder equally, how much would each receive?

2. Assume you are planning to open a sporting-goods store located in the city where you live. You have estimated that a minimum investment of $15,000 will be required. Based on your own financial resources and business experience, what form of ownership would you choose? Outline the reasons for your choice and explain why you rejected the other alternatives.

Student _____

3. Place a check ($\checkmark$) in the appropriate column to indicate whether each of the twelve statements most likely refers to the proprietorship, partnership, or corporation.

	Type of Ownership		
	Proprietorship	Partnership	Corporation
1. The single owner has un-limited liability.			
2. The firm has unlimited life.			
3. Each owner is responsible for the acts of other owners.			
4. Profits of the firm may be taxed twice.			
5. Firm has no existence apart from its single owner.			
6. Every owner has limited liability.			
7. The firm is a legal entity.			
8. The death of any owner brings an end to the firm.			
9. Firm may sell stock to the public.			
10. All decisions can be made without consulting others.			
11. Firm requires written permission of the state to exist.			
12. Divided authority is a common problem.			

Chapter 4

Management and Organization

The preceding chapter was devoted to external forms of organization—the proprietorship, partnership and corporation. Now we turn our attention to the internal management and organization of the business firm.

Any institution—a church, a college, an army, or a business—must be organized and managed if it is to survive. Here we are primarily concerned with business firms, but the principles of management and organization described in this chapter are applicable to most other institutions as well.

KEY QUESTIONS

1. What is management and why is it important?

2. Exactly what do managers do?

3. Are there any principles to serve as guidelines for the development of effective management and organization?

4. What are the three major types of internal organization?

5. Are committees a waste of time?

WHAT IS MANAGEMENT?

A cynic once defined management as the art of getting other people to do your work. There may be an element of truth in this statement, but it would be more accurate to describe management as the process of accomplishing tasks by working through others.

Suppose that ten students work for a college bookstore. One Friday afternoon they are told to restock the bookshelves, unload a shipment of supplies, and clean the floor. If each student decides to do his own thing, the result will be mass confusion. On the other hand, if one student is selected to serve as manager, he can organize the others into groups, divide up the work, and develop teamwork. Through management and organization, the jobs are done faster and better, and no one will miss his Friday night date.

We noted in Chapter 1 that the factors of production—land, labor, capital, and the entrepreneur—are the economic resources used to produce goods and services. The job of the business manager is similar to that of the entrepreneur: to combine land, labor, and capital in the most efficient manner in order to produce maximum output at the lowest cost. In this sense, we may define management as the skillful combining of men, materials, and machines to accomplish organizational objectives.

Still another dimension of management is decision making. The manager's job involves deciding what to do, how and when it should be done, and by whom. One chief executive put it this way: "My job is to make decisions. If I make more good ones than bad ones, the company is likely to earn money. But if I make too many poor decisions, the company suffers and I'll be looking for another job."

The Importance of Management

Without doubt the single most important determinant of the success of a firm is the quality of its management. You want proof? Take a look at Figure 4-1. This chart indicates that nine out of every ten business failures are the result of inexperienced or ineffective management.

As a firm expands in size, the problems of management become increasingly complex. For example, when a firm grows from 10 to 50 employees, the difficulty of maintaining effective management and control may increase *more* than fivefold. The problems of preserving good communications—getting the right word to the right people at the right time—are complicated by increasing size. One executive summed up the problem of size in these words: "Large-scale management is in a battle to the death with complexity. The contestants are joined, and the outcome is still uncertain."

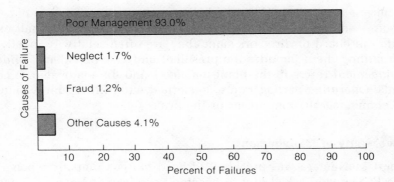

Figure 4-1 Why Business Firms Fail
Source: Dun & Bradstreet, Inc.

Some companies have grown beyond the ability of their managers to control them. The result has often been bankruptcy. In giant corporations with tens of thousands of employees, good management is essential to avoid chaos.

Levels of Management

A large firm may employ hundreds or even thousands of managers operating at different levels within the organization. It is convenient to classify management into three categories: top, middle, and operating management. Figure 4-2 shows a simplified organization chart for a corporation illustrating the three levels of management.

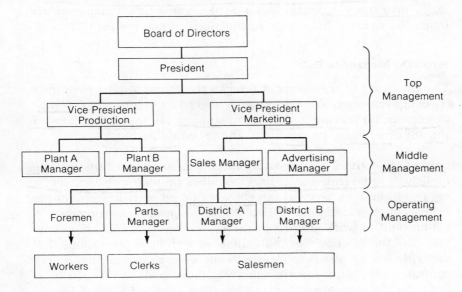

Figure 4-2 Top, Middle, and Operating Management

There is some dispute as to whether a corporation's board of directors should be considered a part of management. We shall exclude the board of directors since they are often relatively inactive. *Top management* includes the president and vice-presidents. *Middle management* refers to the plant managers and the major department heads. *Operating managers* are concerned with direct supervision of the nonmanagerial employees of the firm.

Universality of Management

Robert McNamara was president of Ford Motor Company when John F. Kennedy asked him to become Secretary of Defense. Later McNamara became president of the World Bank. Dwight D. Eisenhower served as head of the Allied Armed Forces in Europe during World War II. After his retirement from the army, he became president of Columbia University. Later he assumed another position of leadership.

There are endless examples of managers who have moved to new jobs in totally different institutions and enjoyed a high degree of success. Indeed, it has been estimated that half of all managers will switch jobs in the next decade. What accounts for the mobility of management? The explanation is that managers, particularly at the upper levels, perform essentially the same functions no matter what type of organization they work for. Therefore, if a man is a good manager in one firm, he will usually do an equally good job with another firm.

The term *universality of management* means that management skills have transferability. The jobs performed by all managers are much the same. What are these functions of management?

What Do Managers Do?

The functions of management refer to the essential jobs performed by every manager. We may identify eight key functions: (1) setting objectives; (2) making policies; (3) planning; (4) organizing; (5) staffing; (6) directing; (7) controlling; and (8) coordinating.

Setting Objectives The most important management function is establishing organizational goals. Objectives provide direction for the organization; they serve as targets to guide all activities within the firm. Without clearly stated objectives, the people in an organization tend to work at cross-purposes; the result is confusion, conflict, and inefficiency. For individuals as well as organizations the first rule for success is to clearly define your goals and then to concentrate every effort toward achieving these goals.

At the top management level objectives tend to be broad in

scope. Robert Townsend, in his book *Up the Organization,* describes how it took Avis Rent-A-Car six months to define its single objective: "We want to become the fastest-growing company with the highest profit margins in the business of renting and leasing vehicles without drivers."[1]

At the lower levels of management, objectives may be more specific. For example, the sales department of a television manufacturer might establish a goal of increasing sales by ten percent within twelve months. At the foreman level, a typical objective might be to reduce worker accidents by one-half in the next month.

The importance of organizational objectives is underlined by Marshall E. Dimock, a long-time student of management:

The first step . . . is the clear determination of objectives, for you cannot make valid detailed plans for either your program or your strategy until you know where you are going. The determination of objectives influences policy, organization, personnel, leadership, and control. Fixing your objectives is like identifying the North Star—you sight your compass on it and then use it as the means of getting back on track when you tend to stray.[2]

Making Policies   A policy is a general rule that guides an organization in achieving its objectives. It goes without saying that policies must be consistent with objectives. Suppose a store has a goal of treating all customers fairly and equally. It might then develop a policy stating that no special price discounts will be offered to any single customer that is not available to all customers.

There can always be too much of a good thing. Some organizations attempt to develop policies to cover nearly every conceivable situation. In other words, they attempt to prepackage all decisions. This practice can kill initiative and stifle incentive. To sum up, policies should be simple, easy to understand, and limited in number.

Planning   The purpose of planning is to define courses of action to achieve objectives. It involves determining *what* should be done, *how* it should be done, *when,* and *by whom.* Objectives provide the framework for all planning.

A simplified example can be used to illustrate the planning process. The XYZ Company has set a goal of doubling production in the next three years. Deciding what should be done to achieve this goal involves examining alternative courses of action—adding to the ex-

[1]Robert Townsend, *Up the Organization* (Greenwich, Conn.: Fawcett Crest, 1970), p. 111.

[2]Marshall E. Dimock, *The Executive in Action* (New York: Harper and Brothers, 1945), p. 54.

isting plant, building a second plant, or perhaps subcontracting work to other firms. After carefully comparing the advantages and disadvantages of each alternative, management may choose the alternative of building another plant.

The "how" part of the plan involves a host of interrelated decisions. How shall the new plant be financed? Where will it be located? What is the best plant layout and design? What steps should be taken to hire and train additional production workers? Planning also requires the development of a detailed timetable to avoid confusion and delay. Each segment of the plan must be carefully scheduled to ensure the smooth execution of the plan. For example, it would be foolish to postpone financing until the last minute, since the lack of funds could delay construction.

Usually one manager is put in charge of executing the plan. This executive is provided with the necessary authority and resources to carry out the plan, and he is held accountable for its success or failure.

Effective planning is a challenging and often frustrating task. Managers engaged in planning should remind themselves of Murphy's Laws:

1. Nothing is as simple as it looks.
2. Everything takes longer than it should.
3. If anything can go wrong it will.

Organizing   Organizing involves arranging men, machines, materials, and work to best carry out plans and achieve objectives. Organization provides the means for translating plans into actions.

As a business firm grows, the need for organization increases. The process of organizing involves identifying those activities to be undertaken, dividing the firm into segments (departments or divisions), and assigning specific activities.

Figure 4–2 shows a firm with two major departments; one is responsible for producing goods and the other for selling them. Each department is further divided into segments, each of which is responsible for specific activities.

Staffing   This management function involves recruiting, hiring, and training the right people to carry out plans. An IBM executive put it this way: "The point is that it's not enough to recruit good men. You must know what needs to be accomplished—your objectives and plans—and make your recruitment decisions in these terms." We shall explore the staffing function in more detail in Chapter 8.

Directing   Managers must supervise the actions of others to accomplish objectives. All institutions consist of human beings, and directing is the management of people. It is the manager's responsibility to ensure that employees are carrying out their assignments in accordance with plans and objectives. The effectiveness of a manager is often measured in terms of how well he works with people.

Controlling The controlling function includes all steps required to ensure that the activities of a firm are conforming to plans. The control process answers the question: How well are we doing? It also involves correcting or modifying activities that do not conform to plans.

Most business firms establish control systems that measure actual performance against established standards and provide information feedback to management. An example is a cost-accounting system. Suppose that plans call for a product to be manufactured at a cost of $1.10, but actual cost per unit is $1.25. Using this information management can attempt to correct the production process, or failing this, adjust the standard cost upward.

Coordinating Coordination means teamwork. No organization can operate efficiently without teamwork. It is the manager's job to ensure that individuals and departments work together toward common goals.

Figure 4–3 summarizes the functions of management. Objectives serve as the starting point for all activities within the firm. Policies are rules that guide behavior. Plans define courses of action to achieve objectives, while organization involves arranging resources and work to carry out plans. Management must hire the right personnel, provide direction and control, and develop teamwork within the organization.

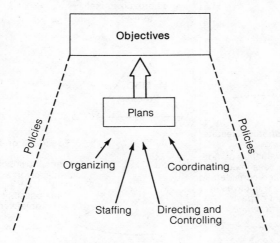

Figure 4–3 The Functions of Management

Management by Objectives (MBO)

We have already described the key role of objectives in guiding the activities of managers and employees in an organization. A growing number of business firms have adopted a formal process for establishing organizational objectives and evaluating performance in terms of these objectives. This process, known as *management by objectives* or *MBO,* is based on the belief that clearly defined objectives are essential for effective group effort.

MBO has been described as a process whereby the members of an organization jointly set objectives that serve as targets for managing the organization. The distinguishing feature of MBO is the emphasis on results. Success is measured in terms of achieving objectives.

How does management by objectives work? Figure 4–4 illustrates the major steps in the process. The first step is establishing specific objectives at every level in the organization. This step requires extensive discussions between managers and their subordinates to develop agreed-upon goals. The emphasis is on participation in goal setting, since the MBO process aims at merging individual goals with those of the organization.

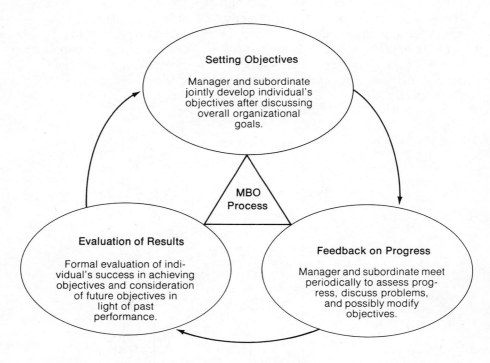

Figure 4–4   The Management-by-Objectives Process

ISSUE PERSPECTIVES ON MANAGEMENT

The following selections are intended to help you capture the flavor of management—to better understand what management is and what managers do.

Management is the marshalling of manpower, resources, and strategy to get a job done.

Marshall E. Dimock, *The Executive in Action* (Harper, 1945).

To make the cooperative efforts of men work and prosper is the task of management. Someone has to have the vision to conceive the need for an enterprise, the skill to mobilize the means of production, the determination to control the enterprise, the leadership to guide people toward objectives, and the financial genius to meet the bills when due. That someone is called a manager. The quality of management spells the difference between success or failure for a business enterprise or for a society.

Robert T. Hof, "Contemporary American Management," *Business Perspectives* (Winter, 1967).

And Moses chose able men out of all Israel and made them heads over the people, rulers of thousands, rulers of hundreds, rulers of fifties, and rulers of tens. And they judged the people of all seasons: the hard cases they brought unto Moses, but every small matter they judged themselves.

Exodus 18:25–26

Success and failure for corporations also stem directly from the qualities of their leaders: Management techniques are obviously essential, but what matters is leadership.

Antony Jay, *Management and Machiavelli* (New York: Holt, 1967).

The best managers think of themselves as playing coaches. They should be the first on the field in the morning and the last to leave at night. . . . A good manager is a blocking back whenever and wherever needed. No job is too menial for him if it helps one of his players advance toward his objective. . . . In business, he identifies company objectives and gets his players to see them as their objectives.

Robert Townsend, *Up the Organization* (Greenwich: Fawcett Crest, 1970).

If there is one secret, above all, of American achievements in productivity, then it is to be found in the attitude of American management. American management engenders an aggressiveness which believes that methodical planning, energetic training, and enthusiastic work can solve any problem.

Opinion of a group of British businessmen after visiting the United States, as quoted by Robert T. Hof, "Contemporary American Management," *Business Perspectives* (Winter, 1967).

Objectives should be qualified for better measurement. For example, a production manager may set a goal of reducing unit production costs by five percent in the next twelve months. Specific objectives serve as the basis for developing plans and strategies aimed at achieving objectives.

An effective MBO program should provide a feedback system to keep each individual posted on his progress in meeting his goals. Many firms schedule regular meetings between managers and subordinates to review progress, solve problems, and assist in planning. At the end of the performance period, a final evaluation is made to measure the extent to which objectives were met. This evaluation serves as a means of recognizing achievement and considering future objectives for the next performance period.

MBO is not a guarantee of success. However, many firms have found that management by objectives is an effective tool for improving planning and control, for increasing effective communications, and for generating enthusiasm and creativity.

PRINCIPLES OF MANAGEMENT

Over the years certain rules of good organization and management have been developed. These principles have evolved through the experiences of thousands of managers in many diverse types of institutions. They provide a set of guidelines for effective management.

Unity of Command

No employee in an organization should report to more than one boss. The unity of command principle is intended to avoid confusion as to which manager is in charge. Without unity of command, there will be conflicting orders, low employee morale, and chaos.

Authority and Responsibility

Authority is the right to make decisions and the power to direct others. The extent of each manager's authority must be clearly defined in order to avoid conflict within the organization.

Responsibility involves being held accountable for accomplishing certain tasks. Everyone in an organization, from the president to the janitor, has certain responsibilities. Each person is answerable to someone in authority for carrying out his responsibilities. It is important that each individual fully understand these responsibilities. For this reason, many firms follow the practice of listing responsibilities and duties in writing.

It is obvious that authority and responsibility are closely related.

It would be foolish to make a manager responsible for a certain activity and give him no authority. The guiding principle is: *Enough authority must be delegated to carry out responsibilities assigned.* In other words, you can't hold a man accountable for activities unless you give him adequate power to control them.

Delegation of Authority

All authority is originally vested in the owner(s) of the firm. Authority is delegated to the president and other managers. Delegation of authority relieves managers of unnecessary work. For example, the president of a large corporation should not spend his time supervising machine operators. Many firms follow the policy of having decisions made at the lowest possible level of management. In other words, the manager closest to the problem deals with it. This policy reduces the work load of top managers and encourages initiative at the middle and operating management levels.

Span of Control

The number of persons reporting to one manager is called the *span of control*. A broad span of control can raise employee morale and improve communications by reducing the number of levels of management. But a broad span of control may also overburden managers and limit the time they have to spend with each subordinate. Figure 4–5 compares two alternative organizations. Company A has a broad span of control while Company B has a limited one. Each firm employs 288 workers. Company A has only two levels of management while Company B uses four levels. Which organizational pattern is better? There is no right answer to this question. It depends on the type of work being done, the skill of the managers, and the need for supervision.

There is general agreement that the span of control should be narrower at the top management level than for operating managers. This is because activities become diverse and problems more complex at the upper levels of an organization. The "rule of seven" states that no more than seven subordinates should report to one man at the top management level. Of course, this is only a rule of thumb. Some firms use a rule of three; others, a rule of eight.

Organizational Stability

Business firms should have the ability to adjust quickly to the loss of key managers. In these days of executive "job-hopping" any organization can expect to lose personnel. A danger to guard against is the "one-man department" headed by an executive who refuses

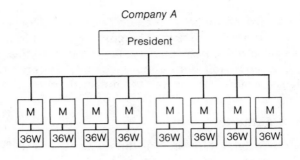

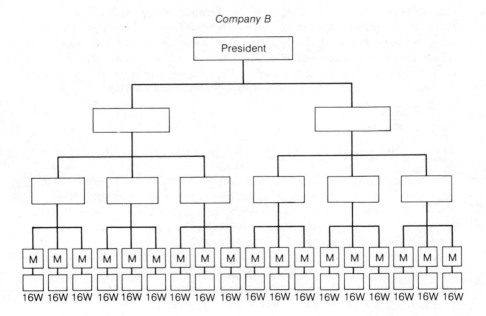

Figure 4-5 Spans of Control in Two Firms

to delegate authority. If he resigns or is incapacitated there will be no one with the experience or knowledge to take his place.

Some corporations establish programs designed to groom junior managers to take over key jobs. Such programs are intended to prevent disruption of operations through the loss of managers.

Organizational Change

No organizational structure should be "carved in stone." In our society, change is the name of the game, and institutions that fail to adapt to change die. For this reason, management must continuously review and revise objectives and plans in terms of changing conditions. The organization of the firm should also be subjected to periodic review to determine if modification or revision is required. For example, one department might be better dissolved, and its functions taken over by another department.

TYPES OF INTERNAL ORGANIZATION

Every firm with more than one person requires some form of organization. In small firms, the organization may be informal. For example, say that Shirley Gomez opens a women's clothing shop with two employees, Marg Chin and Ann Hopkins. Before the first day of business, Shirley says, "Ann, you're in charge of coats and accessories. Marg, you take care of the dresses. Ann, when I'm here ask me any questions you have; when I'm busy, check with Marg." In a few short sentences an organization has been created complete with lines of authority and areas of responsibility.

In larger firms, more complex and formal organization is required. There are three major types of internal organization structures: (1) line; (2) functional; and (3) line and staff.

Line Organization

By far the simplest organization is the line type. There is a straight line flow of authority from the board of directors to the workers as shown in Figure 4-6.

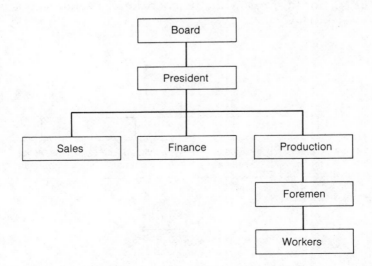

Figure 4-6 Line Organization

The line organization has several advantages. It is easy to understand, and everyone reports to a single supervisor, thereby preserving unity of command. It encourages speedy decisions because only one manager is in charge of each area. Also, "buck-passing" tends to be reduced since responsibility is clearly defined.

The line organization is not without weaknesses. The major disadvantage is that each manager is assumed to be skilled in the many different aspects of his job. For example, the sales manager in Figure 4-6 must make decisions in the areas of advertising, market research, supervision of the sales force, pricing, and so forth. It is unlikely that one person will have the time and knowledge to handle all of these activities effectively. The line organization may also make it difficult to coordinate different functional areas, such as sales, production, and finance, for example.

Although the line organization is widely used by small firms, it is rarely found in large corporations.

Functional or Staff Organization

In the late nineteenth-century, Frederick Taylor, an early student of management and organization, developed the functional or staff organization to overcome the problem of having too many duties for line managers. Each employee reports to several specialists, each of whom is an expert in one part of the worker's job. Taylor's plan is illustrated in Figure 4-7.

The overwhelming disadvantage of the functional organization is obvious: each worker has more than one boss. Unity of command is violated, thereby leading to divided authority, buck passing, and confusion. For this reason, the functional organization is practically never used today.

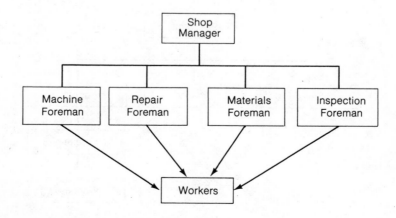

Figure 4-7 Functional Organization

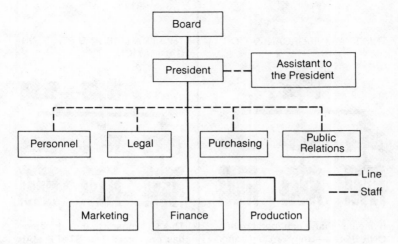

Figure 4–8 Line and ~~Staff~~ Organization
functional

Line-and-Staff Organization

Nearly all large corporations use some form of line-and-staff organization which combines the best features of the line and functional types. Line officers still retain the right to make decisions and issue orders. Staff specialists are available to provide assistance to line officers. Their jobs include solving special problems, interpreting technical information, assisting in planning, and generally supporting line executives. Staff specialists do *not* have line authority. Their function is to provide advice and make recommendations, *not* to give orders. Figure 4–8 shows a typical line-and-staff organization with five staff positions.

The obvious strength of the line-and-staff organization is that unity of command and clearly established responsibility and authority are preserved, while at the same time, expert assistance is available from the staff. This frees line executives from being bogged down in details. If the marketing manager in Figure 4–8 needs to hire five additional salesmen he can get help from the personnel department. If he is negotiating a contract with a customer, legal advice is available from the legal department.

The line-and-staff organization does tend to be expensive because of the added cost of staff specialists. Decision making may be somewhat slowed through the involvement of staff. Another serious problem is that staff officers are often tempted to assume line authority. This can undermine the effectiveness of the line executives and result in confusion and conflict. Figure 4–9 depict's the staff man's functions.

THIS IS A LINE ORGANIZATION.

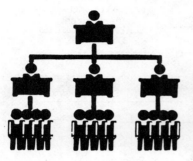

It means that each person has ONE BOSS—Unity of Command.

THIS IS A LINE AND STAFF OR-GANIZATION.

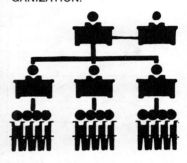

This still means that each person has one boss. The STAFF MAN helps the boss do a more effective job.

THE STAFF MAN investigates, plans, advises, SERVES.

A supervisor directs the work of others. He delegates portions of his authority to others. He needs help on problems involving policy interpretation, company plans, engineering changes, technical information, training, etc. Staff services — THE STAFF MAN — PROVIDE THIS HELP.

THE STAFF MAN doesn't give orders to line — doesn't perform line duties. HE SOLVES SPECIAL PROBLEMS.

Figure 4-9 Who the Staff Man Is and What He Does
Courtesy Exxon Corporation

ISSUE   THE END OF THE ORGANIZATION MAN?

*Be loyal to the company and the company will be loyal to you. After all, if you do
a good job for the organization, it is only good sense for the organization to be
good to you, because that will be the best for everyone.*
                                        William H. Whyte, Jr., *The Organization Man*

The literature of the 1950s and 1960s was filled with references to "the organization man", the individual who worked for a large and soulless corporation
or government agency and totally subordinated his own personal feelings and
desires to the goals of the organization. Corporate conformity was considered
the only road to success for the up and coming manager. However, the past
decade has witnessed a revolt against the conventional symbols of corporate
management, including unquestioning obedience, docile conformity, and the
gray flannel suit.
    This attack on the traditional codes of organizational behavior is hailed by
many as the beginning of a trend toward humanizing social and economic institutions. According to Roger M. D'Aprix, a specialist in employee relations for
Xerox Corporation and author of *Struggle for Identity: The Silent Revolution
Against Corporate Conformity,* "The Organization Man is dead, a victim of
changing values and eye-opening events. I doubt that anyone mourns his
passing."
    What will replace the organization man? Mr. D'Aprix hopes that more en-
lightened corporate managements will strive to create an environment where
employees can gain greater personal satisfaction from their work. Instead of
treating employees as inanimate objects, the successful business organization
will increasingly recognize that employees are individual human beings who
will work hard for goals they understand and accept. Any successful enterprise must provide something of value for its employees to believe in. Therefore, organizations must broaden traditional goals and place increasing emphasis on service to society as a whole. Moreover, there will be growing demands for employee participation in decision making even to the point of
shaping corporate goals and policies.
    Does the end of the organization man signal a better world to come? Per-
haps, but George Melloan of the *Wall Street Journal* raises a provocative
question: "Is it possible that the new demands are merely a cry for indulgence
that eventually will weaken corporate organizations and their ability to accomplish work—which is after all the function they are meant to serve in our economy?" What do *you* think?

References
Roger M. D'Aprix, *Struggle for Identity: The Silent Revolution Against Cor-
    porate Conformity* (New York: Dow Jones–Irwin, 1972), p. 106.

George Melloan, "An Obituary for the Organization Man," *Wall Street Journal,*
    September 7, 1972, p. 13.

William H. Whyte, Jr., *The Organization Man* (New York: Doubleday, 1957), p.
    143.

COMMITTEES

Institutions are rarely managed solely through committees, yet most large organizations make widespread use of a variety of committees. There are, of course, many different types of committees—temporary or permanent, advisory, decision making, or information gathering.

Most managers are either highly enthusiastic about committees or unalterably opposed to them. Opponents claim committees waste time and slow down the decision-making process. Managers who must devote hours to endless meetings do not have the time to carry out their assigned responsibilities. Moreover, committee decisions are, by necessity, compromises. As the saying goes, "A camel is a horse designed by a committee." Finally, it is impossible to pinpoint responsibility for committee decisions. How can you hold an entire group accountable?

On the other hand, proponents argue that committees provide an opportunity to solve complex problems by pooling information. If no one man possesses all the necessary knowledge to make an educated decision, it makes sense to call together a group of individuals and share information. In some cases, many heads are better than one.

It is also argued that committees lead to improved communications. Each member of a committee gains a better understanding of other people's problems and viewpoints. Widespread use of committees also results in broad participation in the decision-making process, which encourages understanding of, and enthusiastic support for, decisions. A man is more likely to support a decision when he has participated in making it.

Is the committee a useful management tool or just a time-waster? Perhaps we should form a committee to come up with an answer.

SUMMARY

Management may be described as the art of working through others to accomplish tasks. Poor management is the major reason for business failure. As firms grow in size they become increasingly complex. This makes effective management essential to avoid chaos.

All managers, regardless of the type of organization, perform eight major functions (or jobs): (1) setting objectives; (2) making policies; (3) planning; (4) organizing; (5) staffing; (6) directing; (7) controlling; and (8) coordinating.

Management by objectives (MBO) is a process used by many business firms to establish organizational objectives and evaluate results in terms of achieving these objectives.

weak

Several principles of management have evolved over the years: (1) no employee should report to more than one manager; (2) enough authority must be delegated to carry out responsibilities assigned; (3) decisions should be made at the lowest possible level of management; (4) too many people reporting to one manager can result in loss of control and overworked executives; (5) business firms should establish procedures to minimize disruption from the loss of key personnel; and (6) any organizational structure should be subject to review and revision.

There are three major types of internal organization. The line organization is simple, easy to understand, and preserves unity of command. However, it requires managers to be skilled in many different areas. The functional or staff organization provides for management by specialists, but it violates unity of command. The line-and-staff organization combines line officers with decision-making authority and staff specialists who give advice and assistance. Line-and-staff organization is common in large corporations.

Committees are useful for pooling information, improving communications, and encouraging widespread participation in decision making. However, committees have been criticized for wasting the time of managers and making "watered-down" decisions.

universal problems

no universal solutions

Student _____

STUDENT FEEDBACK SYSTEM

Directions: Your questions and ideas are important! Here's a chance to get more information and relate your experiences to the materials in the chapter. Answer the following questions and turn in this page to the instructor. Use the reverse side of the page if you need additional space.

1. What topics, problems, and terms found in this chapter require more explanation by the instructor?

2. Do the concepts presented in this chapter agree with your experiences in the business world? Briefly explain why or why not, using examples.

3. Does this chapter suggest any career opportunities to you?

Student _____

REVIEWING MAJOR CONCEPTS

1. How do you explain the fact that former corporation executives are often very successful in managing government agencies?

2. "Many heads are better than one. Therefore, all organizations should be managed through a system of committees." Do you agree or disagree? Explain your answer.

3. Describe two policies in effect at your college.

4. Complete the following table:

Organization	Major Advantage	Major Disadvantage
Line		
Functional		
Line-and-Staff		

5. On which *two* of the eight functions of management would the president of General Electric devote the most time? On which *two* would a production foreman spend the majority of his time?

Student _____

SOLVING PROBLEMS AND CASES

1. You have been hired as general manager and coach of the California Comets, a new professional football team. There are eight management functions listed below. Using your football team, give an example of each function. (*Hint:* What are the objectives of the California Comets?)

    a. Setting Objectives.

    b. Making Policies.

    c. Planning.

    d. Organizing.

    e. Staffing.

    f. Directing.

    g. Controlling.

    h. Coordinating.

2. *Case:* Winton Shoe Company

The production manager of the Winton Shoe Company has ordered several major design changes in the company's line of women's shoes. He claims that the changes (lower heels and simpler buckles) will reduce production costs and at the same time result in a better quality shoe. However, the sales manager is held accountable for any loss in sales. He alone is responsible for achieving sales objectives although he has no control over changes in the product. What principle of management is involved here? If you were the president of Winton Shoe Company, what would you do?

Student _____

3. Draw a line-and-staff organization chart showing the following positions: Foremen, Vice-President for Sales, Board of Directors, Personnel Department (staff), Chief Accountant, Director of Advertising, Vice-President for Finance, District Sales Managers, President, Legal Department (staff), and Vice-President for Production.

4. *Case:* Mercury Machine Tools, Inc.

Two months ago Mr. Vance Edwards became president of Mercury Machine Tools, Inc., known in the industry as MMT. Mr. Edwards had been an executive for one of MMT's major rivals. He decided to spend a week "nosing around" in order to get acquainted with how MMT operates. In talking with his management team and visiting various departments he discovered the following:

a. The marketing vice-president has eleven district sales managers, the advertising manager, and the head of market research reporting directly to him.

b. The foremen in the plant are not permitted to change worker assignments without first checking with the plant manager.

c. The head of the purchasing department (a staff specialist) has been issuing directives to the parts manager who reports to the plant manager.

d. The financial manager is jointly responsible to the marketing vice-president and production vice-president.

e. One of the district sales managers resigned six months ago and no replacement has been found. Meanwhile district sales have dropped 25 percent.

f. The advertising manager and director of market research are feuding and have not spoken to each other for nearly a year.

Mr. Edwards has asked you, his assistant, to prepare a brief report outlining any problems you can find and suggesting possible solutions.

Student _____

5. Interview a corporate manager and find out:

    a. Who develops objectives and policies for the firm?

    b. What is the president's span of control?

    c. What major committees are involved in the management of the corpora-
       tion?

    d. What are the responsibilities of department (or division) heads?

e. Draw an organization chart for the firm.

Part III

The Tools of Management

Chapter 5

Accounting and Budgeting

On your next vacation you visit the faraway land of Zamm. You soon discover the people speak only Zammian, a language you do not understand. Your vacation is spoiled because you cannot talk with anyone.

Sad story? No sadder than the businessman who does not understand accounting—for accounting is the language of business.

This chapter is intended to introduce you to accounting and the related subject of budgeting. It won't make you an instant accountant, but it can help you understand how to use some important accounting tools.

KEY QUESTIONS

1. What is accounting?

2. Who uses accounting information?

3. What is a balance sheet and an income statement?

4. How can you analyze financial statements for fun and profit?

5. Why budget?

ACCOUNTING: WHO NEEDS IT?

You can't tell whether you have won or lost the game unless you know the score. In business, the scoring system is called *accounting*. It involves recording, classifying, and summarizing business transactions and interpreting their impact on the firm. These transactions are expressed in dollars and cents.

Management needs information to make decisions, and the most important source of information is accounting reports. Accounting reports show where a firm has been, where it is now, and where it may be going in the future. These reports reveal how a firm stands financially. They show what a firm owns and what it owes as well as its sales, expenses, profits, or losses.

Management is not the only group interested in a firm's accounting reports. Government requires accounting data on profits, expenses, and property for tax purposes. Commercial banks will rarely make a business loan without first analyzing a firm's financial reports. Suppliers must estimate the financial strength of a business before extending credit. Owners and potential investors study accounting information to evaluate a firm's future prospects. There is no escape: a successful business requires accurate and up-to-date accounting records.

ACCOUNTING STATEMENTS

The two main financial reports are the balance sheet and the income statement. Together they form a picture of a firm's operations and financial condition.

The Balance Sheet

This statement shows the financial condition of a business firm as of a certain date. It is based on the accounting equation:

$$\text{Assets} = \text{Liabilities} + \text{Owners' Equity}$$

Assets are anything of value *owned* by a firm such as buildings, equipment, supplies, and merchandise. Liabilities are debts—what is *owed* by the firm. In other words, liabilities are the creditors' claims on the assets of the business. Owners' equity, sometimes called net worth or capital, reflects the owner's share of the business.

Liabilities appear ahead of owner's equity in the accounting equation and in the balance sheet. This is because liabilities are a preferential right (creditors have first claim on the assets), whereas owners' equity is a residual right. If a firm goes out of business and has to sell its assets, the owner(s) can get only what is left after all the debts are paid off. The residual nature of owners' equity is emphasized when liabilities are transposed to the other side of the equation:

$$\text{Assets} - \text{Liabilities} = \text{Owners' Equity}$$

Figure 5-1 shows the balance sheet for the Hailwood Department Store on December 31, 1974. Two questions: (1) Can you find the accounting equation in the balance sheet? (2) How did the balance sheet get its name?

Notice the balance sheet is divided into five major sections:

Current Assets Current assets are cash and other assets that will be converted into cash in the ordinary course of business. Cash reflects the total of deposits in the bank plus currency on hand. Accounts receivable are debts owed to the store by its customers—in Hailwood's case, mostly customer charge account purchases. Inventory is the amount of unsold merchandise on hand.

Fixed Assets Fixed assets are the permanent or long-term assets of the firm that are not directly converted into cash. Notice in Figure 5-1 that both buildings and equipment are carried at their original cost less accumulated depreciation. Depreciation is the reduction in value of a fixed asset because of wear and tear and obsolescence. Since a fixed asset such as a building has a useful life of several years, the accountant must "write off" or depreciate a portion of its value each year. The $9,000,000 accumulated depreciation shown under the building represents the portion of the $20,000,000 cost that has been written off. The $11,000,000 difference is called the *book value* of the asset. A word of caution: book value has little relationship to actual market value.

The simplest way of depreciating the value of a fixed asset is called the *straight-line method*. To illustrate, suppose the building that houses the Hailwood Department Store cost $20,000,000 when new and had an estimated life of 40 years. The annual depreciation can be found by dividing the cost of the asset by its estimated life:

$$\text{Cost} \div \text{Estimated Life} = \text{Annual Depreciation}$$
$$\$20{,}000{,}000 \div 40 \text{ years} = \$500{,}000$$

How old is the Hailwood building as of December 31, 1974?

Current Liabilities Current liabilities are short-term debts that must be paid within a year or less. Accounts payable consist of debts owed to trade creditors by the firm for the purchase of merchandise, supplies, or other assets on account. Wages payable re-

Figure 5-1

Hailwood Department Store, Inc.

Balance Sheet

December 31, 1974

Assets		
Current Assets		
Cash	$ 700,000	
Accounts Receivable	2,500,000	
Inventory	10,800,000	
Total Current Assets		$14,000,000
Fixed Assets		
Land		9,000,000
Building	$20,000,000	
Less Accumu-		
lated Depreciation	9,000,000	11,000,000
Equipment	5,000,000	
Less Accumu-		
lated Depreciation	3,000,000	2,000,000
Total Fixed Assets		22,000,000
Total Assets		$36,000,000

Liabilities and Owners' Equity		
Current Liabilities		
Accounts Payable	$ 4,400,000	
Wages Payable	170,000	
Taxes Payable	130,000	
Total Current Liabilities		$ 4,700,000
Fixed Liabilities		
Bank Loan (due 1977)	6,000,000	
Mortgage on Building	7,000,000	
Total Fixed Liabilities		13,000,000
Owners' Equity		
Common Stock		
(500,000 shares)	10,000,000	
Retained Earnings	8,300,000	
Total Owners' Equity		18,300,000
Total Liabilities and		
Owners' Equity		$36,000,000

flect money owed to employees, while Taxes payable are liabilities to federal, state, and local governments.

Fixed Liabilities Fixed liabilities are long-term debts that are not due within a year. Hailwood has borrowed $6,000,000 from a bank, and it owes another $7,000,000 debt secured by a mortgage on the store.

Owners' Equity Owners' equity, the owners' share of the corporation, consists of the proceeds from the sale of stock plus profits reinvested in the firm. Common stock represents the investment made by the stockholder. Retained earnings reflect that portion of profits over the years that has been plowed back into the company.

The balance sheet provides a useful picture of the financial strength of a business firm on a specific date. It presents two views of property (or assets). On the left the property owned by the firm is listed. On the right side are the liabilities and owners' equity, which comprise the claims on the property. In accounting, when both sides of a statement are equal, it is said to be "in balance", which explains how the balance sheet got its name. The balance sheet for the Hailwood Department Store may be summarized using the accounting equation:

$$\text{Assets} \quad = \quad \text{Liabilites} \quad + \text{Owners' Equity}$$
$$\$36,000,000 = \$17,700,000 + \quad \$18,300,000$$

The Income Statement   *Know*

The second major financial report is the income statement, sometimes called the operating statement or profit-and-loss statement. It summarizes a firm's operations over a period of time. The income statement lists income and expenses for a particular period, often a year. Figure 5–2 represents a simplified income statement for the Hailwood Department Store covering a period of twelve months.

The single source of revenue for the Hailwood Department Store is the sale of merchandise to customers. The cost of goods sold represents what the store paid for the merchandise which was sold during the year. The difference between sales and cost of goods sold is called gross profit. Operating expenses are listed in some detail so that management can keep track of individual items. Note the depreciation expense which represents the write-off of the building and equipment for the year 1974. Subtracting total operating expenses from gross profit produces net profit before income taxes. After deducting federal income taxes, the firm earned a net profit of $1,420,000 for the year 1974.

Figure 5–2
Hailwood Department Store, Inc.
Income Statement
For the Year Ended December 31, 1974

Sales		$83,000,000
Cost of Goods Sold		60,500,000
Gross Profit		22,500,000
Operating Expenses:		
Wages	$12,200,000	
Selling Expenses	1,300,000	
Administrative Expenses	1,800,000	
Depreciation Expense	1,000,000	
Miscellaneous Expenses	1,900,000	
Interest Expense	900,000	
Taxes	700,000	
Total Operating Expenses		19,800,000
Net Profit Before Taxes		2,700,000
Federal Income Taxes		1,280,000
Net Profit		$ 1,420,000

Net profit (sometimes called net income) may be distributed to the owners (common stockholders) in dividends, reinvested in the business, or both. If the Hailwood Department Store paid dividends of $800,000, this would leave $620,000 in retained earnings for reinvestment.

The income statement reveals the amount of sales income, the expenses incurred to generate the sales, and the resulting profit or loss for the period. It is summarized in the following formula:

Sales − Cost of Goods Sold = Gross Profit − Operating Expenses = Net Profit

FINANCIAL ANALYSIS

Accounting statements provide valuable information on a firm's profitability and financial strength. However, this information must be analyzed and interpreted before it can serve as the basis for management decisions. There are many analytical tools used to explore and interpret accounting statements. Two common techniques are ratio analysis and comparative analysis of income statements. The ratios described below use the data from the financial statements for the Hailwood Department Store (Figures 5–1 and 5–2).

ISSUE   THE BILLION-DOLLAR RIP-OFF: EMPLOYEE THEFT

Each year employees steal somewhere between $10 and $20 billion from business firms. Although exact figures are unavailable, the theft of cash and merchandise probably amounts to $5 billion annually, while kickbacks in the form of under-the-table "gifts" from suppliers to purchasing agents may exceed $6 billion. In addition, embezzlement and theft of industrial secrets account for billions in losses. One expert estimates that 10–15 percent of the price paid for goods and services goes to cover the cost of dishonesty. Other startling facts:

—Employees steal three to four times as much as shoplifters.

—The greatest amount of theft is by supervisors and managers because they have more opportunities for dishonesty.

—Employee crime has nearly tripled in the last ten years.

The reasons employees steal are difficult to pinpoint. Some are pressured by unexpected expenses, others feel they are making up for low pay, while still others have deep psychological motives. In every case, however, widespread employee crime is a reflection of poor management. The failure to establish effective controls coupled with permissiveness and neglect create opportunities for dishonesty at every level in a company.

Experts who specialize in preventing employee thefts offer several suggestions for business firms:

—Honesty begins at the top. Management must set an example and create an atmosphere which encourages honesty.

—Ban all gift-giving and receiving.

—Establish controls and procedures which remove the temptation to steal.

—Set realistic performance standards so that workers won't be tempted to cheat to meet goals.

—Treat employees fairly by rewarding outstanding performance.

Probably the most controversial view of employee theft is offered by Lawrence R. Zeitlin, an industrial psychologist, who claims that stealing is a safety valve for worker frustrations. He believes the main cause of employee crime is job dissatisfaction resulting from dull work, low pay, and little challenge or responsibility. Dr. Zeitlin suggests some firms should consider permitting "controlled theft" by workers to offset job boredom and low wages. "The dishonest worker is enriching his job in a manner that is very satisfactory (for him). The enrichment is costing management, on an average, $1.50 per worker per day. At this rate management gets a bargain. By permitting a controlled amount of theft, management can avoid reorganizing jobs and raising pay." What do you think? Should everyone become a rip-off artist for fun and profit?

References

Mark Lipman, *Stealing* (New York: Harper's Magazine Press, 1973).

Lawrence R. Zeitlin, "A Little Larceny Can Do A Lot for Employee Morale," *Psychology Today,* June 1971, pp. 22–26, 64.

N. Jaspan, "Why Employees Steal," *U.S. News and World Report,* May 3, 1971, pp. 78–82.

Ratio Analysis

A ratio is a convenient means of comparing two quantities. Ratios are used to explore the relationship between various items appearing on the accounting statements. These ratios can be compared to established standards to discover possible weaknesses or potential problems. Among the most commonly used ratios are: (1) the current ratio; (2) equity to debt ratio; (3) net profit as a percent of sales; (4) inventory turnover; (5) rate of return on investment; and (6) profit per share.

Current Ratio The current ratio measures the ability of a firm to pay its short-term debts.

$$\text{Current Ratio} = \frac{\text{Current Assets}}{\text{Current Liabilities}} = \frac{\$14,000,000}{\$4,700,000} = 3 \text{ to } 1$$

For every dollar of current liabilities, the Hailwood Department Store has approximately $3 in current assets. A safe ratio is generally considered to be 2 to 1; a ratio below 1 to 1 is a signal that the firm may experience difficulties paying its short-term debts.

Equity-to-Debt Ratio The equity-to-debt ratio illustrates the relationship between funds from creditors and owners.

$$\text{Equity-to-Debt Ratio} = \frac{\text{Owners' Equity}}{\text{Total Liabilities}} = \frac{\$18,300,000}{\$17,700,000} = 1.03 \text{ to } 1$$

A more conservative ratio would be 2 to 1, and some firms feel it is poor practice to permit the ratio to fall below 1 to 1.

Net Profit as a Percent of Sales Net profit as a percent of sales shows what percent of sales revenue is converted into profit.

$$\text{Profit as a Percent of Sales} = \frac{\text{Net Profit}}{\text{Sales}} = \frac{\$1,410,000}{\$83,000,000} = 1.7\%$$

Out of each dollar of sales, only 1.7¢ is profit; the remaining 98.3¢ is used to pay for the cost of goods sold, operating expenses, and income taxes.

Inventory Turnover Inventory turnover measures how many times a year the average inventory is "turned over" or sold.

$$\text{Inventory Turnover} = \frac{\text{Cost of Goods Sold}}{\text{Inventory}} = \frac{\$61,500,000}{\$10,800,000} = 5.7$$

This formula shows that Hailwood turns its inventory almost once every two months. This turnover would be considered average performance for a department store. Normally the higher the inventory turnover, the greater the net profit.

Rate of Return on Investment Rate of return on investment is the key measure of the efficiency of a business firm. This ratio compares net profit to the stockholders' investment.

$$\text{Rate of Return on Investment} = \frac{\text{New Profit}}{\text{Owners' Equity}} = \frac{\$\ 1,410,000}{\$18,300,000} = 7.7\%$$

The owners of the Hailwood Department Store earned a 7.7% return on their investment in 1974. This return is not particularly high in view of the risks of business ownership.

Profit per Share Profit per share is computed by dividing the number of shares of common stock outstanding into net profit:

$$\text{Profit per Share} = \frac{\text{Net Profit}}{\text{Share of Common Stocks}} = \frac{\$1,410,000}{500,000} = \$2.84$$

Profit per share is a major determinant of a stock's market price.

Table 5-1 shows the average (median) ratios for several types of business firms. Can you explain why the ratios vary so widely for firms in different lines of business?

Table 5-1 Selected Business Ratios, Median Figures for 1971

Line of Business	Current Ratio	Equity to Debt	Net Profits as a Percent of Sales	Inventory Turnover	Rate of Return
Retailing					
Department Stores	2.89	1.18	1.55%	5.6	5.42%
Discount Stores	1.88	.80	1.49	5.2	9.97
Grocery Stores	1.73	1.02	1.00	17.1	10.48
Jewelry Stores	3.16	1.26	2.66	3.0	5.73
Manufacturing and Construction					
Bakery Products	2.07	1.46	1.77%	27.5	6.58%
Household Appliances	2.65	1.03	3.31	4.9	10.29
Heavy Construction	1.98	.98	2.09	—	8.61
Wholesaling					
Auto Equipment	2.70	1.13	2.37%	5.0	9.39%
Fresh Fruits and Vegetables	2.10	1.07	1.20	40.9	9.53

Source: Dun & Bradstreet, Inc.

Comparative Analysis of the Income Statement

It is often informative to compare the results of operations over a period of years. Such comparisons may reveal trends which would not be apparent from one year's results. This type of analysis is more meaningful if accompanied by a percentage breakdown of the income statement. Sales are designated as 100 percent, and all other items are shown as a percent of sales. Figure 5-3 shows abbreviated income statements for Zoe's Candy Company covering a period of three years.

A glance at the income statements suggests that the firm is doing very well; both sales and profits have risen over the three year period. However, closer examination indicates some reasons for concern. Notice that costs of goods sold as a percent of sales has declined each year leading to a larger gross profit margin. This decline could suggest efficient purchasing. On the other hand, operating expenses have been increasing at an alarming rate, more than offsetting the rise in gross profit. As a result, net profit as a percent of sales has been declining. These trends should alert management to examine operating expenses to determine the causes for the rapid increase and to seek ways to control these costs.

BUDGETING

Why Budget?

A budget is a financial tool for planning future operations. Indeed, the very process of creating a budget forces management to make detailed projections about the future. The budget is also a device for management control. It is used to compare actual performance against budgeted standards. This device enables management to identify problem areas and take remedial action. For example, if selling expenses are exceeding budgeted estimates, management can investigate the causes and attempt to correct the situation. To sum up, the budget is both a means of planning for the future and a control device to ensure conformity to plans.

Figure 5-3 Income Statements for Zoe's Candy Company, for the Years 1972–1974

	1972	%	1973	%	1974	%
Sales	$200,000	100	$250,000	100	$320,000	100
Cost of Goods Sold	140,000	70	170,000	68	210,000	66
Gross Profit	60,000	30	80,000	32	110,000	34
Operating Expenses	40,000	20	57,500	23	84,400	26
Net Profit	$ 20,000	10	$ 22,500	9	$ 25,600	8

ISSUE BUSINESS FORECASTING: WHAT DOES THE FUTURE HOLD?

There is a tide in the affairs of men,
Which, taken at the flood, leads on to fortune.

William Shakespeare

Shakespeare, as usual, was right. If you can accurately predict the future, your fortune is made. Of course, no one has a magic crystal ball, but the successful business manager is vitally concerned with what will happen tomorrow, next month, and five years from now. Therefore, he must attempt to predict the future through business forecasting. Forecasts play a key role in developing sales projections, budgeting, inventory control, and marketing strategy.

Business forecasting techniques fall into three broad catagories: subjective forecasting, simple projections, and causal models.

1. *Subjective Forecasting* depends heavily on intuition and experience. Since managers must make forecasts nearly every day, they often rely on educated guesswork that combines a knowledge of important facts plus personal judgement. Subjective methods are quick and inexpensive, and they can be surprisingly accurate for near-term forecasts.

2. *Simple Projections* are essentially extensions of past and current trends. For example, a sales manager may analyze the sales of a product over the last four or five years and use this data to project future sales. This method assumes that conditions will not change much in the future and that past performance is a good indicator of what will occur in coming months or years.

3. *Causal models* employ sophisticated mathematical techniques such as regression analysis that measure the relationship between variables over time. This sounds complicated, but the basic idea is simple. For example, a liquor store owner orders extra beer when a heat wave is forecast because past experience has shown that beer sales increase when the temperature rises. In the same way, a lumber company might develop a model for forecasting the demand for lumber products by correlating sales to consumer incomes, housing starts, and interest rates.

Regardless of the method used, it is easier to predict the immediate future than it is to make accurate long-term projections. Forecasts, no matter how scientific, cannot eliminate uncertainty; but effective forecasting can reduce the range of uncertainty, thereby minimizing the chance of making major mistakes.

Business forecasting can be a difficult and often expensive process, but it is essential for successful business operations. As John Galsworthy warned: ''If you do not think about the future, you cannot have one.''

References

Leonard S. Silk and M. Louise Curley, *A Primer on Business Forecasting* (New York: Random House, 1970).

G. C. C. Parker and E. L. Seguia, ''How to Get a Better Forecast,'' *Harvard Business Review,* March 1971, pp. 99–109.

J. C. Chambers *et al.,* ''How to Choose the Right Forecasting Technique,'' *Harvard Business Review,* July 1971, pp. 45–74.

The budgeting process usually begins with a sales forecast. In large corporations, each department develops a budget which is reviewed, revised, and finally approved by top management. Then a master budget, based on the combined departmental budgets, is developed for the firm as a whole. Frequently, a budget committee reviews all estimates and approves the final projections.

One executive is normally assigned responsibility for administering the budget. He collects data on actual performance, compares performance to budgeted standards, and prepares periodic budget status reports.

Two common types of budgets are the cash budget and the projected income statement. In addition, break-even analysis is a valuable planning tool for budget development.

The Cash Budget

A cash budget is a statement showing projected cash receipts and expenditures over a specified period of time. Figure 5–4 presents a cash budget for Tom Henderson, a college student. At the end of his junior year, Tom wondered if he could afford to return to school next year. He decided to estimate his sources of cash and expenditures for the coming twelve months.

This budget can be used by Tom to control his spending. He knows, for example, that his food and rent should not exceed $75 and $60 a month, respectively.

The cash budget can also highlight the need for additional funds when projected cash expenditures exceed the expected sources of cash.

Projected Income Statement

Another useful tool for budgetary planning is the projected (or *pro forma*) income statement. It shows estimated income and expenses over a specified period. Suppose the management of Zoe's Candy

Figure 5–4 Cash Budget for Tom Henderson, July 1–June 30

Estimated Sources of Cash		Estimated Cash Expenditures	
Bank Balance, July 1	$ 200	Food	$ 900
G.I. Bill	1,000	Rent	720
Part-Time Job	2,400	College Tuition, Fees, Books	880
Total	$3,600	Transportation	400
		Miscellaneous Expenses	600
		Total Expenditures	$3,500
		Cash Balance, June 30	$ 100

Company (see Figure 5-3) wants to develop a projected income statement for 1975. Based on past performance and future projections, management forecasts a sales increase of 25 percent and estimates that cost of goods sold will remain at about 66 percent of sales. Operating expenses are expected to be 25 percent of sales. Figure 5-5 shows a projected net profit of $35,000.

Break-Even Analysis

Businessmen seek to earn profits and avoid losses. The relationships among sales, costs, and profits can be studied through the use of break-even analysis.

The first step is to divide costs into two categories: fixed costs and variable costs. Fixed costs (sometimes called *overhead*) are those costs that do *not* change as the level of production changes. Examples include rent, insurance, bond interest, management salaries, and so forth. Variable costs vary directly with the level of production. Typical examples of variable costs are total wages of factory workers, the cost of materials, and fuel.

Suppose the Carter Widget Company has fixed costs of $60,000 a week and variable costs of $3 per unit. Each unit is sold for $5. The question is: How many units must be produced and sold each week to cover total costs? In other words, how many units are required to break even? The break-even point may be computed using a simple formula:

$$\text{Break-Even Point} = \frac{\text{Fixed Costs}}{\text{Selling Price} - \text{Variable Costs Per Unit}} =$$

$$\frac{\$60,000}{\$5 - \$3} = \frac{\$60,000}{\$2} = 30,000 \text{ Units}$$

The break-even point is 30,000 units a week. If fewer than 30,000 units are produced, the firm will lose money; it will not cover its fixed costs. At any output over 30,000 units a week, the Carter Widget Company will earn a profit. For example, if 40,000 units are pro-

Figure 5-5 Projected Income Statement for Zoe's Candy Company, January–December, 1975

	1974 Results	1975 Projections	1975 Percent of Sales
Sales	$320,000	$400,000	100
Cost of Goods Sold	210,000	265,000	66
Gross Profit	$110,000	$135,000	34
Operating Expenses	84,400	100,000	25
Net Profit	$ 26,600	$ 35,000	9

duced, the profit will be $20,000 ($5 − $3 = $2 × 10,000 units = $20,000).

This analysis can be shown graphically in the form of a break-even chart. The vertical axis in Figure 5-6 shows sales revenues and costs in thousands of dollars. The horizontal axis shows units of output. Fixed costs are illustrated by the horizontal line at $60,000, while variable costs are plotted on top of fixed costs at the rate of $3 per unit of output. Total cost is the sum of fixed costs and variable costs. Therefore, at an output of 20,000 units, total cost is $120,000 ($60,000 in fixed costs + 20,000 units × $3 in variable costs).

The total revenue line is plotted by multiplying the price per unit ($5) by the output. Therefore, when output is 20,000 units, total revenue is $100,000 ($5 × 20,000 units). The break-even point occurs when the total revenue and total cost lines intersect. In Figure 5-6 the break-even point is 30,000 units and $150,000.

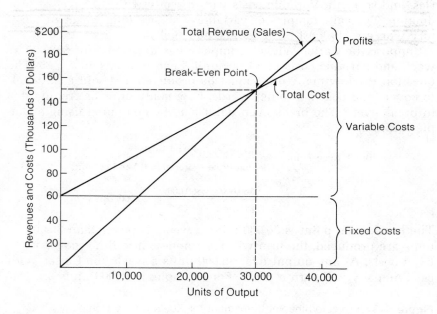

Figure 5–6 Break-Even Chart for the Carter Widget Company

SUMMARY

Accounting is the process of recording, classifying, summarizing, and interpreting business transactions. Accounting reports are used by management, creditors, investors, and various government agencies.

The two major accounting statements are the balance sheet and income statement. The balance sheet reveals the financial condition of the business firm on a certain date. It is organized according to the accounting equation:

$$\text{Assets} = \text{Liabilities} + \text{Owners' Equity}$$

The income statement summarizes the results of operations over a period of time. It shows the firm's income and expenses and the difference between these two which is profit or loss.

Financial analysis provides information for management decision making. Ratio analysis is a convenient method of comparing items from the balance sheet and income statement. In addition, income statements for several years may be compared to identify significant trends.

Budgets are used to plan future operations and as control devices that enable management to compare actual performance to budgeted estimates. A cash budget lists estimated cash receipts and expenditures over a period of months or years. It can serve to highlight the potential need for additional funds. The projected income statement shows estimated income and expenses for a future period.

Break-even analysis is a useful planning tool which illustrates the relationships among sales, costs, and profits. The break-even point, where total revenue just equals total costs, may be found by using the following formula:

$$\text{Break-Even Point} = \frac{\text{Fixed Cost}}{\text{Selling Price} - \text{Variable Costs per Unit}}$$

ISSUE   RISK, INSURANCE, AND THE BUSINESSMAN*

Both individuals and business firms face risks arising from uncertainty about the future. *Risk* refers to the possibility of loss, injury, or damage resulting from unforeseen events. Some, but not all, risks may be reduced or transferred through insurance.

Business firms suffer losses from fire, theft, personal injury, and a variety of other events. Insurance companies sell policies to cover risks in return for an annual payment called a *premium*. The amount of the premium is based on statistical studies which determine the probability of an event occurring. The greater the chance of loss, the higher the premium.

In deciding whether or not to buy insurance, management must consider the financial loss to the business firm should an event occur. If the potential loss is severe, then insurance should be purchased to offset the loss. Some firms elect to reduce the amount of the premium by purchasing deductible insurance. For example, with a $10,000 deductible fire insurance policy, the firm must pay the first $10,000 of damage and the insurance company is liable for the remainder.

The increasingly important field of *risk management* attempts to reduce or transfer the chances of loss through alternatives to insurance. For example, a firm may decide to install a fire sprinkler system in its plant rather than purchase an insurance policy. Sometimes risks can be transferred through contractual agreements where, for example, another firm agrees to take over the responsibility for a particular job. In large firms whose facilities are geographically spread out, self-insurance can save the cost of insurance premiums. In this case, the firm sets up its own insurance reserve fund to pay for possible losses.

In recent years, there has been a tremendous growth in "key man" life and disability insurance to protect the firm against the loss of key personnel. In addition, the increase in stockholders' law suits against inept managers and boards of directors has resulted in expanded liability insurance for officers and directors.

Another major need for insurance arises from the fact that government requires it; for example, workmen's compensation must be carried unless a particular employer is large enough to qualify as a self-insurer. Social security is another type of compulsory national insurance. Interestingly enough, the cost of fringe benefit insurance (group life, health, and disability) corporate pension plans, social security insurance, and workmen's compensation greatly exceeds the cost from most companies of their entire fire and casualty insurance premiums.

*Written by Alex Pappas, a partner in Pappas, Brevet & Associates, Oakland, California. Used with permission.

Student _____

STUDENT FEEDBACK SYSTEM

Directions: Your questions and ideas are important! Here's a chance to get more information and relate your experiences to the materials in the chapter. Answer the following questions and turn in this page to the instructor. Use the reverse side of the page if you need additional space.

1. What topics, problems, and terms found in this chapter require more explanation by the instructor?

2. Do the concepts presented in this chapter agree with your experiences in the business world? Briefly explain why or why not, using examples.

3. Does this chapter suggest any career opportunities to you?

Student _____

REVIEWING MAJOR CONCEPTS

1. Carefully explain the difference between the income statement and the balance sheet.

   balance sheet - shows financial strength at a certain point in time. Probability (how you might do.) income statement - reveals income received, expenses incurred.

2. Name four groups that use business accounting statements.

   Management, Banks, Gov't, Suppliers Owners, investors.

3. Of what value are budgets to management?

   Planning Control Organization & Management

4. Briefly explain the accounting equation.

   Assets = Liabilities + Owners Equity

   A - L = L - L + O.E.

   Assets - liabilities = owners equity

5. If a firm has assets of $250,000 and liabilities of $100,000, what is owners' equity?

$$A = L + OE$$

$$\underset{A}{250,00} - \underset{L}{100,000} = \underset{OE}{\$150,000}$$

6. A firm has owners' equity of $110,000,000 and liabilities of $50,000,000. What is the amount of its assets?

income state vs balance state.

7. A manufacturer purchases a new machine tool for $25,000 which has an expected life of 10 years. Using the straight-line method how much will the machine tool depreciate each year?

Student _____

SOLVING PROBLEMS AND CASES

1. The following information was taken from the accounting records of Over-field's Stationery Store on June 30, 1975.

Accounts Payable	$ 6,000	Accounts Receivable	$ 5,000
Plant and Equipment	20,000	Common Stock	12,000
		(1,000 shares)	
Inventory	12,000	Cash	4,000
Long-term Bank Loan	10,000	Depreciation	4,000
Wages Payable	1,000	Retained Earnings	8,000

a. Prepare a balance sheet for the firm.

b. Compute the current ratio.

c. Compute the equity to debt ratio.

2. From the following data covering the year ended June 30, 1975, prepare an income statement for Overfield's Stationery Store, Inc.

Operating Expenses	$ 40,000
Federal Income Taxes	1,000
Sales	120,000
Cost of Goods Sold	75,000

Using the information in problems 1 and 2:

a. Compute inventory turnover.

b. Compute the rate of return on investment.

c. Compute profit per share.

Student _____

3. Construct a cash budget for the Harper Toy Company using the following estimates: Beginning Cash Balance, $17,000; Payment of Accounts Payable, $35,000; Repayment of Bank Loan, $50,000; Cash Sales, $120,000; Operating Expenses, $82,000; Collection of Accounts Receivable, $13,000.

Estimated Sources of Cash	Estimated Uses of Cash

Do you have any recommendations for the management?

4. The Stark Manufacturing Company has fixed costs of $160,000 a month and variable costs of $12.00 per unit. What is the firm's break-even point if the selling price per unit is $16.00?

How much profit will the firm earn if it sells 55,000 units?

Draw a break-even chart for the Stark Manufacturing Company.

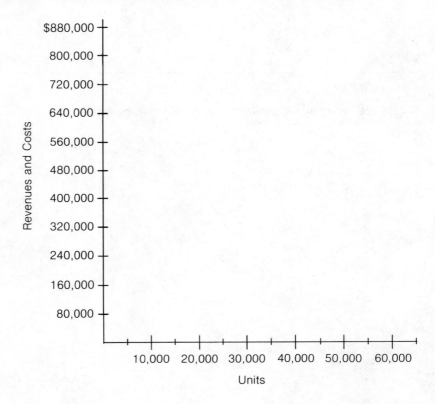

Chapter 6

Statistics and Data Processing

Statistics are facts expressed as numbers. Sound management decisions are based on accurate and timely information, and much business information can be expressed in the form of quantitative data. One purpose of this chapter is to help you become familiar with some statistical concepts and tools typically used by business managers.

Data processing refers to any system for handling and organizing numerical data. Here we are concerned with the use of the electronic computer to process raw data into usable information. Clearly, there is a close relationship between the study of statistics and electronic data processing.

KEY QUESTIONS

1. Where do business statistics come from?

2. What are some of the important tools of statistical analysis and how are they used?

3. How may statistical data be presented to facilitate their use and interpretation?

4. What is electronic data processing and why is it important to businessmen?

5. What does a computer do?

6. How do business firms use computers?

SOURCES OF STATISTICAL INFORMATION

Business statistics may be defined as collecting, analyzing, presenting, and interpreting quantitative data to assist in decision making. Statistical data may originate from sources both inside and outside the firm.

Internal Sources

Much statistical information is available from a firm's own records and reports. Accounting data, employee records in the personnel department, and production and sales reports are valuable sources of statistics. Suppose a manager is developing a new employee-pension plan and needs to know the average age and length of service of employees. This information should be readily available from the firm's personnel files.

External Sources

Many management decisions require information that is not available from internal sources. For example, the manager of a machine-tool company may be faced with the question of whether or not to expand his production facilities. The decision must be based in part on the forecasted level of economic activity. Will the purchases of machine tools rise, remain unchanged, or drop off? The manager can review published reports available from the Department of Commerce and the Federal Reserve Board that analyze present economic conditions and make forecasts of future activity.

   The federal government produces a wealth of statistical information that is of value to businessmen. The annual *Statistical Abstract of the United States* contains hundreds of pages of data. Up-to-date economic statistics are available from the monthly *Survey of Current Business* and *Federal Reserve Bulletin.* In addition, private firms produce thousands of publications containing valuable statistical data.

   If the required information is unavailable from the firm's records or from published reports, it may be necessary to conduct a survey. Surveys normally involve the collection of data through a statistical technique called *sampling.*

Sampling

Suppose a newspaper publisher wants to find out how many subscribers read the comic pages. He could try to question every subscriber, but this would be expensive and time-consuming. Instead he can select a sample—perhaps 500 subscribers from a total of 50,000—to contact. He would expect that the responses from the sample would reflect the reading habits of all subscribers.

Sampling is the process of selecting a small number of items from a large group in order to make generalizations or predictions about the group as a whole (called the *population* or *universe*). Random sampling involves ensuring that each item (or individual) in the population has an equal chance of being selected for the sample.

Sampling has many applications in business. It is used in market research to determine consumer attitudes about new products. Quality-control departments in manufacturing plants often select parts for testing to ensure that performance standards are being maintained. For example, one automobile firm takes every tenth car from the production line for a thorough road test. Auditing is a form of sampling used in checking the accuracy of accounting records.

STATISTICAL ANALYSIS

Raw data are little more than jumbles of numbers. To be of value, data must be processed, summarized, and measured. A widely used tool of statistical measurement is the average.

Averages

An average is a measure of central tendency. It is a summary number used to represent a group of figures. There are three major types of averages: the *mean,* the *median,* and the *mode.*

Suppose the foreman of Department 10 wants to study the amount of overtime worked by his men last month. He collects the data from the payroll department and arranges it in an array—that is, in numerical order from the highest to the lowest—as shown in Table 6–1.

Table 6–1 Hours of Overtime in Department 10 for May

Worker	Hours of Overtime	
Johnson	15	
Black	14	
Chu	11	
Harris	8	
Cohen	8	← Mean = 7.55
Gary	7	← Median = 7
Spinnato	6	
Vatt	6	← Mode = 6
Allen	6	
Poe	2	
Smith	0	
Total	83	

The foreman next decides to compute the mean, which is found by totaling the values and dividing by their number. In this case, he adds the hours of overtime for the department and divides by the number of workers:

$$83 \text{ Total Hours} \div 11 \text{ Workers} = 7.55 \text{ Hours}$$

The mean number of hours of overtime is 7.55 per worker.

The median is the middle value in a group of numbers arranged in numerical order. Since there are eleven workers, the sixth worker divides the group in half, and the median is 7 hours.

The mode is simply the number that occurs most frequently. In our example, 6 hours occurs three times, and this is the mode.

Which average is best? The mean is the most commonly used average, but it is subject to distortion by extreme values. Suppose, for example, four students have the following annual incomes: $1,600, $1,800, $2,200, $2,400. Their mean income is $2,000 ($8,000 ÷ 4 = $2,000). Now a fifth student with an annual income of $27,000 joins the group. The mean income is now $7,000 ($35,000 ÷ 5 = $7,000), a figure that is not representative of the first four students' incomes. In this case the median would be more representative. A good procedure is to compute all three averages for a group of figures.

Index Numbers

Index numbers measure the relative changes in numerical data. Suppose the marketing manager of Conn Paper Products wants to compare the performance of Sales District C to that of the firm as a whole. He can list the sales of the District C and the firm as shown in Table 6–2.

This type of data is difficult to evaluate. It is helpful to convert the dollar sales into index numbers. This conversion is accomplished by first selecting a *base year* (we will use 1970), dividing each year's sales by the base year's sales, and expressing the result as a percentage.[1] The results are shown in Table 6–3.

The use of index numbers makes it clear that District C has outperformed the company as a whole over the five-year period. Between 1970 and 1974, District C increased sales by 114 percent

[1] For District C Sales in 1970:

$$\frac{\$210,000}{\$210,000} = 1 \times 100 = 100\%; \text{ in 1971: } \frac{\$340,000}{\$210,000} = 1.62 \times 100 = 162\%; \text{ etc.}$$

For Company Sales in 1970:

$$\frac{\$1,570,000}{\$1,570,000} = 1 \times 100 = 100\%; \text{ in 1971: } \frac{\$1,850,000}{\$1,570,000} = 1.18 \times 100 = 118\%; \text{ etc.}$$

Table 6-2 Sales of District C and Conn Paper Products, 1970–1974

Year	District C Sales	Company Sales
1970	$210,000	$1,570,000
1971	340,000	1,850,000
1972	350,000	2,200,000
1973	410,000	2,640,000
1974	450,000	2,900,000

while the firm as a whole managed only an 82-percent gain.

The federal government publishes many indexes that measure economic activity. The most widely known is the Consumer Price Index (CPI), which is published every month by the Bureau of Labor Statistics. The CPI measures the changes in retail prices of goods and services purchased by the typical city family. Another important gauge of economic activity is the Index of Industrial Production, which measures changes in the physical output of factories and mines.

PRESENTATION OF STATISTICAL DATA

Most business reports contain numerous statistics. These statistics may be presented in the body of the report, in tables, or in the form of charts. Tables 6-1 and 6-2 represent examples of statistical tables. There are three major types of charts: line charts, pie diagrams, and bar charts.

Line charts are widely used because they are simple to construct and easy to understand. Figure 6-1, which shows the Consumer Price index for the years 1967–1974, is a typical line chart.

Pie diagrams are often used to show different parts of a whole; for example, how a firm's income is spent. Figure 6-2 shows a sample pie diagram.

Table 6-3 Sales Indexes for District C and Conn Paper Products, 1970–1974 (1970 = 100)

Year	District C	Company
1970	100	100
1971	162	118
1972	166	140
1973	195	168
1974	214	182

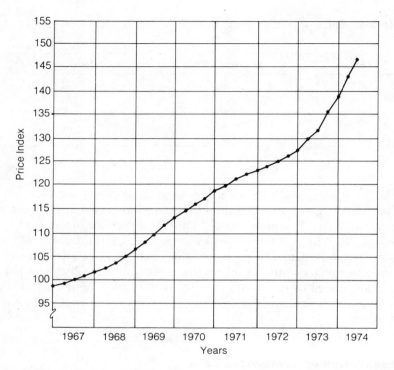

Figure 6–1   Line Chart: Consumer Price Index, 1967–1974 (1967 = 100)
Source: United States Department of Commerce, *Survey of Current Business*.

Bar charts are useful for comparing two or more sets of data. Figure 6–3 shows the net profit for Data–Max, Inc., for the years 1971–1974, and how the profit was distributed among federal income taxes, retained profits, and dividends.

INTERPRETATION OF STATISTICS

All the statistics in the world won't lead to good decisions without accurate interpretation. Needless to say, the interpretation of statistical data is a highly useful management skill. The experienced manager always approaches numerical data with caution, because statistics can lie. They are subject to mathematical errors and human bias. An advertising campaign may claim that three out of four doctors recommend "Product X", but this is not a very convincing statistic if only four doctors were asked for their opinions.

DATA PROCESSING

Data processing refers to any system for collecting, processing, and reporting numerical data. The word *system* means an organized set

Figure 6–2   Pie Diagram
Reprinted with permission of Datamation,® Copyright, Technical Publishing Co., Barrington, Ill. 60010, 1972.

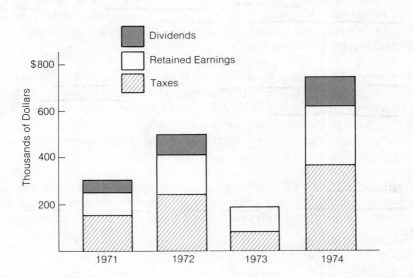

Figure 6–3   Bar Chart

of procedures. In this sense, data processing is thousands of years old. A simple pencil-and-paper bookkeeping system is a method of data processing. The term *electronic data processing* refers to the use of a computer to process quantitative information.

Computer! The very word conjures up images of a mysterious and magical thinking machine. This myth should be dispelled right away. As the former president of Avis put it, "Computers are big, expensive, fast, dumb adding-machine-typewriters."[2]

Why, then, have computers gained such broad use in business and nonbusiness applications? After all, the modern computer was developed only about 30 years ago. The answer is that our society has grown increasingly complex, and as a result there is a rapidly growing demand for accurate and timely information. The computer can provide this information faster, and often at a lower cost, than alternative systems of data processing. Today, nearly all large corporations, and many smaller firms, use computers to perform a variety of jobs.

Computer Components

How does a computer work? Perhaps the easiest way to answer this question is to divide the computer into its component parts. Figure 6–4 illustrates these components. The arrows show the flow of information through the computer.

Input Device The computer must receive both instructions and raw data through some input device. Input may be recorded on punched cards, magnetic tape, punched paper tape, or in magnetic ink on paper documents such as checks. The input unit may be a card reader, a tape reader, a typewriter console, or any device capable of inputting coded data.

Memory The memory, often called the computer's storage, may be viewed as an electronic filing cabinet. Here instructions and data are stored until needed. There are several methods of storing data, such as magnetic core, magnetic drum, and magnetic disk. The capacity of a computer is measured in terms of the size of its memory.

Arithmetic Unit The arithmetic component of the computer is an electronic calculator—it adds, subtracts, multiplies, and divides. In addition, it performs certain tasks of logic such as comparing quantities.

[2]Robert Townsend, *Up the Organization* (Greenwich, Conn.: Fawcett Crest, 1970), p. 18.

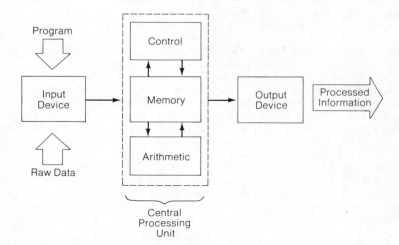

Figure 6–4 The Components of a Computer

Control Unit The control section directs and coordinates the operations of the computer. It may be viewed as an electronic traffic cop that directs the step-by-step processing of data by the computer according to the programmed instructions.

Output Unit Output is data that has been processed by the computer. Output may be recorded in a variety of ways—on paper by a high-speed printer, on magnetic tape, or on punched cards. A more recent development is the use of a special type of television screen called a *cathode ray tube* to project processed information.

The term *hardware* is used to refer to the five components of the computer. The control unit, memory, and arithmetic unit together are called the *central processing unit* or CPU.

Programming

The computer cannot think for itself. In order to do useful work, it requires a detailed set of instructions, called a *program*. The individual responsible for writing computer instructions is called a *programmer*. Computer programs are often referred to as *software*.

The job of programming a computer is complicated by two factors. First, since the computer cannot think like a human being, the instructions must be written in great detail and each step must be in logical sequence. Second, the program must be written in a language which the computer can understand. The two most widely used computer languages are FORTRAN and COBOL. FORTRAN (short for FORmula TRANslation) is primarily used in the area of science and mathematics. COBOL (COmmon Business Oriented Language) finds its greatest application in business data processing.

ISSUE   IS "BIG BROTHER" WATCHING YOU?

In his terrifying novel of the future entitled *1984,* George Orwell described a world without privacy where an all-pervasive government (called "Big Brother") spied continuously on every citizen. Today, a growing number of voices are warning that "1984" is already upon us. The villain, they claim, is the computer that threatens to deprive all of us of our freedom.

Everyone knows the computer is a potent tool for collecting, analyzing, and storing vast quantities of information. But is the computer more than a powerful labor-saving device for reducing tedious work and boosting productivity? Is the computer a monster that will rob Americans of their freedom, humanity, and privacy?

There is little doubt that the expanding use of computers has resulted in a growing volume of information being made available in centralized locations. Think for a moment how much information about you is stored in computer memory devices.

Computers:

—keep track of your birth and hospital records
—record your school and college grades
—compute your wages and process your paycheck
—calculate your taxes and bank balance
—compile your bills and record your "credit rating"
—maintain records of your traffic tickets as well as any criminal arrests and convictions

What worries many people is that more information leads to more power, and this power may be used for evil purposes. Could not this growing pool of information be used to blackmail, coerce, and manipulate human beings? Does not the increasing volume of information impinge upon the individual's right to privacy?

These are difficult questions for which there are no easy answers. However, in the final analysis, it is not so much the computer itself which threatens the right to privacy as it is the morality of the people who control the computer. A computer—indeed, any machine—is neither good nor evil. It is only the men who control the computer who can direct its power toward moral or immoral ends. Thus the problem is not a new one: we must be on our guard against evil men, not evil machines. In this less than perfect world, we must strive to maintain safeguards against infringement of individual rights.*

*For a more detailed discussion of the impact of computers on society, see Stanley Rothman and Charles Mosman, *Computers and Society: The Technology and Its Social Implications* (Chicago: Science Research Associates, 1972).

COMPUTERS IN BUSINESS

The use of computers by business firms is a fairly recent development, beginning less than twenty years ago. Today, virtually no large business operates without the assistance of a computer, and some giant corporations have more than one hundred. How do business firms use computers?

Routine Applications

The majority of computer time is devoted to routine clerical activities that require the processing of large amounts of information rapidly. In accounting, the handling of payrolls, accounts receivable, and accounts payable are relatively easy to adapt to electronic data processing. Consumer services firms such as insurance companies, utilities, and banks use computers to maintain customer records and to handle billing.

Other business applications of the computer include inventory control and production scheduling. Management is continuously seeking to keep the firm's inventory of goods in line with sales. Too little inventory may result in lost sales due to shortages. Too much inventory is expensive to store and increases the risk of being caught with out-of-date merchandise if sales decline. Data from sales reports are fed into a computer which, in turn, makes adjustments in inventory levels. Several computer firms have developed systems that input sales data directly from the store's checkout stand. The computer compares the sales of thousands of items to inventory levels and automatically reorders merchandise. By eliminating delays, this system can reduce inventory costs by thousands of dollars per store.

Another application of the computer is in the area of scheduling production. The computer can keep track of a highly complex production system such as automobile assembly and develop a schedule that will make maximum use of equipment and manpower while avoiding bottlenecks and delays.

Automatic Control Systems

The term *automation* refers to the use of computers to automatically control production processes. An example is the modern oil refinery, which converts petroleum into gasoline, lubricants, and petro-chemicals. A computer is programmed to control the refinery equipment and make automatic adjustments in the refining process to yield the maximum quantities of selected products from the least amount of petroleum.

Automation is based on the *information feedback principle* which permits the computer to give "orders" based on information received from measuring devices that monitor production operations. Figure 6-5 illustrates this principle.

Management Decision Making

Computers have expanded management's ability to make accurate decisions by providing increasing quantities of up-to-date information. This information reduces uncertainty, thereby placing more emphasis on rational analysis and less on intuition and guessing.

An interesting development is the use of *simulation* for management problem solving. This tool allows management to build a computer model of a business operation to compare the consequences of different decisions. For example, suppose an oil company wants to open a new service station in a certain city. It can choose several likely sites and simulate (duplicate) the operation of a model station at each site. The factors that influence profitability such as traffic volume, competition from nearby stations, and operating expenses can be expressed in mathematical terms and fed into the computer. The stations can be "operated" for a period of several years using only a few seconds of computer time. The site whose model offers the greatest potential profit is then selected. Of course, the accuracy of the prediction depends on how closely the model duplicates the real world.

The Future

The use of computers by business firms is bound to expand in the coming decades. New applications are being developed almost daily. Several firms are experimenting with electronic supermarkets. Only one item of each type of merchandise is displayed, thereby saving shelf space. The shopper selects his purchases by keying an input device. The computer totals the bill and prints a list of purchases. Using this list, the merchandise is assembled in the storeroom and delivered to the checkout stand or directly to the shopper's car.

Computer manufacturers are predicting that paper money may be virtually eliminated in the foreseeable future. Instead of receiving a

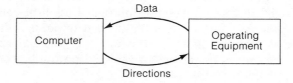

Figure 6-5 The Information Feedback Principle

paycheck, the employee will have his bank account credited with the amount of his earnings. A computer will simultaneously deduct the wages from the employer's account. When the employee wants to make a purchase at a store, he will give the sales clerk an identification card similar to a credit card. The information on the card and the amount of the purchase are fed into a computer that credits the store's bank account and makes an offsetting deduction from the customer's account. In addition, information about the purchase is automatically transferred to the store's computer for inventory and accounting purposes.

SUMMARY

The term *statistics* refers to the collection, analysis, presentation, and interpretation of numerical data. Statistical data may be collected from the firm's own records, from government or nongovernment publications, or by conducting a survey. Most surveys involve sampling. A sample is a small number of items selected from a large group for the purpose of making generalizations about the population as a whole.

Tools for statistical analysis include averages and index numbers. The three types of averages are the mean, the median, and the mode. Index numbers measure relative (or percentage) changes in numerical data.

Statistics are often summarized and presented in tables or charts. Three major types of charts are the line chart, the pie diagram, and the bar chart. Quantitative information must be interpreted with caution because statistics are subject to both mathematical errors and human bias.

Electronic data processing involves the use of a computer to process and modify quantitative data. All computers consist of five major components: (1) an input device; (2) a memory; (3) an arithmetic unit; (4) a control unit; and (5) an output device. The computer needs a detailed set of instructions, called a *program*, to process data. Programs are written in computer languages such as FORTRAN and COBOL.

The use of computers in business continues to expand rapidly. Most computer time is devoted to routine record-keeping activities, particularly the processing of accounting data. Other applications include customer billing, inventory control, and production scheduling. Computers are also used to automatically control production processes, which is often called *automation*. An expanding area of computer utilization is in management decision making. Simulation is a technique for building mathematical models of business activities to test the consequences of different decisions.

ISSUE THE THINKING MACHINES ARE COMING!

What they are, yet I know not,
But they shall be the terrors of the earth.

William Shakespeare, King Lear

In laboratories throughout the world scientists are striving to create artificial intelligence through use of computers with the power to reason and solve problems. Until recently computers have been limited to storing, retrieving, and processing large amounts of data at high speed. Today, most computer scientists predict the development of thinking machines is only a matter of time.

Already there have been a number of successful experiments. A computer using a mechanical arm can select a certain size block from a jumble of blocks on a table. A wheeled computer robot with television camera ''eyes'' can move from room to room performing simple tasks. There are also experiments under way to develop computers that understand spoken language and can simulate speech.

One of the first applications of intelligent computers will be in assembly-line processes that require simple reasoning. In the future, business managers may rely on advice from a computer in making business decisions. The computer will study and analyze all data relevant to the decision before offering a solution. Medical computers that have access to all medical knowledge may assist doctors in diagnosing illnesses and treating patients.

Many scientists and laymen are worried about the potential dangers of artificially created intelligence. Thinking machines might be used to extend the powers of a totalitarian government. For years science-fiction writers have warned that machines may become more intelligent than man and seize control of the world. Of more immediate concern is the growing complexity of computer systems, which may prevent human beings from finding out how a computer solved a problem. Then the solution would have to be accepted or rejected without knowing why.

"Good heavens! It's demanding a human sacrifice!"

Reprinted by permission of Glenn R. Bernhardt.

Reference
William Stockton, ''Do Computers Threaten Freedom?'' *Oakland Tribune,* July 6, 1973, pp. 6–7.

APPENDIX RECOGNIZING A COMPUTER APPLICATION*

Men make machines in order to extend human capabilities. For example, bulldozers, elevators, cars, and power tools extend our muscular capabilities; telescopes and microscopes extend the capabilities of our eyes; and telephones extend our vocal cords and our ears.

Computers are machines that extend our capacity to process information. They have special capabilities that make them into extremely powerful tools. These are:

Memory—they can store large amounts of data, which make them highly suitable as record-keeping tools, and they can also store instructions for later use.

Speed—they can access the data in their memories rapidly, and they can perform elementary operations like addition or multiplication rapidly (a typical time on a fast machine is an addition or multiplication in a millionth of a second).

Capacity to Accept Instructions—unlike an ordinary adding machine which needs you to punch an instruction key after entering each number, a computer is given *all* of its instructions before it begins to do its work.

Capacity to Make Decisions—this allows the program of instructions to specify what to do in a wide variety of cases; the program specifies how to recognize each case and what to do for each one.

Capacity to Control Itself without Human Intervention until a Job Is Finished—this is self-explanatory; compare with an adding machine or automobile where the operator is constantly intervening during the job because the machine does not control itself.

A computer cannot perform a job unless it has a program which tells it what to do. Note that you can change your computer from an inventory control machine to a payroll machine merely by changing the program which controls the computer.

There are two questions which must be answered in judging a potential computer application: (1) Should this job be done at all? (2) If it should be done, should it be done with the aid of a computer? The answer to the second question is yes only if the computer enables you to do the job more easily than with alternative methods or enables you to do jobs which previously were impossible.

When will a job be made possible or easier to do by means of a computer? The answer is, "when you make use of the special capa-

*Written by Ron West, who has been employed as a systems analyst for Bechtel Corporation, San Francisco, and the Lawrence Radiation Laboratory, Berkeley. Used with permission.

bilities of the computer." Thus, good computer applications contain one or more of the following elements:

1. Large amounts of data are to be processed.
2. A large number of individual steps are to be performed in processing. For example, there may be a lot of arithmetic to do. A bank, for example, must make up a monthly statement for each of thousands of customers.
3. The same programs are used regularly once they are written. Inventory control, billing, and manufacturing control are good examples.
4. The same steps are repeated many times.
5. Rapid access to data is required.
6. The data files are accessed frequently by many simultaneous users; for example, airlines reservations.

One word of warning: even if it is easier to do a job with the aid of a computer, it may still be too expensive to use a computer.

Some people worry about whether they can compete with computers. The answer is that we should not try to compete with computers at the things they are designed to do best, but rather to remember that computers are *tools* to aid humans in their pursuits.

Student _____

STUDENT FEEDBACK SYSTEM

Directions: Your questions and ideas are important! Here's a chance to get more information and relate your experiences to the materials in the chapter. Answer the following questions and turn in this page to the instructor. Use the reverse side of the page if you need additional space.

1. What topics, problems, and terms found in this chapter require more explanation by the instructor?

2. Do the concepts presented in this chapter agree with your experiences in the business world? Briefly explain why or why not, using examples.

3. Does this chapter suggest any career opportunities to you?

Student _____

REVIEWING MAJOR CONCEPTS

1. Name two internal sources of business statistics.

2. How are index numbers used?

3. Briefly describe the components of a computer?

4. What is the difference between computer hardware and software?

5. Briefly explain the information feedback principle.

6. Describe three business applications for the computer.

Student _____

SOLVING PROBLEMS AND CASES

1. The students in an accounting course received the following grades on an examination: 67, 98, 54, 72, 78, 84, 75, 72, 65, 93, 72, 70, and 84.

    a. Compute the mean, median, and mode.

    b. If your grade is 75, what is your position in the class?

2. Suppose you want to construct a price index to measure changes in the prices of goods and services typically purchased by college students. You have collected the following data:

Item	1971 Price	1975 Price	Index
Textbook	$8.00	$10.00	
Bus Ride	.20	.25	
Notebook	.25	.25	
Cafeteria Lunch	.60	.90	

    a. In the space provided, compute an index number showing the relative price change for each item. (*Hint:* Assume that 1971 is the base year, and show the 1975 price as a percent of the 1971 price).

    b. Total the index numbers and find the mean.

c. On an average, how much did prices rise between 1971 and 1975?

d. Is your price index an accurate measure of changes in the cost of living for college students? Why or why not?

3. If your college has a computer, find out:

   a. What types of jobs are handled by the computer.

   b. What computer language is used in programming.

   c. Who is in charge of data processing and to whom does he report.

4. Assume you are planning to open a record shop in a nearby city. What types of statistical information would be helpful to you? Where would you find this information?

Part IV

Business Operations

Chapter 7 Finance

In this chapter we will discuss several major topics related to business finance. The first section explores the role of financial management and describes the major sources of funds to support business operations. Then we turn to a challenging problem of corporate finance—the selection of securities to raise long-term funds. In the concluding section of the chapter the viewpoint shifts to that of the investor. Here we are concerned with how the different securities markets operate and with the procedures involved in buying and selling corporate stocks and bonds.

KEY QUESTIONS

1. What do financial managers do?

2. What are the major sources of short-term and long-term financing for business firms?

3. What are the major features of corporation bonds, preferred stock, and common stock?

4. How does corporate management select the type of security to sell for additional funds?

5. How are new issues of securities marketed?

6. How are stocks and bonds bought and sold?

7. Can you beat the stock market?

FINANCIAL MANAGEMENT

Make no mistake about it, money is the lifeblood of business. Inadequate funds will limit a firm's expansion and hinder operations. Indeed, a chronic lack of financial resources can lead to termination of the firm through bankruptcy. Witness, for example, the 1970 financial collapse of the Penn Central Transportation Company, the giant railroad corporation.

Financial management includes all those activities involved in acquiring and using funds to achieve a firm's objectives. The financial manager is concerned with ensuring that adequate funds are available to carry out essential activities. His job involves not only raising money, but also cutting costs, choosing among alternative uses of funds, conserving assets, and keeping records on how funds are used. He is responsible for paying bills, collecting accounts receivable, borrowing money, investing idle cash, and developing financial plans. Depending on the firm, the chief financial officer is known by any of a variety of titles—treasurer, controller, financial vice-president, and so on.

Sources of Short-Term Funds

Short-term funds are used to finance the day-to-day operations of the firm—to purchase inventory, finance accounts receivable, and pay wages and other expenses. The source of much of these funds is debts that must be paid off within a year. In contrast, long-term financing is used to purchase fixed assets such as equipment and buildings. It would be foolish to finance the purchase of a machine tool with a five-year life by borrowing from a bank on a 90-day note. The debt would be due long before the machine had generated sufficient revenues to pay for itself.

The major sources of short-term financing for business firms are: (1) trade creditors; (2) banks; (3) factors; and (4) certain other sources such as sales finance companies, the Small Business Administration, and retained profits.

Trade Creditors   You may recall that the balance sheet lists a current liability called *accounts payable,* which represents short-term debts owed to suppliers. These debts are commonly referred to as *open-book accounts,* and they reflect the purchase of merchandise, supplies, or other assets on credit. The vast majority of business transactions involve purchases on credit, and open-book accounts are the major source of short-term funds.

Suppose Maxwell's Decorators, a retailer in Sacramento, places an order for wallpaper and glue with World Wide Wallcoverings, a distributor. The materials are delivered, and the store receives an invoice (bill), as illustrated in Figure 7–1.

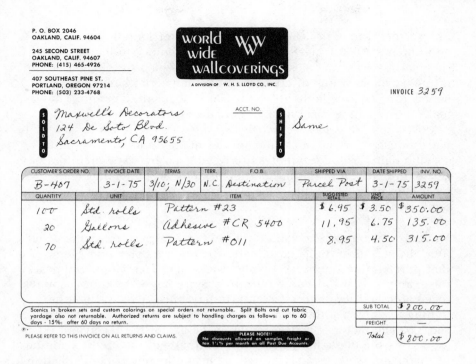

Figure 7-1 An Invoice
Courtesy of W. H. S. Lloyd Co., Inc.

The credit terms on the invoice, 3/10; N/30, mean that if the bill is paid within 10 days of the date on the invoice, the retailer may take a 3 percent cash discount; but the bill must be paid in any case within 30 days. If Maxwell's elects to pay on or before March 10, it will remit $776 ($800 less the $24 discount), but thereafter the entire $800 is due and must be paid by March 30.

The purpose of the cash discount is to encourage early payment. Business firms always try to take advantage of cash discounts because of the substantial savings. In the above example, failure to pay within 10 days means that the retailer has use of the funds for an extra 20 days at a cost of 3 percent. On an annual basis, this is 54 percent interest![1]

Banks   Commercial banks earn interest income by loaning out a part of their customers' deposits to individuals and business firms. Often banks will grant a business firm a *line of credit* to meet short-term financial needs. For example, the Soul Sisters' Dress

---

[1]The real rate of interest is the cost of borrowing money for a year. Using a 360-day "interest year", 3% for 20 days equals 54% for 360 days (360 ÷ 20 = 18 × 3% = 54%). Obviously, it would make sense to borrow funds at up to 53% interest to take advantage of the cash discount.

Shop expects to experience strong demand for its fall fashions. An additional $15,000 is needed to build up inventory to handle the anticipated increase in sales. The dress shop, which has a good credit rating, arranges a line of credit with a commercial bank. The bank agrees to make available up to $15,000 in loans on demand. The loans are repaid as cash income is realized from sales.

Most bank loans are secured by *promissory notes,* which are written promises to repay a certain sum of money plus interest on a specific date. Promissory notes are often used by trade creditors because they are more formal than open book accounts. In Figure 7–2, what sum of money will James Hardy pay to the Taft National Bank on December 31?

Factors Accounts receivable represent charge account debts owed to a business firm by its customers. Factors are collection agencies that purchase accounts receivable at less than face value. Suppose, for example, that the Value Furniture Store has $70,000 in accounts receivable and needs to raise cash to pay bills. A factor may be willing to purchase the receivables at a discounted price, say $60,000. The factor is concerned with the age of the receivables (how long the debts have been outstanding) and the credit standing of the customers. He runs the risk of losing money if the collection expenses (including bad debts) exceed the difference between the face value of the receivables and the purchase price.

It should be noted that some firms borrow money using their accounts receivable as collateral (or security) for the loan. Such loans are made by banks, factors, and finance companies. In this case, the risk of bad debts and collection expenses are borne by the borrower.

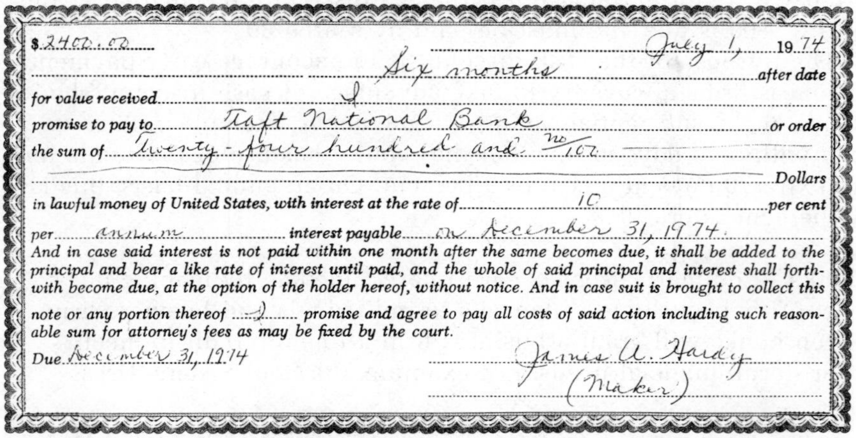

Figure 7–2 A Promissory Note
Courtesy Sam Hopkins Legal Forms Printing Service, Oakland, Calif.

Other Sources   There are a variety of institutions which may provide short-term financing to business. A retailer may sell installment contracts to a sales finance company to raise funds. The retailer obtains these contracts by selling goods to his customers on time-payment plans. Sales or installment contracts are typically used in the purchase of durable goods—automobiles, appliances, and furniture. The sales finance company buys the customer's contract as a discount; that is, at less than its full value. By selling an installment contract the retailer converts credit sales into cash.

The Small Business Administration was created to make loans to small businesses that are unable to secure financing elsewhere. Other government agencies guarantee certain types of business loans made by commercial banks and other financial institutions.

Some companies use retained earnings to meet short-term financial needs. The portion of net profits reinvested in the business may be used for financing current assets or paying current liabilities. However, it is generally considered a good practice to reserve retained earnings for long-term financing.

Sources of Long-Term Funds

Money raised through long-term financing is normally used for the purchase of fixed assets—equipment, buildings, and land. There are three major sources of long-term funds: (1) equity, (2) debt, and (3) internally generated funds. *Equity* refers to ownership. Additional funds may become available through increased investment by the proprietor or partners, or through the sale of more shares of stock by a corporation. Sources of long-term loans include banks, insurance companies, and savings and loan associations. Corporations may borrow by selling bonds to the public.

The phrase *internally generated funds* refers to retained earnings and depreciation. Most successful firms plow back a part of net profits into the business. In addition, depreciation represents a source of funds. Depreciation is an expense representing the estimated annual decline in value of plant and equipment. However, depreciation is a *noncash expense* that is subtracted from income to find net profit. The business firm does not give up any cash for depreciation as it does with other expenses. After all, the plant and equipment being depreciated was paid for when it was acquired. Therefore, depreciation lowers accounting profits without reducing cash income. For this reason, depreciation is considered a source of funds.

How important are internally generated funds? Over the past fifteen years, retained earnings and depreciation have averaged nearly 60 percent of all corporate financing.

Managers must be extremely careful in making long-term finan-

ISSUE HOW'S YOUR DUN & BRADSTREET RATING?

Although Dun & Bradstreet, Inc., has in recent years diversified into publishing, marketing services, and even broadcasting, for most men and women in business D & B is best known as the number one commercial credit rater in the world. Every other month it publishes a giant *Reference Book* which rates nearly 3,000,000 businesses in the United States and Canada. Supplementary books and reports are available on foreign firms. The *Reference Book* and *Business Information Reports* are sold on a subscription basis to thousands of companies who want up-to-date credit information.

A high D & B rating can be as valuable as cash in the bank to a business firm because it opens the door to favorable credit terms. Dun & Bradstreet employs an army of field reporters whose job it is to investigate and rate firms. The rating process involves interviewing a company's management, checking public records and accounting reports, and contacting local banks, suppliers, and other creditors. The rating takes into account the ability of management, the firm's financial strength, its payments record, and the trend of the business.

An example of a typical rating together with an explanation of the Dun & Bradstreet rating system is shown below.

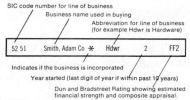

SIC code number for line of business

Business name used in buying

Abbreviation for line of business
(for example Hdwr is Hardware)

| 52 51 | Smith, Adam Co ✳ | Hdwr | 2 | FF2 |

Indicates if the business is incorporated

Year started (last digit of year if within past 10 years)

Dun and Bradstreet Rating showing estimated
financial strength and composite appraisal.

Key to Ratings

ESTIMATED FINANCIAL STRENGTH		COMPOSITE CREDIT APPRAISAL			
		HIGH	GOOD	FAIR	LIMITED
5A	Over $50,000,000	1	2	3	4
4A	$10,000,000 to 50,000,000	1	2	3	4
3A	1,000,000 to 10,000,000	1	2	3	4
2A	750,000 to 1,000,000	1	2	3	4
1A	500,000 to 750,000	1	2	3	4
BA	300,000 to 500,000	1	2	3	4
BB	200,000 to 300,000	1	2	3	4
CB	125,000 to 200,000	1	2	3	4
CC	75,000 to 125,000	1	2	3	4
DC	50,000 to 75,000	1	2	3	4
DD	35,000 to 50,000	1	2	3	4
EE	20,000 to 35,000	1	2	3	4
FF	10,000 to 20,000	1	2	3	4
GG	5,000 to 10,000	1	2	3	4
HH	Up to 5,000	1	2	3	4

**CLASSIFICATION FOR BOTH
ESTIMATED FINANCIAL STRENGTH AND CREDIT APPRAISAL**

FINANCIAL STRENGTH BRACKET

1 $125,000 and Over

2 20,000 to 125,000

EXPLANATION

When only the numeral (1 or 2) appears, it is an indication that the estimated financial strength, while not definitely classified, is presumed to be within the range of the ($) figures in the corresponding bracket and that a condition is believed to exist which warrants credit in keeping with that assumption.

NOT CLASSIFIED OR ABSENCE OF RATING

The absence of a rating, expressed by two hyphens (--), is not to be construed as unfavorable but signifies circumstances difficult to classify within condensed rating symbols. It suggests the advisability of obtaining a report for additional information.

Dun & Bradstreet.
Business Information Systems, Services and Sciences

Reference
Business Information Services (New York: Dun & Bradstreet, 1973).

cial decisions. A poor decision may saddle the firm with problems for many years. For example, a ten-year high-interest loan may be so costly that the borrower is unable to earn profits.

Both proprietorships and partnerships are extremely limited in their ability to raise long-term funds. Banks and other financial institutions are hesitant to make long-term loans to these firms because of their limited life. On the other hand, large and established corporations may raise long-term funds by marketing corporate securities.

Corporate Securities

There are two major categories of corporate securities: stocks and bonds. Stocks may be further divided into preferred stock and common stock.

Although corporations many borrow long-term funds through term loans that mature (come due) in 1 to 20 years, a more common method of debt financing is the sale of bonds.

Bonds A bond may be considered a special type of promissory note with a long-term maturity. Corporations normally sell bonds with maturity (or due) dates of between 5 and 50 years, although the majority of bonds mature in 10 to 30 years.

The bondholder is a creditor of the corporation. Bonds carry promises to repay the amount borrowed (called the *principal*) on a specific date and to pay a fixed amount of interest usually computed on an annual basis. Most corporate bonds are sold in denominations of $1,000 each.

Bondholders stand ahead of stockholders (owners) in case the corporation fails. In other words, if the firm goes bankrupt and if funds are available after paying off current liabilities, the bondholder must be repaid before stockholders receive any payment. In addition, bondholders have a legal right to interest payments. If a corporation fails to pay bond interest, the bondholders may take legal action.

There are many different types of corporate bonds. We shall explore only a few of the major ones.

1. *Registered and Bearer Bonds*. A registered bond has the owner's name on the face of the bond certificate and is recorded in the corporation's books. Interest payments are made by checks mailed to the bondholder. In contrast, bearer bonds (also called *coupon* bonds) carry no evidence of ownership. To receive his interest, the bondholder merely removes a dated coupon attached to the bond. The obvious advantage of the registered bond is that the owner is protected from loss or theft of the certificate.

2. *Mortgage and Debenture Bonds.* Mortgage bonds are secured by property owned by the corporation. Large and successful corporations may sell debentures, which are backed by the general credit of the corporation rather than any specific collateral.

3. *Callable Bonds.* Many bonds contain a *call option,* which permits the issuing corporation to redeem the bond before the maturity date. For example, suppose that in 1965 the XYZ Corporation sold $20,000,000 worth of bonds with a 7 percent interest rate. The bonds mature in 30 years (1995). Each bond has a call price of $1,025 (that is, $25 above the maturity value or par value of the bond). If the XYZ Corporation "calls" the bonds, it must pay the bondholders $1,025 for each $1,000 bond. Should interest rates decline below 7 percent, it may pay the corporation to redeem the bonds and sell a new issue at a lower interest rate.

4. *Convertible Bonds.* Some corporations make their bonds exchangeable for a fixed number of shares of stock. This convertible feature is intended to make the bonds more attractive to investors. For example, a $1,000 bond might be convertible into 20 shares of common stock. If the price of the stock is less than $50 a share, it would not pay the bondholder to convert. However, if the stock price rises above $50 a share, the price of the bond would be expected to increase proportionally. At $60 a share the bond would be worth approximately $1,200 (20 shares × $60 = $1,200). All convertible bonds are callable so that the corporation can force conversion. If bondholders convert their bonds to stock, the corporation is no longer faced with the problem of repayment of the debt.

Figure 7–3 shows a typical corporate bond. Notice that the par value (or maturity value) is $1,000 and the stated rate of interest is 6⅞ percent. When does the bond mature?

Common Stock   Common stock represents ownership of the corporation. The funds received by a corporation from the sale of common stock are not repaid as in the case of bonds. A common stockholder can sell his shares to other investors and receive his investment back, but there is no guarantee against loss.

Par value is the dollar amount printed on the stock certificate. It is a confusing term because there is no relationship between par value and the market price of the stock. To avoid confusion, some corporations issue "no par" stock.

The common stockholder may receive a share of the corporation's profits in the form of dividends. However, the stockholder is not guaranteed a dividend. The board of directors, after considering the amount of profits and the firm's financial needs, may vote to declare a cash dividend. One alternative to a cash payout is a stock dividend, whereby common stockholders receive additional shares of stock instead of a cash payment.

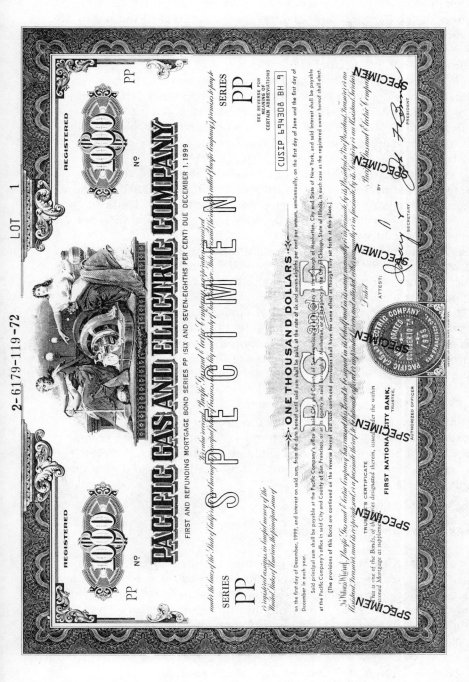

Figure 7-3 A Corporate Bond
Courtesy Pacific Gas and Electric Company

Common stock nearly always carries voting rights. As the voting owners of the corporation, common stockholders elect the board of directors. *Is preferred stock due before Bond holders.*

Preferred Stock   A second type of ownership security is *preferred stock,* which received its name because of certain preferences and priorities over common stock. Should the corporation fail, the preferred stockholders stand ahead of common stockholders for any remaining assets. Moreover, preferred stockholders must be paid their full dividend before common stockholders may receive any dividend.

The dividend on preferred stock is nearly always a fixed amount.[2] Most preferred is sold in denominations of $100 per share. Therefore, the XYZ Corporation's 6 percent preferred would have a dividend of $6 per share. In most cases, preferred stock does *not* carry the right to vote.

Preferred stock may be either *cumulative* or *noncumulative.* In the case of cumulative preferred, missed dividends accumulate and must be paid before common stockholders receive any dividend. Suppose, for example, the XYZ Corporation earned no profits in 1972 and 1973 and did not declare dividends· on its 6 percent cumulative preferred stock in those years. In 1974, a large profit was earned and both preferred and common dividends were paid. Each share of preferred would receive an $18 dividend since $6 per year dividend, missed in 1972 and 1973, accumulated and was paid in 1974. With noncumulative preferred, missed dividends are not carried forward to future years.

Both common and preferred stock represent ownership, while bonds are debt. In a sense, preferred stock stands between common stock and bonds with some of the characteristics of each. Table 7–1 outlines the major features of bonds, preferred stock, and common stock.

MARKETING CORPORATE SECURITIES

In our expanding economy, corporations often require additional long-term funds beyond those available from internal sources. One basic decision is choosing between additional debt or equity. If the firm decides to borrow, it may attempt to negotiate a long-term loan from a bank, insurance company, or other financial institutions. Both debt and equity capital[3] may be raised by selling corporate se-

[2]An exception is participating preferred, which is very rare today.
[3]The term *capital* has several meanings. In economics, *capital* refers to plant and equipment used to produce goods and services. In common business usage, the term refers to the funds available for investment in the firm.

Table 7-1 Summary of Corporate Securities

Bonds	Preferred Stocks	Common Stocks
1. Represent Debt	1. Represent Ownership	1. Represent Ownership
2. Must be Repaid	2. No Repayment	2. No Repayment
3. Pay Interest	3. Pay Dividends if Declared	3. Pay Dividends if Declared
4. Interest is a Fixed Amount	4. Dividends Normally Fixed in Amount	4. Dividends Are Not Limited in Amount
5. Interest is an Expense Paid Before Taxes	5. Dividends Are a Distribution of Profits	5. Dividends Are a Distribution of Profit Paid after Preferred Dividends
6. No Voting Rights	6. Usually No Voting Rights	6. Voting Rights
7. First Claim on Assets	7. Preferred Claim on Assets	7. Last Claim on Assets

curities to the public. Once the decision is made to sell a new issue of securities, there is still the problem of selecting the best type of security—bonds, preferred stock, or common stock. Then management must make arrangements for marketing the new issue.

Selection of Corporate Securities

At this point it is worth reemphasizing that long-term financial decisions are critically important because the firm must live with the consequences for years. Also, keep in mind that management is concerned with the interests of the corporation's owners. Financial decisions are made with an eye toward increasing the rate of return for stockholders, particularly for common stockholders.

In deciding which type of security to sell, management must carefully analyze the firm's financial needs and future prospects in terms of several major factors. These factors include: (1) cost and repayment, (2) taxation, (3) voting control, (4) expected profits, and (5) market conditions.

Cost and Repayment There are advantages and disadvantages to selling both stocks and bonds. Since bonds represent debt, the corporation must pay annual interest charges as well as repay the principal. In the case of stock, no repayment is involved, and there is no legal obligation to pay dividends. However, the sale of additional stock means that profits must be divided among more shares, raising the possibility that profits per share may decline.

Taxation Bonds offer a major tax advantage to the issuing corporation. Bond interest is considered a business expense deductible before paying corporation income taxes. In contrast, dividend payments are not an expense, but a distribution of profits after taxes.

To illustrate the significance of this point, consider a simplified example of two corporations with identical sales and expenses, except that one pays annual bond interest of $50,000 and the other dividends of $50,000. Figure 7-4 shows that interest is deducted prior to computing the corporation income tax. As a result, Corporation B pays twice as much income tax as Corporation A. This is one reason that the sale of new issues of corporation bonds has far exceeded financing by stock in recent years.

Voting Control If additional shares of common stock are sold, existing owners may lose voting control of the corporation. On the other hand, bonds do not carry voting rights, and most preferred stock is nonvoting.

Expected Profits Many firms such as public utilities enjoy steadily rising sales and earnings year after year. These firms can afford to sell large quantities of bonds because income is available to meet fixed charges—that is, interest and repayment of principal. On the other hand, the sales and profits of steel and construction companies tend to fluctuate with changes in economic activity. A firm with unstable income cannot afford a high debt to equity ratio because in poor years it may have difficulty in meeting fixed charges.

As a general rule, bonds should not be sold unless the expected rate of return from the investment of proceeds exceeds the interest rate. For example, suppose the XYZ Corporation sold $10,000,000 of 8-percent bonds to finance the construction of a new factory. The expected increase in after tax earnings from the factory is $1,000,000 a year which exceeds the annual interest payment of $800,000 (8 percent of $10,000,000). The difference of $200,000 reflects an increase in earnings for the stockholders. The process of increasing profits by investing borrowed funds at a rate of return higher than the interest rate is called *trading on equity* or *leverage*.

Figure 7-4 Tax Treatment of Interest and Dividends

Corporation A - $50,000 in Interest		Corporation B - $50,000 in Dividends	
Sales	$600,000	Sales	$600,000
Expenses	500,000	Expenses	500,000
	100,000	Profit Before Taxes	100,000
Less: Bond Interest	50,000	Income Tax (50%)	50,000
Profit Before Taxes	50,000	Net Profit	50,000
Income Tax (50%)	25,000	Less: Dividends	50,000
Retained Profit	$ 25,000	Retained Profit	$ 0

Market Conditions   If stock prices are rising and investor confidence is high, it may be relatively easy for a corporation to sell a new issue of stock. On the other hand, when stock prices are falling, corporate bonds may be more attractive to investors. When interest rates are high, a corporation may be forced to pay a high rate of interest on its bonds to attract investors. In 1967, large corporations could sell bonds with a 5 percent interest rate, but four years later the same firms were forced to pay 8½ percent. Obviously, the higher the interest rate, the greater the interest expense.

How Corporate Securities Are Marketed

The sale of a new issue of corporate securities to the public normally involves an *investment banker,* also called an *underwriter.* The primary job of an investment banker is to market new securities to the public.

   After careful analysis, the management of the Hailwood Department Store has decided to raise additional long-term capital by selling $5,000,000 of cumulative preferred stock at $100 per share. The investment banking firm of Dobbs and Dartmore is invited to underwrite the new issue. Dobbs and Dartmore first conducts a thorough investigation into the financial condition and operations of Hailwood, using a team of accountants, merchandising experts, and financial analysts. If everything is found to be in good order, the investment banking firm enters into negotiations to purchase the preferred stock for resale to the public. A key area of negotiation is the *spread,* which is the difference between the price paid for the stock by the underwriter and the market price. In this case, the two firms agreed to a 5-percent spread amounting to $250,000 (5 percent of $5,000,000). The spread represents a fee paid to the investment banker to cover expenses and provide a profit.

   Another area to be settled is the dividend rate on the preferred stock. The underwriter wants a high dividend to make the stock attractive to potential buyers, while Hailwood's management would prefer a low rate. After studying comparable preferred stocks of other corporations, it is decided that a dividend of $8 per share is appropriate.

   The investment banker assists in gaining approval of the issue from various government agencies including the Securities and Exchange Commission. Dobbs and Dartmore also agree to help in the preparation of the *prospectus,* a booklet that provides detailed information on the Hailwood Department Store and the new issue of preferred stock. Under federal law, each potential buyer of the new stock must be provided with a copy of the prospectus.

   When all arrangements are complete, Dobbs and Dartmore will give Hailwood's management a check for $4,750,000 ($5,000,000 less the spread of $250,000) in return for 50,000 shares of $8 cumulative preferred stock.[4]

In marketing the stock the investment banker will notify stock-brokers throughout the country and offer them a commission for selling the stock to their customers. If the public fails to buy all 50,000 shares, the investment banker may be forced to hold on to the remainder until market conditions improve.

THE SECURITIES MARKETS

You will recall that one of the advantages of owning corporate securities is the relative ease of transferring ownership. Billions of dollars of stocks and bonds are bought and sold daily in securities markets. These markets include organized stock exchanges and the over-the-counter market, and they involve a variety of financial institutions such as brokerage firms, investment companies, and security dealers.

Stock Exchanges

A stock exchange is a market place where corporate securities are bought and sold. The exchange itself does not purchase or sell securities; rather, it provides facilities for its members to trade stocks and bonds for their customers.

The New York Stock Exchange (NYSE) is the largest and the best-known exchange. It has 1,366 members, each of whom own a "seat" on the exchange. Most of the seats are owned by brokerage firms that represent customers in buying and selling securities. The NYSE lists about 1,500 stocks and 1,300 bonds. These securities are not new issues, but are stocks and bonds already sold by corporations. In other words, stock exchanges do *not* provide funds for corporations.

In order to have its securities listed on the New York Stock Exchange, a corporation must meet certain requirements as to minimum size and financial resources and be approved by the board of governors of the exchange. Other major exchanges include the American Stock Exchange and Pacific Stock Exchange.

Over-the-Counter Market

Only about 4,500 different securities are listed on organized exchanges, but over ten times that number of stocks and bonds are

---

[4]In most states, corporations are required by law to give existing stockholders first preference in purchasing new issues of securities. This preference, called *privileged subscription,* is ignored here in order to keep the example simple.

traded over-the-counter. These unlisted securities include government and foreign bonds, most insurance company and bank stocks
and bonds, as well as many securities of medium-sized and smaller
corporations. The over-the-counter market consists of about 4,000
security dealers who buy and sell securities for their own accounts.
Each dealer normally maintains an inventory of several unlisted
stocks and bonds. He makes a market by standing ready to buy and
sell these securities.

There are two prices for over-the-counter securities, the *bid* and
the *ask*. For example, the common stock of the XYZ Corporation
may be quoted at 25 bid and 26 ask by a dealer on a particular day.
This means that the dealer is willing to buy the stock at $25 per
share and to sell it for $26 a share. The difference between the bid
and ask prices represents the dealer's mark-up or gross profit.

Brokerage Firms

A stockbroker buys and sells securities for his customers and
charges a commission for this service. Large brokerage firms are
normally members of the New York Stock Exchange and other
major exchanges. Some brokerage houses also serve as over-the-
counter dealers. In addition to buying and selling listed and unlisted securities for customers, some brokers also act as investment
bankers in underwriting new issues.

Brokerage firms provide a variety of services to their customers.
They collect and distribute financial information and provide research reports on corporate securities. Most brokerage houses make
loans to customers who maintain margin accounts. Buying on margin means that the customer need not come up with the full cash
amount of the transaction. For example, if he buys 100 shares of a
stock at $20 a share, the amount due is $2,000 (omitting commissions and taxes). If the margin rate is 70 percent, he must deposit
$1,400 (70 percent of $2,000) and the broker will lend him the remainder.

Opening an account with a brokerage firm is a relatively simple
process similar to opening a checking or savings account with a
bank.

A Typical Transaction

Suppose you want to purchase shares of General Electric common
stock, which is listed on the New York Stock Exchange. You call or
visit your broker and ask him for a quote on GE common. Using an
electronic quote machine connected to the floor of the NYSE, he
discovers that the last sale of General Electric was at 61¼ ($61.25
per share). You decide that you can afford to purchase 100 shares.

This is called a *round lot*. Anything less than 100 shares is an *odd lot*. You then enter an order to buy 100 shares of GE *at the market*—that is, at the best price available when the order is received. A *limit order* sets a maximum price you are willing to pay—say $61 per share. Of course, a limit order may not be filled if there are no sellers at the limit price.

Your market order is sent to the floor of the NYSE by teletype where a floor broker employed by your brokerage firm takes it to the trading post where General Electric is bought and sold. At the trading post, the floor broker asks for a quote on GE and discovers it is 61 bid and 61¼ ask. This means that there is a seller willing to take $61.25 a share for his stock and a buyer willing to pay $61.00 a share. Your floor broker bids 61⅛ and another broker representing a seller accepts the bid. Confirmation of the purchase is teletyped back to your broker's office. The entire process has probably taken less than five minutes.

You have purchased 100 shares of General Electric common stock at a net cost of $6,112.50 ($61⅛ per share × 100 shares). To this amount you must add your broker's commission plus federal and state taxes which will bring the total cost to $6,193.76.[5]

Investment Companies

A popular way to invest in corporate securities is through the purchase of investment company shares. Investment companies sell their securities to the public and invest the proceeds in the stocks and bonds of other companies.

Investment companies may be either closed-end or open-end. A *closed-end investment company* sells its securities only when first organized. Thereafter, the securities are traded over-the-counter or on an organized exchange. *Open-end investment companies,* better known as *mutual funds,* are by far the more popular type. Mutual fund shares are sold on a continuous basis—that is, the fund issues new shares whenever there are buyers. The money received from the sale of shares is used to purchase the securities of other corporations. The value of the mutual fund shares is based on the value of the securities which it owns. Suppose, for example, that on December 12, 1974, the Go-Go Fund owns a portfolio of common stocks with a current market value of $2,700,000. If the fund has 90,000 shares outstanding, the liquidation price of each share is $30 ($2,700,000 ÷ 90,000 shares = $30 per share). This is the price that the shareholder would receive if he wanted to sell his Go-Go Fund shares on December 12.

---

[5]Brokerage commissions vary with the dollar amount of the transaction. The average rate is approximately 2 percent. Taxes amount to only a few cents a share.

There are two major advantages of investing in a mutual fund: diversification and professional management. Since the investor's money is spread among many different securities, the risk of losing the entire investment is minimized. The managers of the open-end investment company keep a close watch on the fund's portfolio and make purchases and sales intended to increase the value of the fund's shares. To some extent, the individual investor is relieved of the necessity of keeping close watch on his investment.

Mutual funds also have certain disadvantages. When purchasing shares, the investor must pay a commission, called a *front-end load,* which amounts to about 9.3 percent.[6] In addition, there is an annual management fee, which usually averages ¼ of 1 percent of the portfolio's value.

Stock Quotations

More than thirty million Americans own corporate securities and the number is growing daily. Since many of these investors want timely information on their investments, financial news reporting has expanded rapidly over the past few decades.

Most newspapers present a daily summary of stock transactions on major exchanges. This summary may appear confusing at first glance, but with a little practice it is easy to read. Figure 7–5 presents a portion of the stock quotations for the New York Stock Exchange together with a section-by-section explanation.

Buy Philosophy: purpose-timing-amount of money
what
How

Can You Beat the Market?

One way to make (and lose) money is to purchase corporate securities. Basically, there are two types of security buyers—speculators and investors. The speculator is interested in quick profit. He usually buys a company's stock which is subject to wide and rapid price changes with the hope of buying low and selling high in a relatively short period of time (a few hours, days, weeks, or at most, a few months). The investor is interested in long-range appreciation (growth) of his funds. He normally purchases a portfolio of securities in several corporations, and often holds these securities for years with the objective of steady (if not spectacular) appreciation and/or income.

The individual considering the purchase of stocks or bonds should first determine his objectives. Is he primarily interested in current income, steady appreciation, or fast profits? Investment objectives must relate to the individual's personal circumstances—his

[6]A few funds do not charge a commission and are called *no-load funds.*

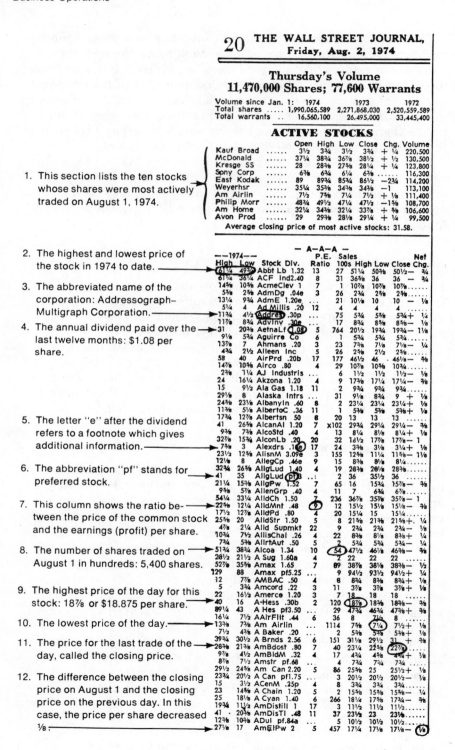

1. This section lists the ten stocks whose shares were most actively traded on August 1, 1974.

2. The highest and lowest price of the stock in 1974 to date.

3. The abbreviated name of the corporation: Addressograph–Multigraph Corporation.

4. The annual dividend paid over the last twelve months: $1.08 per share.

5. The letter "e" after the dividend refers to a footnote which gives additional information.

6. The abbreviation "pf" stands for preferred stock.

7. This column shows the ratio between the price of the common stock and the earnings (profit) per share.

8. The number of shares traded on August 1 in hundreds: 5,400 shares.

9. The highest price of the day for this stock: 18⅞ or $18.875 per share.

10. The lowest price of the day.

11. The price for the last trade of the day, called the closing price.

12. The difference between the closing price on August 1 and the closing price on the previous day. In this case, the price per share decreased ⅛.

Figure 7–5 How to Read Newspaper Stock Quotations

financial resources, knowledge, personality, and willingness to accept risk. It is important to understand that there is a close relationship between the potential profit from an investment and the degree of risk involved. In other words, the greater the potential
profit, the higher the risk of loss.

Successful investors and speculators carefully evaluate a possible
investment before committing their funds. They attempt to answer
a variety of questions through careful research. In what type of industry does the firm operate and what are the future prospects for
the industry? What products and/or services does the firm produce? What is the corporation's earnings record? Does the firm
have good management? What has happened to the price of the
stock or bond over the past few years?

If you think it is easy to make a quick fortune on the stock market, perhaps you should consider the advice of Bernard Baruch, one
of the most successful speculators of all time:

If you are ready to give up everything else—to study the whole history and background of the market and all the principle companies whose stocks are on the board as carefully as a medical student studies anatomy—if you can do all that, and, in addition, you
have the cool nerves of a great gambler, the sixth sense of a kind
of clairvoyant, and the courage of a lion, you have a ghost of a
chance.

SUMMARY

Financial managers are primarily concerned with acquiring sufficient funds to finance operations and using these funds to achieve
the firm's objectives. Short-term funds are employed in financing
the day-to-day operations of the firm, while long-term funds are
normally invested in fixed assets.

The major source of short-term funds is from open-book accounts
which are debts owed to trade creditors. Most trade creditors offer
a cash discount for early payment of the amount owed. Banks may
extend a line of credit to established firms that specifies the maximum amount the bank will loan. Most bank loans are secured by
promissory notes, which specify the repayment date and the rate of
interest.

Factors are companies that purchase accounts receivable at a discount. Other sources of short term funds include sales finance companies and various government agencies such as the Small Business
Administration.

Long-term funds are available from owners, creditors, and internal sources such as retained earnings and depreciation. Corporations may sell additional shares of preferred and common stock or
bonds to raise long-term capital.

Bonds are formal, interest-bearing debts with long-term maturities. Bondholders stand ahead of stockholders in their claim to the assets of the corporation, and bondholders have a legal right to interest payments. Registered bonds, which have the name of the bondholder recorded on the certificate and in the corporation's books, are protected from loss or theft, but bearer bonds are not. Mortgage bonds are secured by property owned by the corporation, while debentures are backed only by good credit standing of the firm. Many corporate bonds may be redeemed prior to maturity by paying a call price. Some bonds are convertible into shares of stock.

Common stockholders are the voting owners of the corporation. As such, they bear the greatest risks, but enjoy the greatest opportunities for gain if the corporation is profitable. Dividends are a distribution of profits paid to stockholders at the discretion of the board of directors.

Preferred stock, another type of ownership security, enjoys preferences over common stock as to assets and dividends. In most cases, preferred stock is nonvoting, and the dividend is limited to a fixed amount.

In deciding which type of corporate security to sell to raise additional capital, management must consider the problems of cost and repayment, the tax treatment of interest and dividends, the effect on the voting control of the firm, the amount and stability of future earnings, and current market conditions. New issues of stocks and bonds are normally marketed through an investment banker, who purchases the securities from the issuing corporation and resells them to the public.

Corporate securities are traded on organized exchanges and over-the-counter. The most famous exchange is the New York Stock Exchange which provides facilities for its members to buy and sell stocks and bonds for their customers. In contrast, the over-the-counter market consists of roughly 4,000 security dealers who trade for their own accounts.

A stockbroker acts as an agent for his customers in the purchase and sale of corporate securities. He charges a commission on each transaction. Brokerage houses often act as over-the-counter dealers and some serve as investment bankers. In addition, brokerage firms make loans to their customers on margin accounts.

Investment companies sell securities to the public and reinvest the funds in the stocks and bonds of other corporations. Open-end investment companies, better known as *mutual funds,* are the most popular type. They sell shares on a continuous basis, as opposed to closed-end investment companies, which only sell securities when first organized. Investment companies offer the investor diversification and professional management.

Corporate securities are purchased by both speculators and investors. The speculator attempts to earn a quick profit by buying low and selling high within a short period of time. On the other hand, the investor is interested in long-range appreciation and/or current income. Successful investors and speculators carefully study possible purchases in light of their own objectives.

Fortunes have been made and lost in the stock market. Successful investing is more a matter of careful study, knowlege, and skill than it is of luck. On the other hand, good luck never hurt anyone.

APPENDIX BONDS: PREMIUMS, DISCOUNTS, AND YIELDS

There is a market for corporate and government bonds just as there are markets for food, houses, and other goods. The price of a bond is determined by the forces of supply and demand. Depending on the circumstances, a bond may sell at par value, at a discount, or at a premium.

Par value, sometimes called *face value,* is the amount printed on the bond certificate; in the case of corporate bonds, it is usually $1,000. This is the amount of money which will be repaid to the bondholder when the bond matures or comes due. A discount price is any price below par value, while a premium price refers to any price above par value.

What factors determine the price of a bond? The degree of risk influences what investors are willing to pay for a bond. In estimating risk, investors consider the size and earnings of the corporation issuing the bond. Two securities research firms, Moody's Investor's Service and Standard & Poor's, rate bonds according to their quality or safety. These ratings, beginning at the top, are AAA, AA, A, BBB, BB, B, etc. The lower the quality of the bond, the greater the risk.

The price of a bond also varies according to other interest rates in the economy. If interest rates are rising, bond prices tend to decline since investors can find more attractive returns elsewhere. Inflation also tends to depress bond prices. A rapid rise in prices reduces the buying power of the dollar, thereby eroding the value of bonds.

Yield measures the rate of return from investing in a security. The yield on a bond may be computed using a simple formula:

$$\text{Yield} = \frac{\text{Dollar Amount of Interest}}{\text{Bond Price}}$$

The dollar amount of interest is the stated rate of interest on the bond certificate multiplied by the par value. For example, a $1,000 par value bond issued by the ABC Corporation matures in 10 years and has a stated rate of interest of 8 percent. The dollar amount of interest is $80 (8 percent × $1,000 = $80). Therefore, if a bond is selling at par value, its yield is the same as the stated rate of inter-est.

Suppose, however, the ABC bond is selling at a discount, for ex-ample, $800. In this case, the yield may be calculated as follows: Yield = $80/$800 = 10 percent. The amount of the discount, $200, is a bonus to the investor since the ABC Corporation must pay the bondholder $1,000 when the bond matures in ten years. This bonus, in effect, increases the bond yield. Since the ABC bond matures in ten years, the amount of the discount averages $20 a year ($200 ÷ 10 years = $20). Adding the $20 discount to our yield formula we get:

$$\text{Yield} = \frac{\$80 + \$20}{\$800} = \frac{\$100}{\$800} = 12.5\%$$

When a bond sells at a premium, its yield is less than the stated amount of interest. If the ABC Corporation bond is selling at $1,100, then the yield is: $80/$1,000 = 7.27 percent. Of course, the investor who pays $1,100 for the bond will receive only $1,000 when the bond matures. Therefore, he is paying a penalty of $100.

The price of a bond and its yield move in opposite directions. When the bond price goes up its yield goes down, and when the price declines the yield increases. The yields for other securities, such as common and preferred stock, may be calculated in much the same way as bond yields.

Student _____

REVIEWING MAJOR CONCEPTS

1. Briefly, why are long-term financial decisions considered more important than short-term financial decisions?

2. What are internally generated funds?

3. Explain why short-term funds should not be used to finance the purchase of fixed assets.

4. What is the difference between cumulative and noncumulative preferred stock?

5. From the viewpoint of the corporation, what tax advantage do bonds have over stock?

6. Why do public utilities normally have higher debt-to-equity ratios than steel companies?

7. What are the major advantages and disadvantages of buying mutual fund shares?

8. Briefly, what does an investment banker do? What risk does the investment banker assume in underwriting an issue of securities?

9. True or False? Stock exchanges are a major source of long-term financing for corporations. Explain your answer.

10. The potential profit from any investment is directly related to the degree of risk. Explain this statement in terms of the following investments.

   a. A bank savings account paying 4-percent interest and insured by an agency of the federal government.

   b. A General Motors 6-percent debenture bond.

   c. The common stock of a small electronics firm that is experimenting with commercial applications of laser beams.

Student _____

SOLVING PROBLEMS AND CASES

1. *Case:* Vargas Hardware Store

   On September 15, 1974, Vargas Hardware received a shipment of lawn-mowers together with an invoice for $1,200. The terms on the invoice were 2/20; N/60.

   a. If Vargas pays the bill on or before October 5, how much does the store owe?

   b. If Vargas elects to wait until October 30, how much should be paid?

   c. If Vargas can negotiate a short-term loan from a bank at an annual interest rate of 10 percent, would it pay to borrow funds and take the discount? Explain why or why not.

2. *Case:* Zenith Widget Company, Inc.

   The Zenith Widget Company has decided to go out of business due to declining sales and profits. After selling its assets and paying off current liabilities, $3,000,000 in cash remains. The firm's outstanding securities are shown below:

Common Stock	$2,000,000
Bonds	1,600,000
Preferred Stock	1,200,000

   a. How much will the owners of each type of security receive?

   b. What would your answer be if the remaining cash were only $1,000,000? Explain.

3. Suppose you own a 6-percent convertible bond callable at 103 ($1,030). The bond is convertible into thirty shares of common stock which has a current market price of $36 per share. If the corporation calls the bond, what should you do? Explain your decision.

4. *Case:* Home Run Products Company

Spike Hanson is the owner and manager of the Home Run Products Company, a small but profitable manufacturer of baseball equipment. Recently he has become concerned about his firm's shortage of cash. Since sales are expected to increase rapidly in the next few months, he feels that additional funds are needed to purchase more inventory and meet operating expenses. A simplified balance sheet for the firm is reproduced below.

Cash	$ 5,000	Accounts Payable	$ 10,000
Accounts Receivable	80,000	Note Payable to Bank	15,000
Inventory	30,000	Taxes Payable	5,000
Fixed Assets	100,000	Spike Hanson, Capital	185,000
	$215,000		$215,000

Mr. Hanson has turned to you, his accountant, for advice. What suggestions do you have for raising additional funds?

Student _____

5. *Case:* Fun-Rite Toys, Inc.

In 1970, Fun-Rite Toys sold 10,000 shares of $8 cumulative preferred stock at $100 per share. The $8 preferred dividend was paid in 1970. The firm experienced losses for the next three years due to poor economic conditions plus increased competition. No dividends were declared on either common or preferred stock during 1971, 1972 and 1973. In late 1973, a new line of toys was introduced that proved highly successful. Profits for 1974 reached record levels, and the board of directors declared $600,000 in dividends. How much did the preferred stockholders receive?

6. *Case:* Barton Machine Tools, Inc.

Late in 1974, the Finance Committee of Barton Machine Tools was considering the best source of long-term funds to finance the purchase of a
foundry that would cost $12,000,000. The financial vice-president had pre-
pared a report that estimated that the new foundry would increase the
firm's pre-tax profits by an average of $4,000,000 each year for the next
24 years. However, this estimate did not include the cost of the funds
needed for the purchase. The committee members were in full agreement
that the foundry would be a good investment, but there was some
difference of opinion as to how the $12,000,000 should be raised.

One committee member recommended that Barton issue debenture bonds,
which he felt could be sold at an 8-percent interest rate. The head accountant proposed a $9 cumulative preferred stock issue, while two other
committee members favored the sale of additional shares of common stock
at the current market price of $20 a share. The current common stock divi-
dend is $1.00 per share.

Barton Machine Tools had earned profits every year for the past twenty
years with the exception of 1958. Dividends on common and preferred
stock have been paid each year since 1965. The firm's current capital
structure is shown below:

5% Mortgage Bonds due 1984	$ 1,000,000
$7 Noncumulative Preferred	5,000,000
Common Stock (1,000,000 shares)	10,000,000
Retained Profits	8,000,000

As assistant to the president, you have been asked to write a brief report
analyzing the alternatives and presenting your recommendations.

Student _____

7. *Case:* Harriet Silvers

Harriet Silvers is a young stockbroker recently employed by a leading brokerage firm. One afternoon, a Mr. Martin Kingman introduced himself and
asked Harriet to suggest some "hot" common stocks.

In talking with Mr. Kingman, Harriet learned that he had recently retired at
the age of 65 from his job as sales clerk with a department store. He lives
with his wife in a small apartment near the brokerage office. His income
from social security and a pension fund is $450 a month. In addition, he
has a savings account of $15,000 on which he earns 4 percent interest.

Mr. Kingman mentioned that he wants to "make a little quick money on the
market" by investing his $15,000 in common stocks. He feels that his prof-
its from the stock market will permit him to live more comfortably on his
retirement income.

What advice should Harriet offer to Mr. Kingman?

Chapter 8

Personnel

Business is people. Every organization consists of groups of people—employees and managers—working together. Psychologists have long recognized that each human being is a unique combination of abilities, aptitudes, and personality traits. In short, no two individuals are exactly alike. This fact makes personnel management—the management of people—a challenging and vital part of every manager's job.

This chapter deals with the people part of business. It is divided into three major sections: human relations, personnel management, and labor relations.

KEY QUESTIONS
1. How are human beings motivated?
2. What factors influence employee morale?
3. What is leadership?
4. What are the responsibilities of the personnel department?
5. How did the American labor movement develop?
6. What is collective bargaining and how does it work?
7. What methods are used by unions and employers in labor-management conflicts.

HUMAN RELATIONS

Morale is to all other factors as four is to one.

Napoleon

The success of a business is largely dependent on the degree to which its employees are motivated to carry out assigned duties and work toward achieving the firm's objectives. Until a few decades ago, businessmen often viewed workers as little more than commodities to be purchased at a low price and worked hard for long hours. However, a few managers, concerned for the workers' welfare, made efforts to increase wages, improve working conditions, and boost morale. The result was often astonishing gains in productivity. It began to dawn on employers that treating workers like human beings could pay off in dollars and cents! Today, managers are increasingly concerned with the relationship between employee morale and productivity.

The Hawthorne Experiments

The human relations movement gained impetus from the Hawthorne Experiments conducted by Elton Mayo of Harvard University at the Hawthorne Works of the Western Electric Company during the 1920s and 1930s. The research began as an attempt to measure the effect of illumination on worker output, but the experiments were broadened to include changes in rest periods, working hours, and other conditions. The researchers were astonished to find that however they changed working conditions production increased, even when the working conditions were deliberately changed for the worse. Mayo and his associates concluded that the workers involved in the experiments enjoyed the attention they received, and their feeling of increased recognition and status motivated them to boost output. It appeared that social and psychological factors might be more important than physical working conditions in determining productivity! The widespread publicity given the Hawthorne Experiments caused many managers to rethink their approaches to personnel management.

Motivation and Needs

One of the most widely accepted theories of human motivation was developed by Abraham Maslow.[1] According to Maslow, human beings are motivated by needs which are arranged in the form of a hierarchy illustrated in Figure 8-1. Basic needs are physical or material in nature—the need for food, clothing, and shelter are exam-

[1]A. H. Maslow, *Motivation and Personality* (New York: Harper and Row, 1954), pp. 80–106.

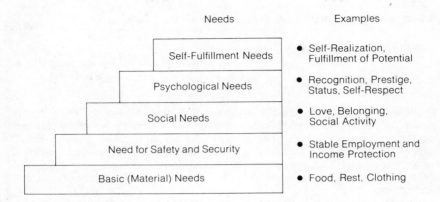

Needs	Examples
Self-Fulfillment Needs	● Self-Realization, Fulfillment of Potential
Psychological Needs	● Recognition, Prestige, Status, Self-Respect
Social Needs	● Love, Belonging, Social Activity
Need for Safety and Security	● Stable Employment and Income Protection
Basic (Material) Needs	● Food, Rest, Clothing

Figure 8-1   Maslow's Hierarchy of Needs

ples. A hungry man is motivated to seek food. A secure job and insurance are ways of satisfying safety needs. When these material needs are satisfied, human behavior is influenced by social and psychological needs which include recognition, social acceptance, self-respect, as well as self-realization through a sense of accomplishment.

Up to the middle of the twentieth century, most workers were motivated by monetary incentives; that is, by money to meet basic needs. However, the substantial increase in per capita income over the past few decades has meant that the vast majority of workers can now satisfy their material needs. This ability to satisfy basic needs has placed increased emphasis on psychological and social needs as the prime motivators of human behavior. For this reason management must rely on effective human relations practices to motivate workers.

Morale

Morale refers to a worker's attitude toward his job and the firm. Morale is determined by the extent that an employee's work satisfies his needs. Obviously, there is a close relationship between employee morale and productivity. Effective managers attempt to improve morale by identifying worker needs and undertaking activities to fulfill these needs.

Although morale is intangible and difficult to measure, there are some indicators which can be used to gauge the level of employee morale. Labor turnover measures the number and frequency of employee resignations. A high rate of labor turnover is often a signal of low morale. Increasing absenteeism suggests declining morale, as does low productivity. A drop in productivity should alert management to possible morale problems. Frequent strikes are another indicator of worker dissatisfaction.

ISSUE JOB ENRICHMENT: THE END OF WORKER BOREDOM?

We have run out of dumb people to handle those dumb jobs.
> Robert Ford, Personnel Director,
> American Telephone and Telegraph Company

Today you hear a great deal about *worker alienation,* a term that refers to the growing number of workers who are "turned off" by their jobs. Many men and women are complaining that their jobs provide no satisfaction or personal fulfillment. Management has listened to these complaints with growing concern, for worker alienation is often reflected in declining productivity, rising absenteeism, and increasing labor turnover, all of which can dramatically boost labor costs.

For years the key to increasing productivity was thought to be specialization—the breaking down of all work into small component parts, assigning each worker a tiny task, and relying on assembly-line processes. Specialization has been carried to great extremes in both factories and offices. Today, however, there is growing recognition that the advantages of specialization may be more than offset by worker boredom and alienation. More and more business firms are turning to job enrichment programs to overcome worker dissatisfaction.

Job enrichment may be described as the reshaping of jobs to provide workers with more variety, responsibility, interest, and sense of accomplishment. At the Saab and Volvo automobile plants in Sweden, traditional assembly lines are virtually eliminated, and work teams put together entire segments of cars. The teams are responsible for inspection and the quality of workmanship. In many offices in this country, clerical workers are being given broader and more diverse duties and encouraged to make decisions without consulting their supervisors. In some firms, job enrichment has not been limited to office and factory workers but extended to include sales, professional, and managerial personnel.

Many job enrichment programs have proved highly successful in boosting morale, improving quality, and reducing errors. Absenteeism and labor turnover have shown dramatic improvement. However, not every program has been an unqualified success. Some managers feel that sharing responsibility and increasing worker freedom threatens their status and authority. Moreover, there has been growing opposition from labor union leaders who often see job enrichment as a plot for getting more work out of fewer workers.

References
Roger Ricklefs, "Boredom Fighters Put Variety in Many Jobs, Find Productivity Rises," *Wall Street Journal,* August 21, 1972, p. 1.

Byron E. Calme, "Wary Labor Eyes Job Enrichment," *Wall Street Journal,* February 26, 1973, p. 11.

Harry Bernstein, "A Campaign to Sell Americans on Work," *San Francisco Chronicle,* December 29, 1972, p. 10.

It is management's responsibility to build good morale by providing a work climate that motivates workers by meeting their needs. This, of course, is not always an easy task. However, a good human relations program begins by recognizing the social and psychological needs of human beings.

What factors tend to build morale? This is a complex question, and space does not permit a comprehensive answer. However, it is possible to identify a few factors which contribute to good morale.

Recognition   It goes without saying that human beings want their efforts to be recognized and acknowledged. A few words of encouragement and praise can be very effective in boosting an employee's morale. Many large firms publish house organs—company newspapers or magazines—that contain articles and announcements about employees and their jobs. Is there anyone who does not like to see his name in print?

Recently a textile firm sponsored a daily music program on a local radio station that was piped into the company's offices. Instead of commercials, spot announcements praised the work of outstanding employees. Management claimed that productivity increased by 125 percent as a result of the program.

Preserve Self-Respect   An individual's dignity and self-esteem influence his attitude toward work. A supervisor must be careful not to needlessly damage an employee's self-respect. One rule of thumb is to praise publicly, but criticize privately. A public reprimand causes an employee to lose face before his fellow workers, and it may result in permanent hostility and poor morale.

Stressing Job Importance   Workers engaged in assembly-line operations often perform the same simple task thousands of times a day. These employees may come to feel like cogs in a giant machine, and as a result, morale may decline. Management can undertake a program to emphasize to the worker the importance of his job by relating his task to the operation of the completed product. For example, workers who install automobile brakes might be shown a motion picture stressing the prevention of automobile accidents through properly functioning brakes.

Good Communications   Some managers think of communications as getting "the word" to the workers. But effective communications is more than a one-way street. Employees must be able to transmit their problems and suggestions to management without being confronted with excessive delays and red tape.

Good communications involves transmitting understanding. Whenever possible, employees should be given the reasons for an order. Suppose, for example, the manager of a department store issues the following directive to all store personnel: "Effective next Monday, this store shall open one hour later and close one hour later." This announcement is likely to generate hostility since no explanation is offered for the change and because the employees were not consulted about the later hours.

The lack of effective communications can lead to rumors which are likely to cause anxiety and undermine morale. When an organization is undergoing change, management should endeavor to keep all employees informed of the latest developments in order to reduce rumors.

While on the subject of communications, it is worthwhile noting that one of the most important skills that a manager can develop is the ability to listen. It is a natural tendency for a human being to hear only what he wants to hear. To fully understand what is being communicated, the listener should attempt to put himself in the speaker's shoes. This means adopting the speaker's frame of reference to fully perceive his meaning.

Prompt Handling of Complaints and Grievances   Closely related to good communications is effectively dealing with employee complaints and grievances. In the first place, management should welcome workers' requests to discuss grievances because getting the problem out into the open is the first step toward solving it. The very act of voicing a complaint serves as a safety valve. Unexpressed grievances tend to become internalized and cause frustration out of proportion to the problem.

Some firms have adopted an open-door policy for handling grievances whereby the worker may take his complaint up the chain of command until he is satisfied. For example, if a production worker is not satisfied with his foreman's solution to the grievance, he next takes it to the plant supervisor and so forth. Other firms submit unresolved grievances to arbitration, a procedure described later in the chapter.

The Key Role of Leadership

Leadership may be defined as the act of persuading and directing others so as to gain their enthusiastic participation and support. In one sense, all managers are leaders. No single factor has more influence on employee morale than the leadership of the supervisor. The manager's actions create the atmosphere in which his subordinates operate. His methods of issuing orders, his fairness and consideration, and even his sense of humor will influence worker behavior.

Styles of leadership are based on certain assumptions as to how people are motivated and how they react to work. Douglas McGregor has categorized such assumptions into two theories which he

Table 8–1 McGregor's Theory X and Theory Y

Theory X	Theory Y
1. People dislike work and will avoid it if possible.	1. People do not hate work; it's as normal as rest or play.
2. Most people must be directed, coerced, and threatened with punishment to make them work toward company objectives.	2. People don't have to be coerced or threatened. They will commit themselves to mutual objectives and work hard to achieve them if their needs are satisfied in the process.
3. People dislike responsibility, have little ambition, and want security above all.	3. Under the right conditions people will seek responsibility and bring to bear all their energy, imagination, and creativity in solving business problems.

calls Theory X and Theory Y.[2] These theories are summarized in Table 8–1.

Theory X, which McGregor calls the traditional view, assumes that organizational objectives are not compatible with human goals. In contrast, Theory Y suggests a participative approach to management, which emphasizes the involvement of employees in the decision-making process so that they will be more highly motivated.

McGregor suggests that the Theory Y approach is the more desirable one for managers to adopt. However, recent research suggests that the Theory X approach works well under some circumstances and ineffectively in others.[3] The same is true for Theory Y. The best approach seems to depend on the nature of the work being done and the needs of the people involved. In organizations where work and procedures are formalized and the tasks to be accomplished are predictable, Theory X may prove the more appropriate approach. Theory Y appears to work better where there is an emphasis on innovation and problem solving.

Styles of leadership range from totally autocratic to democratic. Some managers believe that the autocratic manager who makes all the decisions and gives orders that are carried out without question is outdated. They may prefer participative leadership, where subordinates are encouraged to involve themselves in the decision-making process while the leader attempts to develop group consensus. Obviously there is an infinite variety of leadership styles, each of which will work in different circumstances. The most appropriate leadership style depends on the personality of the leader, the nature

[2]Douglas McGregor, *The Human Side of Enterprise* (New York: McGraw–Hill, 1960).
[3]See, for example, John J. Morse and Jay W. Lorsch, "Beyond Theory Y," *Harvard Business Review,* May–June 1970, pp. 61–68.

of the subordinates, and the type of work being performed. For example, the leadership style that is effective for an assembly line foreman might be totally ineffective in managing a group of scientists in a research laboratory.

The truth is that very little is known about leadership. Good leaders come in all shapes, sizes, colors, and sexes. We do know two things about leadership: (1) leaders lead, and (2) leadership is critically important to the success of any enterprise.

Perhaps the ultimate in leadership was described 25 centuries ago by the Chinese poet Lao-tzu:

A leader is best when people barely know he exists,
Not so good when people obey and acclaim him,
Worse when people despise him.
Fail to honor people, and they fail to honor you.
But a good leader, who talks little,
When his work is done, his aim is fulfilled,
The people will say, "We did it ourselves."

Improving employee morale is not something that can be accomplished overnight. It is a long-range process that involves all levels of management. An effective human-relations program entails convincing employees that the firm is sincerely concerned with their welfare and recognizes their importance as human beings. It is *not* enough to pay lip service to these goals; actions speak louder than words. Good human relations require time and commitment, but the results are well worth the effort.

PERSONNEL MANAGEMENT

In a broad sense, the management of personnel is the responsibility of every manager in an organization. However, most large firms have a personnel department to provide specialized services relating to employees. It should be noted that the personnel manager is a staff position whose primary responsibility is to provide assistance in personnel matters to other departments. Typically, the personnel department is concerned with (1) hiring, (2) orientating, (3) training, (4) evaluating, and (5) compensating employees.

Hiring

The hiring process begins with a careful analysis of the position to be filled. This study is used to develop *job specifications,* which describe the qualifications needed to perform the job.

Recruiting is the process of actively seeking out prospective employees and encouraging them to apply for open positions. Recruiting may involve classified advertising (see Figure 8–2), the use of employment agencies, and visits by company recruiters to schools and colleges.

ISSUE THE OTHER SIDE OF THE COIN: ARE MANAGERS TREATING EMPLOYEES LIKE SPOILED BRATS?

The proliferation of programs designed to improve employee morale and motivation through better communications and "more humane" management may have been carried too far. The following comments were made by Robert F. Six, president and chief executive officer of Continental Airlines, when accepting the "Man of the Year" award from UCLA's Executive Program Association:

> It has been my observation that a desperate management in a frantic effort to implement employee communication frequently treats its people like spoiled brats. The use of brainstorming sessions, of management chats, of this endless search for a two-way street whereby employer and employee may vent their souls and fall in love with each other misuses work time and shows depressingly small success.
>
> So, too, does the ancient plea that "My door is always open—bring me your problems." This is guaranteed to turn on every whiner, lackey and neurotic on the property. If you enjoy playing priest or psychiatrist, this is great fun, but it has nothing to do with the motivation of the employees.
>
> May I suggest that there are many millions of workers who actually, honest-to-God, like their jobs and are proud of their skills? Accepted doctrine seems to insist that employees hate work, hate the boss and have to be cuddled and cajoled into punching a clock because they would much rather be down at the library improving their minds or out on the beach playing in the sand.
>
> Ladies and gentlemen, despite what you hear, most people enjoy going to work in the morning. Honest! They find their tasks interesting—even challenging—their fellow workers like-minded people with whom they can share occupational concerns. Many grow to be their friends. The cadence of the job has a healthy rhythm. Their rewards are tangible and satisfying. *

*Reprinted by permission of Mr. Six.

PERSONNEL ASSISTANT

Expanding and stable San Francisco Bay Area headquartered corporation seeks individual with recruiting and unemployment compensation experience. Typing ability desirable. Excellent salary, benefits and opportunity to progress with a leading company. Our employees are aware of this advertisement. Please send complete resume and salary history to:

Box 529 K, Wall St. Journal, Palo Alto

ASSISTANT CONTROLLER

Large, Independent Oil Company needs Assistant Controller. Southwestern Location. Ideal qualifications will be B.A., M.B.A., C.P.A. plus 10 years heavy experience in management of Accounting functions. Oil industry experience preferable. Responsibilities to include data processing and credit in addition to accounting. Must be able to manage without close supervision. Reports to Corporate Controller headquartered in distant City. Applicants submit resumé and salary history to:
Box 526 K, Wall Street Journal, Palo Alto
Equal Opportunity Employer

Figure 8-2 Management Recruiting
Reprinted by permission of the *Wall Street Journal.*

The selection of new employees is a very important process. Many firms find their freedom to fire unsatisfactory employees is severely limited by union contracts and company policies. Therefore every effort must be made to hire the right individual for the position or the company may be stuck with an unsatisfactory employee for many years.

The selection process normally begins with the *application form,* which provides information on the applicant's personal characteristics, work experience, education, and so forth. The application form serves as a screening device for eliminating those applicants who obviously do not have the necessary qualifications for the position. A typical application form is shown in Figure 8–3.

The most important part of the hiring process is the *interview.* Face-to-face contact with the applicant permits the interviewer to gain additional information not available from the application form and to generally evaluate the applicant's qualifications for the position. Some firms use a series of interviews beginning with a preliminary or screening interview and ending with a final selection interview.

Many employers are making increasing use of *testing* in the selection process. There are various types of tests designed to measure different characteristics.

1. *Performance Tests* are used to measure skills such as typing and shorthand accuracy and speed.

2. *Aptitude Tests* attempt to determine an individual's potential proficiency for certain types of work such as clerical or assembly jobs.

3. *Personality Tests* try to measure motivation and personality traits of the applicant. Such tests are often criticized for being invalid and subject to misinterpretation.

Orientation

The purposes of orientation are to introduce the new employee to his work environment and to ensure that he is familiar with company policies and procedures. An employee is usually apprehensive when he takes a new job. An orientation program can ease this apprehension by explaining to the worker what is expected of him and by introducing him to his fellow workers. An effective orientation program can reduce labor turnover by helping new employees adjust quickly to the work environment.

Training

The purpose of training is to provide employees with the knowledge and skills to perform their duties effectively. Training methods

Victor Corporation
Employment Application

FOR OFFICE USE ONLY
DATE EMPLOYED _____
TITLE _____
SALARY _____
ENGAGED BY _____
TITLE _____

NAME	LAST	FIRST	INITIAL	SOCIAL SECURITY NUMBER
ADDRESS	STREET	CITY	STATE	ZIP CODE

TELEPHONE NUMBER	MINIMUM SALARY REQUIREMENT	DATE AVAILABLE	DATE OF BIRTH	AGE
POSITION DESIRED			HEIGHT	WEIGHT

MILITARY SERVICE DATA	BRANCH OF SERVICE	DUTIES
DATE OF INDUCTION	DATE OF DISCHARGE	RANK AT DISCHARGE	TYPE OF DISCHARGE

LAW VIOLATIONS List any law violations for which you have been arrested or convicted. Indicate when, where and disposition of each case.

EDUCATIONAL RECORD (NAME AND ADDRESS)	CIRCLE LAST GRADE COMPLETED	DID YOU GRADUATE?	DATE OF LEAVING
LAST ELEMENTARY SCHOOL	1 2 3 4 5 6 7 8		
LAST HIGH SCHOOL	9 10 11 12		
JUNIOR COLLEGE	MAJOR FIELD	DEGREE	
COLLEGE OR UNIVERSITY	MAJOR FIELD	DEGREE	
COLLEGE OR UNIVERSITY	MAJOR FIELD	DEGREE	

EMPLOYMENT DATA List positions starting with most recent.

COMPANY NAME	FROM: MO. YR.	BEGINNING SALARY	JOB TITLE
ADDRESS	TO: MO. YR.	ENDING SALARY	JOB DUTIES
CITY	STATE	REASON FOR LEAVING	
SUPERVISOR			
COMPANY NAME	FROM: MO. YR.	BEGINNING SALARY	JOB TITLE
ADDRESS	TO: MO. YR.	ENDING SALARY	JOB DUTIES
CITY	STATE	REASON FOR LEAVING	
SUPERVISOR			
COMPANY NAME	FROM: MO. YR.	BEGINNING SALARY	JOB TITLE
ADDRESS	TO: MO. YR.	ENDING SALARY	JOB DUTIES
CITY	STATE	REASON FOR LEAVING	
SUPERVISOR			

TWO PERSONAL REFERENCES (NOT RELATIVES OR PERSONS YOU HAVE WORKED FOR)

NAME	MAILING ADDRESS	STATE	TEL. NO. IF KNOWN	BUSINESS OR PROFESSION

Signature _____ Date _____

Figure 8–3 An Employment Application Form

vary from firm to firm. Probably the most common method is *on-the-job training* where an employee attempts to develop skills while actually performing a job. Often an experienced worker will be assigned to provide guidance and assistance.

Vestibule training takes place in a special area away from the job site. Necessary materials and equipment are available for practice. The advantage of vestibule training is that the trainee is not subjected to on-the-job distractions and pressures.

Some firms use *formal classroom training,* particularly in management development programs. A variety of instructional techniques including lectures, discussions, role-playing, and audiovisual presentations may be used.

Evaluating

Most large organizations have developed formal procedures for rating the performance of employees. The purpose of evaluation is to provide information for determining wages and salaries and for promotions. In addition, an effective evaluation process can serve to assist employees in recognizing and overcoming their shortcomings.

Compensating

Wage and salary administration is one of the most complex responsibilities of the personnel department. A fair and equitable system of compensation is a major determinant of employee morale. Interestingly enough, studies have shown that the relative differences in compensation paid to various workers is often more important than the absolute size of the paycheck. This is because an employee tends to measure his status by comparing his income to that of other workers.

There are several methods of compensation:

Time Rate   Time-rate systems pay workers according to the amount of time spent on the job. For example, the employee may be paid at a rate of $4 per hour for a 40-hour week and $6 per hour for overtime above 40 hours.

Piece Rate   Piece-rate systems base the employee's pay on his output. There is a built-in incentive for the worker to increase his production. An example is a system that pays a worker at the rate of 10 cents per unit. If the worker produces 300 units a day, he earns $30; if his output increases to 370 units, his earnings would be $37 per day. The piece-rate system is commonly used to compensate salesmen who work on a commission basis.

Profit Sharing   Profit sharing is used by some firms to encourage increased production, reduce labor turnover, and promote employee loyalty. A portion of after-tax profits are set aside for distribution to workers in the form of a bonus. Profit-sharing plans have met with mixed results. If profits decline, worker bonuses are reduced and morale may drop. Moreover, such plans may result in lower earnings for stockholders.

Fringe Benefits Fringe benefits refer to noncash payments, which often take the form of company-paid health, accident, and life insurance; pension plans; rest periods; paid holidays and vacations; company-subsidized cafeterias; and a variety of other benefits. In recent years, fringe benefits have grown increasingly important. Today, fringe benefits account for more than 25 percent of labor costs, and this share is growing.

The personnel department may also undertake many other activities such as developing health and safety programs, administering transfers and separations, maintaining employee records, and handling labor relations.

LABOR RELATIONS

A specialized area of personnel management is *labor relations*, which refers to management's relations with labor unions. In many American industries, all or nearly all of the workers are union members. Wages and conditions of employment are negotiated through a process called *collective bargaining*. What unions are and how they operate is best understood by briefly reviewing the historical development of labor unions in the United States.

The American Labor Movement

Even before the Revolutionary War, groups of craftsmen banded together in an attempt to improve their bargaining position with employers. However, most early unions failed, largely because of internal conflicts and the strong opposition of employers. In 1886, a cigar maker named Samuel Gompers helped to found the American Federation of Labor (AFL), which was a voluntary association of craft unions. Except for one year, Gompers was president of the AFL until 1924. He was a staunch believer in *business unionism,* a philosophy based on three guidelines: (1) unions should be organized by crafts such as carpenters and machinists; (2) labor should focus on "bread-and-butter" issues such as higher wages, better working conditions, and shorter hours; and (3) unions should operate within the framework of the capitalist system and not become deeply involved in politics.

Union membership grew steadily until by 1920 there were five million members. However, in the 1920s employers launched a concerted counterattack against the unions, and by the end of the decade membership had dropped to barely three million workers.

In the 1930s the turning point came for the American labor movement. The Great Depression led to the election of Franklin Roosevelt and a Democratic congress with strong labor support. The fed-

ISSUE WHAT'S YOUR JOB PSYCHOLOGY?

A job is more than a way of earning a living; it is a means of achieving self-esteem, status, and personal satisfaction. Of course everyone wants a job which is rewarding and satisfying. Your job success depends to a large extent on your attitudes and personal characteristics—that is, on your job psychology.

A job represents a contract between an employer and an employee that entails responsibilities for both parties. The employer has an obligation to pay the employee what he is worth, to provide opportunities for advancement, and to reward superior performance. The employee's responsibility begins with a commitment of time, energy, and effort to the firm's success. In other words, he should identify with the firm's goals.

When you take a job, the first thing to find out is what is expected of you in terms of performance and behavior. Your first question should be "What can I contribute?" not "What's in it for me?" Be realistic enough to recognize that no job is exciting and satisfying all the time. Your employer expects you to get the job done on time even if it is difficult and unpleasant. In short, he expects you to produce! After all, you are accepting his money. Taking a job without a commitment to deliver to the best of your ability is a rip-off.

Probably the single most important reason for job failure is the inability to get along with others. Your interpersonal relations with your coworkers can make or break you. A little courtesy and kindness can go a long way. Don't act superior, even if you think you are. Remember that acts of hostility toward others are usually a reflection of your own feelings of dissatisfaction or inadequacy.

Another determinant of job success is your personal image—how others view and react to you. Your image depends on a number of factors, including your appearance, tact, poise, and honesty. Obviously, the way you dress as well as your personal grooming influence the reactions of coworkers, customers, and your employer. Most firms have an easily recognized appearance model. If you feel your dress and grooming are no one's business but your own, then you had better find a job where these factors are unimportant.

Tact is skill in not offending others. Try to develop an awareness of people's feelings and sensitivities. A good rule to keep in mind is that no one likes to be criticized. Poise is a combination of confidence (but not overconfidence) and dignity that engenders respect from others. It is a reflection of personal competence and self-assurance mixed with humility. In short, poise is the ability to laugh at oneself and yet not be a fool.

If you were an employer, would you hire or promote a dishonest person? Of course not! Be worthy of other people's trust. Remember your reputation for personal honesty will follow you throughout your career.

Technical skill and intellectual brilliance are rarely key factors in job success. Far more important are the employee's attitudes and personal characteristics. Do you have a positive job psychology?

Reference

Philip W. Dunphy, "Career Adjustment and Development," in *Career Development for College Students* (Cranston, R.I.: The Carroll Press, 1969), pp. 217–228.

eral government encouraged union growth and passed a series of laws that were favorable to organized labor. In 1935, a group of labor leaders broke with the AFL and formed the Congress of Industrial Organization (CIO) to organize workers in mass-production industries such as steel, automobiles, and rubber. In the next ten years, the number of unionized workers increased five-fold, and by 1973 union membership stood at nearly 20 million.

In 1955, after twenty years of competition, the American Federation of Labor and the Congress of Industrial Organization merged to form the AFL–CIO. Major independent unions include the Teamsters, United Auto Workers, and United Mine Workers.

Types of Unions   There are two major categories of unions—craft and industrial.

1. *Craft unions* consist of skilled workers organized by crafts or trades such as electricians, plumbers, and musicians. Most craft unions are associated with the AFL.

2. *Industrial unions* are organized on an industry-wide basis and their members are normally semiskilled or unskilled production-line workers. Examples of industrial unions include the United Rubber Workers and United Steel Workers. The majority of industrial unions are associated with the CIO.

Unions: Problems and Prospects   The tremendous growth of the labor movement during the 1930s and 1940s has slowed in recent years. Figure 8–4 shows union membership and the percent of the total labor force that is unionized. It is interesting to note that the percent of the labor force belonging to unions reached a peak of about 25 percent in the early 1950s, and in the last twenty years union membership has failed to keep pace with the growth in the labor force.

There are several factors that explain why unions have not matched the rapid growth in membership achieved during the 1930s and 1940s. The major strength of the unions has always been among blue-collar workers—that is, skilled craftsmen and production-line employees. However, the structure of the American work force has changed drastically in the past few decades. The blue-collar work force has declined in relative importance, while the number of white-collar workers, which include office workers, sales personnel, and most government employees, has grown at a rapid pace. The unions have spent millions of dollars in attempts to organize white-collar workers. These efforts have been successful in some cases—for example, many government employees have joined unions. But the fact remains, the vast majority of white-collar workers remain unorganized.

Figure 8–4 Union Membership, 1930–1972
Source: United States Department of Labor, Bureau of Labor Statistics, *Handbook of Labor Statistics, 1973.*

The public's attitude toward unions has changed. In the 1930s many people viewed the unions as underdogs fighting for worker rights against selfish "fat-cat corporations." But the growing wealth and power of many unions caused the public to become less sympathetic. This change in attitude was reflected in labor laws passed in the 1940s and 1950s that sought to limit union power and check the corrupt practices of a few union leaders.

Today many craft unions in the construction trades are under attack for discrimination against racial minorities. Some politicians and businessmen have charged that unions have acted to reduce productivity and encouraged inflation through restrictive work rules and excessive wage demands.

What does the future hold for unions? Some people predict that organized labor will experience another period of rapid growth as increasing numbers of white-collar workers are persuaded to join unions. Others believe that unions will lose membership as the blue-collar work force continues to shrink in relative importance. What do you think?

Labor Laws

Federal, state, and local governments have passed hundreds of laws that have influenced labor–management relations. Three important pieces of labor legislation are the Wagner Act, the Taft–Hartley Act, and the Landrum–Griffin Act.

Wagner Act   In 1935, Congress passed the National Labor Relations Act, commonly known as the Wagner Act. This law was intended to encourage the growth of unions by guaranteeing workers the right to organize and bargain collectively. Prior to the passage of the Wagner Act, employers were free to fight unions with almost any method including firing union members, using strikebreakers and armed guards, and by refusing to meet with union representatives.

The Wagner Act also established the National Labor Relations Board (NLRB), a three-member government agency, to investigate charges of unfair labor practices and to hold elections to determine if the majority of workers in a particular plant want to be represented by a union.

Taft–Hartley Act   After World War II, organized labor called a series of major strikes aimed at securing large wage increases. Public opinion turned antiunion, and in 1947 Congress passed the Labor Management Relations Act, commonly called the Taft–Hartley Act. The law was an attempt to correct some of the abuses of organized labor and to restore the balance of power between unions and business firms.

The Taft–Hartley Act outlawed certain unfair labor practices by unions. The closed shop, which prevents employers from hiring nonunion members, was made illegal, as was the practice of featherbedding, which requires employers to pay for work not performed. Secondary boycotts, described later in the chapter, were also outlawed.

The Taft–Hartley Act also contains a provision that permits the President of the United States to secure a court order postponing a strike for 80 days whenever the strike threatens the national health and safety. This is known as the *80-day "cooling-off injunction,"* and it requires striking workers to return to work.

The most controversial part of the Taft–Hartley Act is Section 14b, which permits individual states to pass laws prohibiting the union shop. These so-called "right-to-work laws" make it illegal for a worker to be forced to join a union to keep his job. At this time, nineteen states have "right-to-work" laws, but none of these states is highly industrialized.

Landrum–Griffin Act During the 1950s a congressional committee investigated charges of racketeering and corruption on the part of some labor leaders. As a result, the Labor Management Reporting and Disclosure Act, also known as the Landrum–Griffin Act, was passed in 1959. This law requires unions to report the handling of union funds, particularly financial arrangements with union officers. It attempts to ensure the democratic participation of union members in the election of officers and the conduct of union affairs. For example, the secret ballot is required in union elections.

Collective Bargaining

The process by which representatives of labor and management attempt to settle their differences through negotiations is called *collective bargaining*. This process requires that the union be recognized by management as the bargaining agent for the employees. Under the Wagner Act, such recognition may be granted voluntarily by management, or when the majority of workers vote to be represented by a union. The degree of union recognition, which may vary considerably from firm to firm, is defined by what are called *shop agreements*.

Shop Agreements There are four major types of shop agreements.

1. The *closed shop* requires that management hire only workers who are already union members. Obviously, from the union's viewpoint this is highly desirable because the union essentially controls all hiring. The Taft–Hartley Act declared the closed shop illegal, but it still persists in some industries.

2. The *union shop* permits employers to hire nonunion workers, but all workers must join the union within a specified period of time, usually thirty days after being hired.

3. Under an *agency shop* agreement workers need not join the union but nonunion members are required to pay union dues.

4. An *open shop* reflects no formal recognition of the union by management. Workers may join the union or not, at their option.

The Labor Contract The purpose of collective bargaining is to sign a labor contract. The labor contract is simply a list of rules and procedures that govern the relationship between management and employees. The major provisions covered in most labor contracts include: (1) the life of the contract; (2) union recognition and the shop agreement; (3) wages and hours; (4) fringe benefits; (5) provisions for holidays, vacations, and overtime; (6) layoffs and seniority; and (7) grievance procedures.

Mediation and Arbitration   Should labor and management be unable to reach agreement on the labor contract or some other item of dispute, a third party may be asked to intervene. In *mediation,* a neutral third party listens to the arguments from both sides and attempts to get labor and management to settle their differences. Although the mediator may recommend solutions, neither party is bound to accept those recommendations.

Arbitration is similar to mediation except that both labor and management agree to be bound by the decision of the arbitrator. In other words, the arbitrator acts as judge and jury, and his decision is binding on both parties.

Arbitration is commonly used as the last resort in settling grievances. A typical procedure calls for management to select one arbitrator, labor another, and a third arbitrator is selected by the other two. After hearing both sides of the dispute, the board of arbitrators vote to determine a solution.

Labor–Management Conflict

It is inevitable that some disputes between labor and management result in open conflict. Workers feel that they have a right to higher wages, improved working conditions, and job security. On the other hand, management also feels that it has certain prerogatives such as the right to introduce new equipment, to change production procedures, and to hire and fire workers. These different viewpoints often lead to conflicts that involve direct pressure being exerted by both sides.

Union Pressure   The most important union weapon is the *strike*. The walkout strike where workers leave their place of employment is the most widely used. The sit-down strike, where workers remain on the job but refuse to perform work, and the slowdown strike, which involves reducing production, have both been declared illegal by the courts.

Picketing occurs when workers parade in front of their place of employment carrying signs stating that a labor dispute is in progress. Members of other unions will often refuse to cross a picket line, thereby bringing additional pressure on management. There are two major types of boycotts. In a *primary boycott* union members refuse to purchase an employer's products until he concedes to their demands. A *secondary boycott* involves taking action against a second firm not involved in the labor dispute in order to bring indirect pressure on an employer. Suppose, for example, that the shoemaker's union is striking the ABC Company, a shoe manufacturer. The union then pickets retail shoe stores that carry ABC shoes to force the stores to stop buying from the ABC Company.

Because the secondary boycott involves an "innocent" third party, it was declared illegal under the Taft–Hartley Act.

Management Pressure The employer's equivalent of the strike is the *lockout*. Management refuses to allow workers to enter the plant until they drop some demand or halt some activity.

The *injunction* is a court order, obtained by an employer, which prohibits a union from engaging in some activity. Prior to the 1930s, the injunction was management's main weapon against unions, but legislation has severely limited its use.

The *blacklist* is a secret list of union members and organizers which is used by firms in an industry to prevent these people from being hired. Although the blacklist is considered an unfair labor practice under the Wagner Act, it is still used in a few nonunionized industries.

Another illegal antiunion weapon is the *yellow-dog contract* under which a worker is required to sign a contract promising not to join a union as a condition of employment.

The publicity given to strikes by the news media may lead people to conclude that most collective-bargaining sessions break down and lead to open conflict. This is far from true. The vast majority of labor contracts are negotiated and signed with little fanfare and publicity. Our system of collective bargaining is far from perfect, but it is workable.

SUMMARY

The Hawthorne experiments led many managers to recognize that worker motivation and morale influence productivity. According to Maslow's hierarchy of needs theory, human beings are motivated by both material and nonmaterial needs. Of particular importance are psychological and social needs, which include recognition, social acceptance, and self-respect.

Some of the major indicators of worker morale are labor turnover, absenteeism, productivity, and the number of grievances. Management can help to build high morale by praising good performance, preserving employees' self-esteem, stressing job importance, establishing good communications, and providing for the effective handling of grievances.

Leadership is the art of gaining the enthusiastic participation and support of others in achieving the leader's goals. Styles of leadership differ according to the leader's personality, the type of work being performed, and the education and skills of the employees. McGregor's Theory X and Theory Y represent two contrasting views of how people are motivated and how they react to work.

Most large organizations have a personnel department, which is responsible for assisting other departments in the areas of hiring, orientating, training, evaluating, and compensating employees. The selection process is critically important because a firm may be saddled with an unsatisfactory employee for many years. This process normally includes screening, interviewing, and testing.

The term *labor relations* refers to the relations between employers and unions. The American labor movement experienced its most rapid growth in the 1930s and early 1940s largely as a result of favorable government legislation and the successful organizing of workers in mass-production industries. In 1955, the American Federation of Labor and the Congress of Industrial Organizations merged to form the AFL–CIO. About two-thirds of all union members belong to unions that are associated with the AFL–CIO. Craft unions consist of skilled workers organized by trade, while industrial unions are organized on an industry basis and include semiskilled production workers. The future growth of American unions depends on their ability to organize the white-collar work force.

The Wagner Act (1935) guaranteed workers the right to organize and bargain collectively and established the National Labor Relations Board. The Taft–Hartley law (1947) sought to limit unfair labor practices by unions, provided for a presidential 80-day "cooling-off injunction," and permitted states to pass "right-to-work laws." The Landrum–Griffin Act (1959) required unions to report their financial activities and attempted to guarantee union members' rights.

Collective bargaining refers to negotiations between labor and management for the purpose of signing a labor contract. The bargaining process may include mediation or arbitration, both of which involve the assistance of neutral third parties.

The shop agreement defines the degree of union recognition by management. Four major types of shop agreements are the closed shop, the union shop, the agency shop, and the open shop.

Both unions and management attempt to exert pressure during labor conflicts. Unions may call a strike, picket, and use boycotts. Employers may lockout workers or seek a court injunction against the union. In the past, some firms have used blacklisting and the yellow-dog contract to oppose union organizing efforts.

ISSUE UNION SHOOTOUT: UFW VS. THE TEAMSTERS

Not all union conflicts are with employers. Some of the bitterest labor battles have been jurisdictional disputes over which union will represent a group of workers. Such is the case in the long-running feud between the United Farm Workers (UFW) and the International Brotherhood of Teamsters (IBT) over which will be the bargaining agent for the newly organized agricultural laborers.

The dispute appears to have all the features of a classic battle between David and Goliath. David, of course, is the tiny UFW under the inspired leadership of César Chávez who has spent over a quarter of a century struggling to create a union for farm workers. Opposing Chávez is the 2.4-million-strong IBT, the largest and wealthiest union in the United States.

By 1971, Chávez appeared to have won the battle. The UFW had signed 150 contracts with growers covering 40,000 workers. This success was partly a result of strong public sympathy for *la causa*—the cause—which enabled Chávez to launch a series of effective boycotts against nonunion grapes and lettuce. There was also substantial support from prominent political figures such as Robert and Ted Kennedy. Perhaps even more important was the backing of the 13.5-million-member AFL–CIO, which donated $1.6 million to the UFW.

Beginning in 1973, however, the UFW suffered a series of crushing setbacks as most growers elected to sign new contracts with the Teamsters. UFW membership dwindled to barely 6,500 workers. The IBT was anxious to organize farm workers because field strikes affect the livelihood of the truck drivers and cannery workers who are already Teamster members. The growers charged that Chávez was a poor union administrator and an inflexible bargainer who was more interested in creating a social revolution than operating his union efficiently. Chávez claimed that the IBT and the growers were conspiring to destroy the UFW and that the Teamsters were guilty of coercing workers and using illegal organizing methods.

The main difference between the UFW and IBT contracts is the hiring-hall system where workers are assigned jobs by union representatives on a seniority basis. Chávez has always insisted that hiring halls are essential to protect the union. The growers claim the hiring halls are inefficient and workers oppose their use, because families are broken up as members are sent to different farms. The new IBT contracts call for a return to the use of labor contractors to handle hiring. Chávez charges that the contractors are often corrupt.

Complicating the entire picture is the fact that agricultural workers are not covered by national labor laws such as the Wagner and Taft–Hartley Acts. This means that the National Labor Relations Board is not empowered to hold secret elections to determine which union the workers favor. Chávez wants an election and predicts 90 percent of the workers would vote for UFW. On the other hand, he does not favor bringing farm workers under the national labor laws because the Taft–Hartley Act bans the secondary boycott, which has been the UFW's most effective weapon.

The UFW is on strike and César Chávez has called for a nationwide boycott of Teamster-harvested products. This may well be the decisive battle in the long war between the IBT and the UFW.

References

William Wong, ''Struggle in the Fields,'' *Wall Street Journal,* June 29, 1973, p. 26.

''Tug of War Over the Farm Hands,'' *U.S. News and World Report,* September 17, 1973, pp. 96–98.

Student _____

REVIEWING MAJOR CONCEPTS

1. What was the major conclusion drawn from the Hawthorne experiments? Why were the Hawthorne experiments important?

2. Why are social and psychological needs probably more important than material and safety needs in motivating most American workers?

3. Why should management be interested in employee morale?

4. Would you prefer to be paid on a piece-rate or on a time-rate basis? Explain why.

5. Why has labor union growth slowed in recent years?

6. Do you expect American unions to grow or decline in membership in the next ten years? Why?

7. What is the difference between a craft union and an industrial union? Give an example of each.

8. Briefly describe the major provisions of the following laws:

   a. Wagner Act.

   b. Taft–Hartley Act.

   c. Landrum–Griffin Act.

9. What does the National Labor Relations Board do?

Student _____

10. "Right-to-work laws" essentially outlaw the union shop. Would you vote for or against such a law for your state? Explain why.

11. Many labor contracts have a seniority clause providing that "the last man hired shall be the first fired." Why do unions favor such a provision? Do you think a seniority clause is fair? Why or why not?

12. Which of McGregor's two theories do you think accurately reflects most people's attitudes toward work? Explain your choice.

Student _____

SOLVING PROBLEMS AND CASES

1. *Case:* Perez Auto Parts

Emanuel Perez is the hard-driving owner and manager of a successful wholesale auto parts firm with over 100 employees. Mr. Perez started his business twenty-five years ago working out of his garage with his wife as his only assistant. Working sixteen to twenty hours a day, he built a profitable business that sells auto parts to auto repair shops and service stations in a middle-sized western city.

Mr. Perez pays his workers top wages, but he has always opposed such fringe benefits as paid vacations, coffee breaks, and health insurance. His workers are not unionized, and he recently fired a worker whom he suspected of being a union organizer.

Recently Mr. Perez noticed that the number of deliveries per driver had been declining. He immediately went out to the work area and bawled out the foreman in front of several drivers. In recent weeks, several employees have quit and absenteeism has been rising.

Yesterday, Mr. Perez learned that four drivers have been trying to persuade the other employees to join the Teamsters Union. His first reaction was to "fire the troublemakers". He told his wife, "Workers today are soft and lazy. I pay top wages and I expect hard work. What's wrong with those guys anyway?"

If you were Mrs. Perez, what would you say to your husband?

2. *Case:* Work–Rite Tools, Inc.

Work-Rite Tools produces garden implements ranging from power lawn mowers to simple hand tools. The company operates two plants, one located in the Watts section of Los Angeles and the other in the suburbs of Portland, Oregon.

Mr. Franklin Hilgard, Work-Rite's president and chairman of the board, has been active for many years in the civil rights movement. Over 70 percent of the employees in the Watts plant are black, and the company has actively recruited black managers, many of whom are in their twenties and hold college degrees.

Last week, fifteen black managers led by Mr. Victor Stark, assistant production manager for the Watts plant, held a press conference in which they made the following charges:

a. Many workers and managers in the Watts plant are paid less than those in the Portland plant for the same job.

b. Nonminority people have been promoted over qualified blacks.

c. Work-Rite Tools buys from only a very few minority-owned suppliers.

d. The company has been increasing employment at the Portland plant while laying off workers at the Watts plant.

Mr. Stark's group demanded that the company stop these practices immediately and, in protest, all fifteen called in sick the next day.

Mr. Hilgard, the president, refused to discuss the demands until the black managers returned to work, and he gave them twenty-four hours to report back to their jobs.

It is now twenty-four hours later, and the managers have not returned. You are the personnel manager of Work-Rite and Mr. Hilgard has asked for your advice. Incidentally, you are a black man. What do you suggest?

Student _____

3. *Case:* The Green Food Company

Mr. Hal Hardy has just been promoted to Plant Manager of a food processing factory owned by the Green Food Company. Reviewing the past
performance of the plant, Mr. Hardy found that worker productivity has
been low, and the plant has been struck by the union several times despite
the fact that wages and fringe benefits are generally higher than those paid
by other companies in the area.

Mr. Massey, the former plant manager, maintains that the union leaders
"are nothing but a bunch of troublemakers". He openly boasts that at the
last contract negotiation he "tricked" the union representatives into taking
less than the company was prepared to offer. Mr. Massey had also issued
instructions to his foremen to "ignore or take a hard stand on worker
grievances to prevent the employees from becoming a bunch of chronic
complainers."

The labor contract for the plant expires in two weeks. The union is already
talking about another strike.

What action should Mr. Hardy take?

Chapter 9   Marketing

Marketing, sometimes called distribution, is the payoff for business. Marketing activities generate the income necessary to meet expenses and provide profits. To put it bluntly, efficient production may be desirable, but effective marketing is essential.

From the consumer's point of view, marketing means the right goods are available at a convenient time and location at a price he is willing to pay. Marketing has been described as delivering a standard of living to consumers.

There are several ways of studying the broad area of marketing. This chapter attacks the subject from the manager's viewpoint.

KEY QUESTIONS

1. What is marketing and how important is it in our society?

2. Is the consumer king?

3. How do managers develop a marketing strategy for the business firm?

4. What roles do middlemen (retailers and wholesalers) play in distributing goods and services?

5. What considerations influence the use of advertising and personal selling in promoting products?

6. What role does price play in marketing goods and services?

THE KEY ROLE OF MARKETING

Marketing has been defined as all activities involved in moving goods from the producer to the consumer. This definition encompasses a host of activities such as advertising, personal selling, retailing, wholesaling, market research, storage, transportation, and so forth. However, in a sense this definition is limited. In recent years, many businessmen have broadened their view of marketing into what has been termed the marketing concept.

The Marketing Concept

Prior to about 1950, most managers considered marketing as the simple process of selling the goods and services produced by the firm. Emphasis was placed on production, not distribution. However, in the rapidly expanding economy following World War II, it became increasingly apparent that the major challenge had shifted from producing goods to marketing them. In order to support mass-production industries, it has become necessary to develop mass markets. For this reason, many firms have become marketing-oriented—that is, they have placed primary emphasis on marketing.

The marketing concept holds that business firms must focus on determining consumer needs and then develop a marketing strategy for fulfilling those needs. In other words, the business firm must become consumer oriented, for the failure to meet consumer needs can lead to failure. The consumer is king!

The Importance of Marketing

Approximately 50 percent of the retail price of goods and services you buy represents marketing costs. For some goods, such as fashion merchandise, marketing costs are much higher.

Does marketing cost too much? If consumers would be satisfied with a limited number of standardized products sold at a few centralized locations, then marketing costs could be slashed. But the American consumer wants both variety and convenience and he is willing to pay for them.

Today, more than one-quarter of the labor force is engaged in marketing activities, and if current trends continue, this proportion should grow. For one thing, this means there are an increasing number of career opportunities in marketing.

MARKETING MANAGEMENT

Some managers have carried the marketing concept one step further by suggesting that marketing considerations should control (or at least influence) all other business functions including production and finance. They argue that marketing is the essential function because it alone brings in the bread.

Marketing Strategy[1]

The purpose of marketing is to satisfy the needs of a group of consumers with a product. The task of the marketing manager is to develop a plan or strategy consisting of two parts:

1. *Identifying the target market*—the group of consumers at which the firm will aim its marketing efforts; and
2. *Developing a marketing mix*—the combination of tools that the firm will employ to satisfy the target market.

The Target Market

No business firm can hope to satisfy all consumers. Consumers fall into groups according to age, income, geographic location, sex, marital status, and so forth. It may also be possible to *classify consumers* according to social and psychological characteristics such as desire for social acceptance, personal pride, and need for status. Market research is employed to define these market segments. The marketing manager then selects the target market—those groups of consumers which offer the greatest potential for his firm.

The Marketing Mix

Once the target market is determined, the next step is to select the best combination of marketing tools for hitting the market. These tools may be divided into categories called *"The Four P's":*

1. *Product.* Here we are concerned with developing the best product (either a good or service) to satisfy the consumers in the target market. Included in this area are decisions about packaging and branding.
2. *Place.* This category includes all the institutions and activities necessary to move the product to the target consumers. It involves choosing the right channels of distribution for the product.
3. *Promotion.* The major promotional tools are advertising and personal selling. The purpose of promotion is to inform the target

---

[1]Many of the concepts presented in this and following sections were developed by Alfred R. Oxenfeldt, "The Formulation of a Marketing Strategy", in E. J. Kelly and W. Lazer, *Managerial Marketing: Perspectives and Viewpoints* (Homewood, Ill.: Richard D. Irwin, 1958), pp. 264-271. A comprehensive examination of marketing strategy may be found in E. J. McCarthy, *Basic Marketing: A Managerial Approach,* 3rd Ed., (Homewood, Ill.: Richard D. Irwin, 1968).

consumers (as well as selected wholesalers and retailers) about the firm's product and to persuade them to purchase it.

4. *Price.* The fourth *P* refers to establishing the right price, which will make the product attractive to consumers as well as profitable for the company.

The concept of marketing strategy is summarized in Figure 9-1. The starting point is the identification of the target market or those consumers at which the firm will aim its marketing efforts. The marketing mix involves developing the right product, with the right promotion, sold in the right place, at the right price to satisfy the target consumers.

CONSUMERS: THE TARGET MARKET

The success of any business firm depends on its ability to satisfy consumer needs. It follows that all a business firm must do to be successful is to discover what consumers want and provide them with it. Of course, this is easier said than done. First, consumers are human beings, and each individual has unique needs. Second, consumer wants tend to change over time. Finally, consumers may have difficulty in describing what they want.

Consumer wants and behavior differ according to social class, income, age, sex, marital status, education, and other factors. The marketing manager may classify consumers into groups according to these factors.

Suppose, for example, we take two families, A and B. Family A consists of a successful doctor and his wife, both in their late fifties

Figure 9-1 Marketing Strategy: The Consumer Target and the Four P's

with married children and an annual income of $35,000. Family B includes a young truck driver, his wife, and three small children, with a family income of $9,000 a year. Which family would be the best market for luxury cars? for diapers? for country club memberships? for toys? for new homes? for laundry detergents? for vacation trips to Europe?

Market Research

Gathering and analyzing information about consumers is called *market research*. Large firms may spend millions of dollars on market research to determine consumer wants and define their target markets. However, all businessmen attempt to learn who their customers are and what they want.

For several years, Henri Duprès worked as a French chef in several Berkeley, California, restaurants. Now he has saved enough money to open his own French restaurant. He first wants to learn what type of people dine at quality French restaurants, what dishes they enjoy, and how much they are willing to pay for a meal. He is also concerned with the best location for his restaurant, how it should be decorated, and the type of promotion he should use.

Mr. Duprès's research efforts include a visit to the library to study census data published by the federal government. He finds a great deal of information on incomes, occupations, education, and age groups broken down by geographical areas in and around Berkeley. He next plots the location of existing French restaurants on a map using the telephone book as a reference. He also visits several French restaurants and talks with the managers and customers.

Henri Duprès's marketing research efforts were informal and inexpensive. However, after gathering and studying the information, he is in a better position to define his target market and develop an effective marketing mix.

A carefully planned marketing strategy based on market research cannot guarantee success, but it can reduce the chances of failure.

Types of Markets

Markets may be divided into two broad categories: final consumers and industrial users. The final consumer purchases goods and services to directly satisfy his needs. Industrial users buy products such as raw materials, equipment and supplies used in the processing of other goods.

Final consumer markets tend to be large in size and are often spread geographically throughout the country. The market for toothpaste is an example. On the other hand, industrial users tend to be relatively few in number and geographically concentrated. If a firm produces specialized machine tools used in manufacturing domestic automobiles, its market would be limited to the four major automobile makers located in and around Detroit.

The buying motives of consumers and users differ substantially. In general, final consumers tend to be motivated by emotional or psychological factors such as prestige, fear, and pride. For example, many cosmetics and body-care products are aimed at the individual's desire to be attractive to the opposite sex. In contrast, industrial users are primarily concerned with rational considerations such as reliability, economy of operation, assurance of continuous supply, and availability of service.

It should be apparent that the marketing mixes aimed at final consumers and industrial users vary significantly due to the different characteristics of the two markets.

PRODUCT

A product may be viewed as a combination of consumer satisfactions and benefits. Strange idea? Not at all. If a man purchases a new Ford Thunderbird does he think of the car as a certain number of pounds of steel, aluminum, rubber, and other materials? Of course not. He views the car in terms of the benefits it conveys to him—transportation, comfort, prestige, and status. In other words, consumers buy a product because of the satisfactions they expect to gain from it.

Product planning and development is the process of creating new products and improving existing ones. Market research aimed at determining what consumers want is the basis of product development. In this sense, marketing precedes production.

Our society is characterized by accelerating change. Developments in technology are making possible a host of new products. Today you can purchase a pocket-sized electronic calculator for under a hundred dollars, while only a few years ago electronic calculators were heavy and bulky and cost a thousand dollars or more. An entire new market is opening up. In a few years, nearly every student may own his personal calculator.

Changes in technology have been matched by rapid changes in consumer tastes and incomes. This means that business firms must develop new products in order to survive. If the market changes, the product must change. The Model-T Ford hardly meets the needs of today's consumers.

Product planning and development is a difficult and hazardous process. It has been estimated that three out of four new products fail to earn a profit. The classic example is the Edsel, which cost Ford Motor Company an estimated $200,000,000.

The process of developing and introducing a new product may require years of careful research and testing. Often business firms will market test a new product in one city or section of the country to gain firsthand information on consumer reactions. If these reactions are unfavorable, the firm may abandon the product or redesign it. Test marketing may also help the firm to develop place, promotional, and price strategies.

PLACE

Even the best product will not sell unless it is available at the time and place consumers wish to buy it. The marketing manager must determine where and how the product should be distributed to reach the target market.

Channels of Distribution

The routes that products take as they move from the producer to the consumer (or user) are called *channels of distribution*. These channels often involve middlemen—wholesalers and retailers—who perform a host of marketing services. Four major channels of distribution are shown in Figure 9–2.

Producer——▶Consumer   At first glance this channel would appear to be the cheapest and most efficient means of distribution. However, for consumer goods, it is relatively unpopular and expensive. Several firms such as Avon, Fuller Brush, and Amway have been highly successful in distributing their products door-to-door. These firms enjoy vigorous selling from their sales forces, and their products command a premium price.

Figure 9–2   Channels of Distribution

Some manufacturers sell consumer goods from their own retail outlets. See's Candies is an example. Other firms employ direct mail distribution using catalogs and magazine advertising to solicit orders.

Direct selling from the manufacturer to the user is very common in the industrial market. Since industrial users are few in number and often geographically concentrated, a manufacturer can reach the market through his own sales force with relative ease.

Producer⟶Retailer⟶Consumer   This channel is used when retailers purchase in large quantities or when the product has a high dollar value. Retail chains such as Safeway, Sears, and Woolworth prefer to purchase directly from manufacturers and to undertake the services normally performed by wholesalers. The producer may employ salesmen to contact retailers directly when the sales volume justifies the expense. Furniture and appliance manufacturers typically use this channel.

Producer⟶Wholesaler⟶Retailer⟶Consumer   This is the most common channel of distribution for many types of consumer goods. When a product such as cigarettes requires widespread distribution to many different retailers it is economically efficient to use wholesalers. The wholesaler provides a sales force for the manufacturer. Since the wholesaler may distribute thousands of different products, the marketing cost per item may be very low. Because most wholesalers operate in a limited geographic area, producers often employ salesmen to contact the wholesaler.

Producer⟶Wholesaler⟶Wholesaler⟶Retailer⟶Consumer Sometimes a manufacturer cannot afford to maintain even a small sales force to contact wholesalers. He may distribute through certain types of wholesalers such as agents who sell to other wholesalers. A manufacturers' agent may represent several producers of noncompeting goods. He contacts wholesalers and major retailers in a territory which may cover several states. In essence, the manufacturers' agent is the producer's sales force working on a commission basis.

There is no law requiring a producer to use only one channel of distribution. Many firms distribute through two or more channels at the same time. For example, a cake-mix manufacturer may sell his product directly to large food chains and use wholesalers to reach the small grocery stores.

Retailing

Retailing is the sale of merchandise to final consumers. Today there are approximately 1,800,000 retailing firms with combined annual sales of nearly $500 billion.

It would appear from these figures that retailing is a small-scale operation with the average retailer having sales of about $275,000 a year. However, the averages are deceiving. Only 5 percent of the retailers account for over 50 percent of the total sales. This means the vast majority of retailers are small, but a few giant firms account for a major proportion of sales. The "big-time" retailers include the chain stores, some of which have hundreds of outlets.

What are the advantages of large-scale retailing? In the first place, large retailers have a buying advantage. They purchase merchandise in volume, thereby realizing quantity discounts—lower costs per unit. The chain stores also enjoy an advertising advantage since they can spread the cost of advertising over many stores. For example, if Safeway operates ten stores in a city, a $1,000 newspaper ad costs only $100 per store. Large retailers have the added advantage of specialization of management. For example, the department store gets its name from the fact that merchandise is divided into departments, each of which is managed by a buyer. By concentrating on one type of merchandise such as kitchenware, the buyer can become highly knowledgeable about his customers' needs, the best sources of supply, and the most effective merchandising methods.

Small retailers also have some advantages which may include a close relationship with their customers, extensive services, and specialized merchandise. Many women prefer to buy their clothing from small dress shops because of the distinctive styles and the personal attention.

Retailing is subject to very rapid changes, and the firm which fails to adapt to change is likely to face declining sales and profits. The past thirty years have witnessed the decentralization of retailing as stores have followed their customers to suburban locations. The downtown shopping areas have experienced declining sales coupled with rising costs. Shopping centers with plenty of parking and one-stop shopping have proved to be very popular with consumers, but not all shopping centers have been successful. Self-service retailing was initiated by the supermarkets and then copied by discount houses, variety stores, and other retailers. The trend toward self-service has forced manufacturers to spend large sums on advertising in order to presell consumers before they enter the store.

It was once popular to classify retailers by types—such as general stores, supermarkets, specialty shops, discount houses, and so forth. However, the distinction between types of retailers is fading largely due to *scrambled merchandising*. Prior to World War II, most retailers tended to specialize in one type of merchandise. Grocery stores sold food. But no more. Today the rule is scrambled merchandising—the mixing of many different types of merchandise together in one store. Supermarkets sell hardware, toiletries, and clothing as well as food. Drug stores carry cameras, small appliances, and automotive supplies. Today the aggressive retailer is likely to add any line of goods which offers an attractive profit. Scrambled merchandising leads to increased competition, and some single-line retailers have been unable to survive.

A relatively new and increasingly popular retailing institution is the catalog showroom that sells appliances, jewelry, and other hard goods. The customer preshops at home using a mailed catalog and then buys the merchandise at a warehouse. Operating costs are low. Very little space is devoted to display, and shoplifting losses are drastically reduced. The typical discount house has shoplifting losses amounting to 6.5 percent of sales while losses for catalog showrooms average only 0.5 percent.

Wholesaling

The wholesaler performs a variety of marketing activities in moving goods from the producer to the retailer. Wholesalers also sell to industrial users and other wholesalers. What services do wholesalers offer to retailers and producers?

Wholesaling Functions Wholesalers maintain a sales force to contact customers. Distributing through wholesalers may be the most economical channel for many manufacturers. One drawback, however, is that wholesalers do not provide vigorous sales effort for individual products.

Often wholesalers will store and deliver merchandise for manufacturers and retailers. This relieves the manufacturer of transportation and warehousing problems. The retailer can keep his inventory low by depending on the wholesaler for rapid delivery of small quantities of merchandise. Furthermore, wholesalers often extend credit and provide merchandising assistance to retailers.

Some retailers and manufacturers prefer to bypass the wholesaler and deal direct. It must be emphasized that the wholesaler may be eliminated, but wholesaling functions cannot be eliminated. When a manufacturer sells direct to a retailer, one or the other must undertake the jobs performed by the wholesaler. For example, Safeway acts as its own wholesaler by maintaining extensive warehousing facilities and a fleet of delivery trucks.

Types of Wholesalers There are dozens of different types of wholesalers operating in many industries and handling a variety of merchandise. However, most wholesalers fall into two general categories—merchant wholesalers and agent middlemen.

ISSUE FRANCHISING: THE MAGIC FORMULA FOR SUCCESS?

Here's an easy question: What do Holiday Inns, McDonald's, Colonel Sanders Kentucky Fried Chicken, and Rexall Drug Stores have in common? Right! All are franchised operations. Today franchising is one of the fastest growing trends in retailing.

What is a *franchise?* Basically, it is an agreement which gives an independent businessman (called the *franchisee*) the right to distribute standardized products or services in a certain area. The *franchisor* is usually a successful corporation that offers proven methods of operation, a widely advertised brand name, training, and supervision to the franchisee. In return, the franchisee normally agrees to purchase equipment and supplies from the parent company and to pay an annual fee based on sales. In addition, most franchise agreements call for an initial investment that ranges from $1,000 to $200,000 or more.

From the standpoint of the small businessman, the major advantage of franchising is that it reduces the chances of failure. However, a franchise is no guarantee of success. Dozens of franchisors have failed, and even the strongest franchise cannot overcome a poor location or incompetent management.

Should you consider investing in a franchise? First ask yourself if you have the temperament to work within the rigidly proscribed rules laid down by the parent company. In many ways a franchisee is not his own boss. If you do have the background and personality for this type of business, the next step is to find the right franchise.

A good starting point is to write the National Association of Franchised Businessmen for information and advice. Then visit franchise shows and study the various packages and products, but don't be in a hurry to sign a contract. Beware of the "fast-buck operators" who are more interested in selling expensive equipment than in successful franchises. It's a good idea to talk with existing franchise holders about their operating problems and the actual assistance offered by the parent company.

When you have narrowed the choice down to one or two good prospects, it's time to perform a detailed financial analysis of projected sales, expenses, and profits. You might want to hire an experienced accountant to help with financial planning. Finally, franchise contracts can be highly detailed and confusing. Before you sign one, be sure to obtain legal assistance from a good attorney.

Keep in mind the advice offered by *Changing Times* magazine. "There are two things you ought to know about buying a franchise: It's a great way to go into business and it's a quick way to lose your shirt."

References

"The Burger that Conquered the Country," *Time,* September 17, 1973, pp. 84–92.

"What It Takes to Succeed in the Franchise Business," *Changing Times,* May 1970, pp. 25–28.

1. *Merchant Wholesalers* take title to the merchandise they sell. This means they purchase goods for resale. Most, but not all, merchant wholesalers offer a full line of services to manufacturers and retailers. Although costs vary with the type of merchandise and the services provided, merchant wholesalers typically charge 10 to 25 percent of the retail price.

2. *Agent Middlemen* are limited service wholesalers who do not take title to the merchandise they sell. An example is the manufacturers' agent who represents several producers. He covers a sales territory and charges a commission of roughly 5 percent of sales. Another type of agent middleman is the broker who negotiates transactions between buyers and sellers for a commission.

In determining the type of wholesaler to use, both the manufacturer and the retailer must measure the services offered against the costs. It is foolish to pay for unneeded services.

Figure 9–3 illustrates how the wholesaler simplifies the movement of goods from the producer to the retailer.

PROMOTION

> *Doing business without advertising is like winking in the dark.*
> *You know what you are doing, but nobody else does.*
> Daniel J. Boorstin

Promotion refers to any method of persuading or informing consumers about the product, place, or price. There are two main promotional tools—personal selling and advertising. Personal selling, the most widely used type of promotion, involves face-to-face or telephone contact between the salesman and the customer. Advertising is nonpersonal selling on a mass basis.

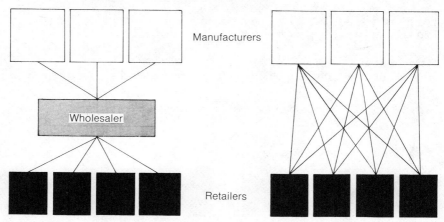

Manufacturers

Wholesaler

Retailers

Figure 9–3   How Wholesalers Help

The Promotional Mix

Every marketing manager must decide the best method of promotion—through advertising, personal selling, or some combination of the two. Most firms use both personal selling and advertising, but place primary emphasis on one of the tools. The promotional mix is the combination of advertising and personal selling used by a firm.

What determines the promotional mix? Basically, there are two considerations: the target market and the nature of the product. For example, in the industrial market, personal selling is the dominant promotional tool because the target market tends to be small and concentrated while the product may be expensive and complex. The market is relatively easy to reach with a sales force, and the customers want detailed information and assistance that can only be provided through personal contact. Would a business firm purchase a $2 million computer by clipping a coupon from a magazine advertisement?

Advertising is often the major promotional tool in the consumer market where there are many thousands of buyers and the product is usually simple and inexpensive. The promotional mix for laundry detergents is dominated by advertising due to the huge market, low price, and simple product.

Personal Selling

There are several advantages to promoting a product through personal selling. A salesman can focus his efforts by calling only on good prospects. In contrast, much advertising is wasted because it reaches individuals who have no interest in the product. In this sense, advertising is like a shotgun while personal selling is a rifle.

The salesman can tailor the sales message to the customer, demonstrate the product, answer questions, and close the sale.

The key disadvantage of personal selling is the high cost per contact. A good salesman may cost $25,000 a year or more in compensation and expenses. Since the salesman can only call on a limited number of prospective customers, the cost per call may be prohibitively high.

Advertising

When a firm is attempting to reach a large and widespread market, it is almost forced to rely on mass selling through advertising. Over the past twenty years, spending on advertising has tripled to over $25 billion a year. Although advertising through mass media such as network television and large circulation magazines can be expensive, the cost per contact may be very low. For example, if a firm spends $100,000 to sponsor a television program that reached ten million viewers, the cost per viewer is only a penny.

Types of Advertising Advertising tends to fall into two broad categories, product and institutional. *Product advertising* primarily aims at informing and persuading consumers about a good or service. *Institutional advertising* attempts to create a favorable image for the business firm. Some retail stores use institutional advertising to increase customer goodwill by stressing the store's prestige, personal service, and quality merchandise. The "Ford-Has-a-Better-Idea" campaign combines both institutional and product advertising.

The Advertising Agency Most advertising campaigns are planned with the help of an advertising agency, which provides specialized assistance in creating *copy* and selecting *media*. The term *copy* refers to the advertising message, both written and visual material. Media is the means of delivering the advertising message to the target consumers. The agency may also perform market research and assists in developing marketing strategy.

Advertising agencies are normally paid 15 percent of the media price for their services. Suppose, for example, the XYZ Corporation spends $1,000,000 to purchase advertising space in magazines. The magazine bills the XYZ Corporation for the cost of the space and remits 15 percent or $150,000 to the agency employed by XYZ. In other words, the agency, although employed by the advertiser, is compensated indirectly by the media.

Advertising Media In planning an advertising campaign, the marketing manager attempts to select the best media to reach the target consumers. He must also consider which media is most effective in presenting the advertising message. The most popular advertising media are newspapers, television, direct mail, magazines, and radio. Advertising expenditures by medium are shown in Figure 9–4.

1. *Newspapers* are the most widely used advertising medium. They offer widespread coverage in specific geographic areas, since a large percentage of households subscribe to a newspaper. Moreover, newspaper advertising is highly flexible because ads can be submitted and printed within a few hours. For these reasons, most retail advertising is carried in newspapers.

One disadvantage of newpapers is the lack of reader selectivity by interest group. Newspapers are read by all different types of people, and it is difficult to reach a specific target market without wasted circulation. Why doesn't Rolls Royce advertise in local newspapers?

2. *Direct Mail* is highly selective. It can be used to zero in on the target consumers. The effectiveness of direct mail advertising is

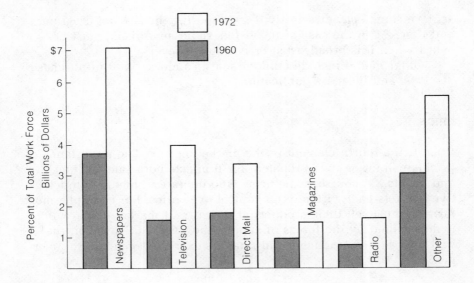

Figure 9-4 Spending on Advertising by Medium, 1960 and 1972
Source: *Statistical Abstract of the United States* and *Advertising Age*.

largely dependent on the mailing list. Some firms specialize in selling mailing lists broken down by location, income, age, occupation, special interests, and other characteristics. A good mailing list permits the advertiser to direct his advertising message at prime prospects.

The major disadvantage of direct mail advertising is "waste paper circulation." This means that many people throw away the advertisements unopened.

3. *Television* is the fastest growing advertising medium. Since television appeals to two senses—sight and hearing—the impact of the advertising message is increased. Television can be used to reach a limited geographic market through local stations. Some selectivity by interest group can be achieved through program and time selection.

The key drawback of television advertising is its cost. One minute spots on prime time network television can cost $100,000 or more. However, the cost of local commercials is much less.

4. *Magazines* are published for nearly every special interest group, enabling the advertiser to pinpoint his target market. Moreover, magazines can print high-quality color advertisements and each copy may be read by several consumers. Magazines tend to be an inflexible medium since copy must be submitted one to two months before publication.

5. *Radio* offers the advertiser a relatively low-cost medium with geographic selectivity through local stations. It is also possible to

achieve some listener selectivity by choosing the station, program, and time. As in the case of television, radio advertising must be heard when it is broadcasted or it is lost forever.

6. *Other media* include outdoor signs, catalogs, point-of-purchase displays, and business publications.

PRICE

Price is the fourth element in the marketing mix. The importance of pricing cannot be overestimated, for it affects both sales volume and profits. Of course, some firms who operate in highly competitive markets have virtually no control over price. For example, most farmers must sell their products at the current market price, which is determined by the forces of supply and demand. However, the vast majority of producers and retailers exercise some control over price.

Pricing Considerations

A basic law of economics is that more of a product will be sold at a low price than at a high price. For this reason, some firms rely on low price to generate sales. This is the strategy used by discount houses and many supermarkets that are willing to accept a lower profit margin in order to gain increased volume.

Let's take an example. You will recall that the gross profit margin (or mark-up) is the difference between the selling price of a product and its cost. It is usually expressed as a percent of the selling price; for example, a product selling for $1.00 that costs 70¢ would have a mark-up of 30 percent. Suppose the Super-Value Toy Store can generate sales of $200,000 with an average gross profit margin of 30 percent and $500,000 with a 20-percent margin. The difference between the 30-percent and 20-percent mark-ups represents a 10-percent price reduction.

Sales	×	Gross Profit Margin	=	Gross Profit
$200,000	×	30%	=	$ 60,000
500,000	×	20%	=	100,000

In this case, the lower profit per dollar of sales is more than offset by the increase in sales. The result is an increase in gross profit.

Another factor influencing price is cost. Over the long run, prices must be high enough to permit the firm to cover its costs. Consistently selling below cost results in losses which will ultimately lead to failure.

Competition also affects prices. A single service station in a small isolated town can charge a high price for gasoline, but a dealer lo-

ISSUE ADVERTISING: CONSUMER FRIEND OR FOE?

Nearly each new year brings a record in business expenditures on advertising. This mass-marketing tool has proven to be highly effective in promoting a wide variety of goods and services. But is advertising beneficial or harmful to the buying public? A growing number of critics, including many consumer advocates and economists, are convinced that advertising is generally wasteful and misleading. On the other hand, the defenders of advertising are quick to claim that both individual consumers and society as a whole realize significant benefits from advertising. Their main arguments fall into four major categories.

1. Advertising provides valuable information to consumers. How can shoppers make intelligent buying decisions unless they have information about product features, prices, and buying locations? According to *Printers' Ink,* a trade magazine, "advertising is the most economical way of bridging the gap between the man with an idea, a product, or a service for sale and the man who can benefit from buying it."

2. Advertising promotes competition by making it easier to introduce new products and services to the buying public.

3. Advertising leads to lower production costs and therefore to lower prices by encouraging mass production. Without advertising, many firms would not generate sufficient sales volume to realize the advantages of mass production.

4. Advertising pays for mass media. "Free" radio and television as well as most of the costs of newspapers and magazines are paid for through advertising expenditures.

The critics are unconvinced by these arguments. They claim most advertising is not informational but persuasive. For example, the majority of television commercials are designed to persuade consumers to buy without providing significant information. Some detractors complain that much advertising is misleading and attempts to manipulate consumers through emotional appeals.

Some economists believe advertising increases rather than reduces the price of goods. They point out that most advertising is competitive—that is, intended to increase the sales of one brand at the expense of another. Therefore, competitive advertising campaigns often cancel each other, but the costs are passed on to the consumer in the form of higher prices.

The critics also blame advertising for the "dismal programming" offered by the television networks. They argue that most people would prefer pay TV if the right programs were available.

Finally, the opponents believe advertising reduces the level of competition in our economy. According to Ralph Nader and Aileen Cowan, "competition in the marketplace is rapidly being reduced to competition in advertising as businessmen spend more and more money on inflated and deceptive claims rather than improving products or lowering prices. The result is both the exploitation of the consumer and the undermining of serious, meaningful competition."

There you have the arguments. Is advertising your friend or foe? More to the point, do you favor less advertising by business firms?

References

Ralph Nader and Aileen Cowan, "Claims without Substance," in Ralph Nader, ed., *The Consumer and Corporate Accountability* (New York: Harcourt Brace Jovanovich, Inc., 1973), pp. 90–97.

"What Advertising Is, What It Has Done, and What It Can Do Now," *Printers' Ink,* September 8, 1967, pp. 39–60.

cated in a city with hundreds of service stations must gear his price to meet competition.

Some firms are able to charge higher prices because of superior product or promotion. Fuller Brushes command premium prices because of the high product quality plus vigorous promotion through door-to-door selling.

Pricing Strategies

Two extreme pricing strategies are skim-the-cream pricing and penetration pricing.

Skim-the-Cream Pricing This strategy involves charging a high price in order to achieve large profits per unit. Skim-the-cream pricing is typically used when a firm introduces a new and unique product with strong consumer appeal. IBM followed this strategy when it brought out the Selectric typewriter.

Skim-the-cream pricing offers several advantages. A high price may suggest superior quality to the consumer, thereby enhancing the image of the product. Since consumers welcome price reductions, a high initial price may be lowered at a later date to broaden market appeal.

Penetration Pricing Charging a very low price for products may permit a firm to capture a significant proportion of the total market in a very short period of time. Moreover, penetration pricing discourages competitors from entering the industry. Japanese television manufacturers have used low price to gain a major foothold in the American market.

THE MARKETING MIX

You will recall that the marketing mix is that combination of product, place, promotion, and price aimed at reaching the target market. It would be a serious mistake to think that there is an ideal marketing mix for any market. Business firms are continuously experimenting to improve their marketing strategies. In fact, firms in the same industry may have vastly different mixes. Revlon and Avon both manufacture cosmetics and toiletries, but each firm uses different place, promotion, and price strategies.

Often a unique marketing mix can be very profitable. In the highly competitive washing machine market, Maytag Company earns a 13-percent return on sales, which is three times the industry average. Maytag's product strategy emphasizes quality, reliability, and service. The company is slow to introduce new models until major engineering improvements are developed. Maytag's machines sell for around $350, a hundred dollars more than its competitors' top models. Distribution is through a sales force that calls directly on selected retail dealers. These retailers are given a high profit margin in return for which they are expected to carry a sizable inventory of Maytag parts and train their servicemen to repair Maytag machines. Consumer advertising emphasizes quality and reliability.

The result of this successful marketing strategy is a 14-percent return on investment, one of the highest of any firm in the United States.

SUMMARY

Marketing is all the activities necessary to move goods from the producer to the consumer. The marketing concept holds that business firms should concentrate on discovering consumer needs and then focus on fulfilling these needs.

Marketing strategy consists of two steps: (1) identifying the target market, and (2) developing the marketing mix. The target market is the group of consumers which the firm wishes to serve. The marketing mix refers to developing product, place, promotional, and price strategies to reach the target consumers.

Consumer needs differ according to age, sex, occupation, social class, income, and psychological factors. Market research is used to gather and analyze facts about consumers. Two broad types of markets are final consumers and industrial users.

Business firms must create new products in order to meet changing consumer needs. Product planning and development is difficult and expensive. To reduce the chances of failure, many firms test new products in a limited market before committing themselves to full production.

Channels of distribution are the routes which goods take as they move from the producer to the retailer. These channels often include retailers and wholesalers.

Large retail firms are growing in importance due to their advantages in purchasing, advertising, and specialization of management. The field of retailing is subject to rapid changes, and retailers must adapt to these changes in order to survive.

Wholesalers perform a variety of services for both producers and retailers. These services include selling, storing, transporting, and financing. Some manufacturers and retailers prefer to bypass the wholesaler, but this requires undertaking the wholesaler's functions. The two major categories of wholesalers are: (1) merchant wholesalers, who take title to the merchandise they sell and typically offer a broad range of services, and (2) agent middlemen, who do not take title to merchandise but only perform the selling function.

Promotion is informing and persuading consumers about a firm's product, place, or price. The combination of personal selling and advertising used by a firm is called the *promotional mix*. It is determined by the target market and the nature of the product.

Personal selling is effective in tailoring the sales message to the individual customer, but the cost per contact is high. Advertising is often used to reach consumer markets which consist of large numbers of potential customers. Product advertising aims at selling a good or service, while institutional advertising attempts to create a favorable image for the firm.

Advertising agencies assist in creating copy and selecting media. The major types of media are newspapers, direct mail, television, magazines, and radio.

Price influences both sales volume and profits. Two major pricing strategies are skim-the-cream and penetration pricing.

There is no perfect marketing strategy and business firms are constantly adjusting their marketing mixes. The profitability of a firm largely depends on its success in identifying consumer needs and developing effective product, place, promotional, and price strategies to meet these needs.

Student _____

REVIEWING MAJOR CONCEPTS

1. Briefly explain the marketing concept.

2. What are the two steps in developing a marketing strategy?

3. What advantages do large chain stores enjoy over small retailers? Does the small retailer have any advantages?

4. Why has the trend toward self-service retailing encouraged manufacturers to spend more on advertising?

5. What are the advantages and drawbacks of franchising to the franchisee?

Business Operations

6. What services do wholesalers perform?

7. "You can eliminate the wholesaler, but you cannot eliminate his functions." Explain this statement.

8. What two major considerations influence the promotional mix?

9. Identify the major advantages and disadvantages of personal selling and advertising.

10. Explain how a retailer might increase total profit by cutting price.

Student _____

SOLVING PROBLEMS AND CASES

1. *Case:* Honda Motorcycle Company

In 1960, a Los Angeles advertising agency called GB&D was selected to represent Honda Motorcycle Company of Japan. The firm was asked to create a marketing strategy designed to sell Honda Motorcycles in the United States. The marketing budget for this job was quite small.

In 1960, GB&D had to face up to the fact that total sales for all brands of motorcycles in the country were only 40,000 units, of which Honda's share was just over 5 percent. Honda had only 137 dealers in the United States. Added to this was the generally unfavorable image of hare-brained youths in black leather jackets speeding around the countryside on cycles.

Honda and GB&D had one thing in their favor: a first-rate product. It was decided to shy away from the prevailing "black leather jacket" motorcycle image and create an entirely new idea in the two-wheel field. Motorcycling was to be promoted as a very pleasant and healthy activity for the entire family.

GB&D's initial marketing strategy aimed at identifying Honda's prime markets. Who were its best prospects, and where were they located? The advertising agency did its market research the hard way: interviewing field men, dealers, purchasers, and "the man on the street".

GB&D decided to try a region-by-region advertising campaign using magazines for its main medium. The campaign stressed the joys of motorcycling for everyone, particularly the family. The agency also started an extensive dealer-education campaign to improve dealer selling methods and service.

In two years, Honda's share of the market increased from 5 to 52 percent; its dealer network went from 137 to 767; and sales from $979,000 to $17 million.

a. Why did the advertising agency (GB&D) use market research?

b. Why do you think GB&D started with a region-by-region marketing campaign instead of going for the entire national market at once?

c. From a marketing standpoint, what was wrong with the "black leather jacket" image of motorcycling that prevailed in 1960?

d. What were the roles played by advertising and personal selling in marketing Honda motorcycles?

Student _____

2. *Case:* Hardin Homes

In 1946, James Hardin, a former carpenter, was discharged from the Army and decided to go into the business of building homes. He knew that World War II had created a tremendous shortage of houses, and millions of returning servicemen would be seeking low-priced homes. Mr. Hardin also believed that he could use mass-production techniques in building homes, thereby substantially reducing construction costs.

By using his accumulated savings and borrowing from banks, mortgage companies and the Federal Government, Mr. Hardin raised enough capital to buy 500 acres of land and begin construction. Instead of painstakingly erecting one house at a time, he broke down the construction process into 26 steps, and built whole blocks at one time. A separate crew was assigned to each step, and moved from one unfinished house to another performing it. Handsaws were banished, and all parts were precut with power saws. By sticking to one basic design, Mr. Hardin was able to price his houses at under $8,000.

Marketing the homes was relatively simple. When a few model homes were completed, an advertisement was placed in the local newspapers and several salesmen were hired. The response was overwhelming. People willingly made down payments on homes that would not be completed for months. The salesmen had little to do but stand behind counters and take orders.

During the next ten years, Mr. Hardin built three huge "developments", each containing between 5,000 and 10,000 homes. Following his same "magic" formula of low-priced, mass-produced, standard homes, Mr. Hardin continued to meet with success. However, in 1960, a fourth housing development ran into trouble. Although crowds continued to flock to see the model homes, actual sales fell off alarmingly. Mr. Hardin was at a loss to see what was wrong.

Mr. Hardin talked the problem over with his son, Frank, who was majoring in business administration at the local college. Frank offered the following advice: "Dad, you are behind the times. People no longer want to buy small, identical homes. They want variety. Also, you should spend more money on marketing and create a new image for your homes."

Mr. Hardin pointed out to his son that variety costs money. His efficient, mass-production techniques were based on standardized design. As he put it, "If I start offering larger, individual homes, my construction costs will zoom, and I'll have to raise my prices. My success during the past ten years has been based on low prices and good value."

What should Mr. Hardin do? Develop a plan of action, with specific recommendations, for Mr. Hardin to follow.

3. *Case:* Mel Roberts

Mel Roberts is a wealthy inventor who recently developed an electronic mouse trap that lures mice and rats with an ultrasonic tone (which cannot be heard by the human ear) and kills them instantly with a tiny laser beam. Mel has tested his invention, which he calls ''Rat-Zap,'' and found it foolproof. He has contracted with a manufacturer to produce the trap at a cost of $15 each.

Mel is uncertain how to market the product and he has asked your advice. Outline a marketing strategy for Rat-Zap.

Student _____

4. *Case:* Van Meter Candy Company

The Van Meter Candy Company, located in San Francisco, California, is a family-owned firm that produces inexpensive hard candies and chocolates. The firm is managed by two brothers—Herman, who supervises production, and Adolph, who handles sales. The firm sells its entire output to chain supermarkets and variety stores headquartered in the San Francisco area. The candy is resold to consumers by the pound or in packages with the retailer's brand name.

Last year the company's employees voted to be represented by a union and won a 25-percent wage increase. In order to offset rising production costs, the brothers invested all available cash in automated equipment. The new equipment doubled production capacity and reduced per unit manufacturing costs when the plant is operated at full capacity.

The company is now faced with the problem of marketing the increased output. No funds are available to employ additional sales personnel. Adolph Van Meter wants to expand distribution, but he is uncertain how this can be accomplished.

What suggestions can you offer the Van Meter brothers?

5. What advertising media are the following firms likely to use? Briefly explain your choices.

   a. A small manufacturer of fishing rods.

   b. A department store located in a city of 50,000.

   c. A large whisky distiller.

   d. A dress shop specializing in high-fashion merchandise.

   e. A stock-brokerage firm with four offices located in a large city.

Chapter 10   **Production**

Production means making things. In a broader sense, production is the creation of goods and services by combining men, materials, machines, and management.

Production managers perform the same functions as managers in other parts of the firm. However, they are particularly concerned with decisions relating to location and design of plant facilities, selection of production equipment, planning and control of production operations, and materials handling.

This chapter provides a brief overview of the American production system, describes the different types of production processes, and introduces the major phases of production management.

KEY QUESTIONS

1. What factors account for the tremendous productivity of American industry?

2. What are the major kinds of production?

3. What factors influence plant location?

4. How are plant layout and equipment determined?

5. How are production processes planned and controlled?

6. What is motion and time study, and how is it used?

7. How are raw materials and supplies purchased?

8. Why is inventory control important?

PRODUCTION: A BIRD'S-EYE VIEW

Chapter 1 pointed out that Americans enjoy the highest standard of living in recorded history. What accounts for our high level of national wealth? A good part of the answer lies with the tremendous productivity of American industry. This productivity is based on several factors: (1) large-scale production, (2) mechanization, (3) standardization, (4) specialization, and (5) diversification.

Large-Scale Production

Bigness can mean efficiency. In the United States, three-quarters of total production is accounted for by five hundred giant corporations, most of which own and operate several huge plants. Large-scale mass-production permits the cost of expensive equipment to be spread over many units of output. Suppose, for example, that a machine tool costs $1,000,000. If the firm produces only 100,000 units, the cost per unit of the machine is $10. However, if production is 2,000,000, the unit cost of the machine is only 50 cents.

Large-scale operations also encourage specialization of labor, which leads to increased productivity. Moreover, giant corporations can spend millions of dollars on research to develop improved products and to streamline production.

Of course, bigness is not an unmixed blessing. For one thing, management problems become increasingly difficult and complex as firms grow in size.

Mechanization

Mechanization means the substitution of machinery for manpower. Obviously, the more capital equipment a worker has at his disposal, the greater his productivity. Capital investment per worker in the United States exceeds $30,000, the highest figure in the world. Management substitutes machinery for men when it reduces costs.

Automation is an extension of mechanization. The essence of automation is machines directing machines. It involves the use of electronic computers to control operating machines through information feedback systems.

Standardization

The term *standardization* actually has two related meanings: (1) making parts interchangeable, and (2) limiting the number of types and sizes of a product. Standardization is a necessary ingredient of mass production. Each left fender for a Ford Pinto is identical to all others. This keeps down inventory costs for dealers as well as for the manufacturer. Standardization also permits long production runs, which reduce manufacturing costs and improve quality.

ISSUE AUTOMATION: IS YOUR JOB NEXT?

For progress there is no cure.

John Von Neumann

In broad terms, automation refers to any use of computers or other self-regulating devices that replace human control over processes or machines. Does this mean that automation displaces human beings? Does God make little green apples?

There is little doubt that automation is causing dramatic social changes. Some observers fear that the computer is increasing productivity so rapidly that the nation's economy cannot create new jobs fast enough for the people who are displaced. They foresee a future with massive technological unemployment where a large percentage of the work force is permanently without jobs. However, before we push the panic button perhaps we should consider the other side of the story.

In the first place, the computer industry is creating thousands of new jobs each year in manufacturing, programming, and maintaining the expanding number of computers. Beyond this, automation creates jobs indirectly by boosting productivity and workers' incomes. The result is a growing demand for goods and services, which generates more output and employment. Today, for example, the increasing demand for services has created millions of jobs for beauticians, salesmen, lawyers, airline stewardesses, and repairmen.

Automation is twisting the structure of the labor market by putting more emphasis on brainpower and less on musclepower. There is an expanding demand for technicians, managers, and accountants while job openings for unskilled or semiskilled workers are dwindling.

In the long run, automation offers another bonus—more leisure time. This will mean shorter working hours, longer vacations, and earlier retirements. The increased free time will further boost the demand for leisure-time products and services.

If you are concerned about losing your job to automation, now is the time to protect yourself through a carefully planned program of education and training. Also, when choosing a career, be sure to consider the probable long-term impact of automation on alternative occupational fields.

References

Stanley Rothman and Charles Mosman, *Computers and Society: The Technology and Its Social Implications* (Chicago: Science Research Associates, 1972).

Gilbert Burck, *The Computer Age and Its Potential for Management* (New York: Harper & Row, 1965).

Specialization

Years ago managers discovered that productivity could be boosted by dividing work into simple jobs or tasks and assigning workers to perform each job over and over again. Specialization of labor permits an unskilled worker to become expert in performing a simple task in a few days.

Unfortunately, specialization is not an unmixed blessing. It can lead to boredom and inefficiency because workers lose interest in their jobs. For this reason, some firms have initiated job-enlargement programs which assign employees a variety of tasks. One electronics company has its workers assemble entire components, requiring twenty or more different operations.

Diversification

Many firms continuously seek to add new products in order to expand sales and profits. Ford's Mustang and Pinto were introduced to gain broader market appeal. Diversification may also lead to better utilization of plant, equipment, and by-products. For example, Armour and Company brought out Dial Soap to utilize animal by-products from its meat-packing operations.

The opposite of diversification is *simplification*, which means eliminating products that are no longer profitable. In the early 1970s, General Electric stopped producing computers, electric fans, vacuum cleaners, blenders, integrated circuits, and television camera equipment. The objective of this massive simplification program was to abandon markets in which GE was not earning satisfactory profits. In fact, between 1970 and 1973, General Electric's profits nearly doubled.

PRODUCTION PROCESSES

The word *production* may conjure up images of huge automobile assembly plants pouring out thousands of cars daily. But production means more than assembly. To understand the scope of production, it is useful to define five production processes: (1) extraction, (2) analytic, (3) synthetic, (4) fabrication, and (5) assembly.

Extraction

The extraction process involves taking materials from the earth or water. Typical examples include mining of coal and iron ore. Drilling for petroleum and claiming salt from sea water also represent extraction.

Analytic

The term *analytic* refers to the process of breaking down a material into component products. An example is oil refining, in which crude petroleum is broken down into oil, gasoline, petro-chemicals, and other products. In meat packing, a steer carcass is divided into various cuts of meat; even the bones and hooves are separated and sold for feed and glue.

Synthetic

The opposite of analytic is *synthetic,* which means to chemically combine several materials into a product. Steel is produced by combining iron ore, coke, manganese, and other materials at high temperatures. The production of glass is another example of the synthetic process.

Fabrication

When a material has its form changed, it has been fabricated. Typical examples are converting cotton into thread and sheet steel into shaped body panels for automobiles.

Assembly

When different parts are put together to form a final product we have an assembly process. An obvious example is the television production line, on which various circuits, tubes, and other components are assembled to produce a TV receiver.

MANUFACTURING SYSTEMS

Manufacturing refers to the production of goods in factories or plants. Manufacturing may be divided into two broad categories: (1) mass production, and (2) custom production.

Mass Production

Mass production is the manufacture of standard products in large quantities. The purpose of mass production is to reduce unit costs through long production runs, emphasizing mechanization, standardization, and specialization. Mass production requires heavy investment in equipment and a limited range of products.

Custom Production

Custom production is manufacturing products to customer specifications. Custom manufacturers are often called *job shops* because each order or job is usually different. The costs of production are high due to short production runs and the problems of scheduling and setting up for each different job.

PRODUCTION MANAGEMENT

The job of the production manager is to produce goods of acceptable quality in the most efficient manner. This requires the careful planning, organizing, and controlling of production operations. The production manager must make decisions regarding a host of factors that influence the production process. These factors include: (1) plant location, (2) plant layout, (3) production equipment, (4) production planning and control, (5) make or buy decisions, (6) job design, and (7) quality control.

Plant Location

The location of physical facilities may be a critically important decision for the business firm. Once the decision is made, it is difficult and expensive to change location. For some companies, the location of the plant may make the difference between success and failure. The major considerations in selecting plant locations are: (1) nearness to market, (2) nearness to raw materials, (3) availability of labor, and (4) other factors such as transportation, taxes, and community facilities.

Nearness to Market When a firm produces perishable goods or when the transportation cost of finished goods is high, the primary factor determining plant location may be nearness to the market. Bakeries tend to be located close to their customers. Automobile manufacturers have followed the practice of locating assembly plants near large population centers. It is less expensive to ship parts to these plants than to transport assembled automobiles to the market.

Nearness to Raw Materials When raw materials used in production are heavy or bulky, it is likely the plant will be located near to the source of these materials. For this reason, canneries and frozen food plants are usually located near agricultural areas. Why are there so many oil refineries in Texas?

Availability of Labor A century ago the American textile industry was concentrated in New England. Today, most textile plants are located in the southeastern part of the country. One reason for the move was to get nearer to the source of raw cotton. Another factor was the availability of a large supply of inexpensive, nonunionized labor in the South.

When the production process requires highly skilled workers, their availability may determine location. This is one reason that many electronics firms are located near universities.

Other Factors   Plant location is influenced by a host of other considerations, including power supply, taxes, transportation facilities (highways, railroads, and airports), climate, land cost, and community services. Some localities are willing to give business firms major tax concessions for building a plant in their communities. Why?

Plant Layout

Layout refers to the arrangement of equipment and facilities in the plant. The objective of plant layout is to attain maximum production efficiency by speeding the flow of work and materials.

Planning the layout of a factory begins with an engineering study to determine the number of men and machines and the amount of space needed for production. Cardboard templates and scale models may be used in planning the layout design. More recently, computers have been employed to determine the most efficient arrangement of floor space.

There are two basic types of layouts—process and line. The choice between the two depends on the nature of the production system.

Process Layout   Process layout is typically found in custom production where a variety of different products are manufactured to customer specifications. In the process layout, machines of the same type are grouped together in a section of the factory. Figure 10–1 presents a simplified process layout.

The dotted line shows the progress of a typical order; each number represents a different operation. Figure 10–1 illustrates the major disadvantages of the process layout—excessive materials handling as the order moves from department to department and the need for large amounts of storage space for goods in process.

Line Layout   In mass production manufacturing, machines are arranged according to the sequence of operation rather than by separate sections. This has the advantages of reducing handling and saving space. However, the line layout is inflexible; once established, it is difficult to alter. Moreover, the breakdown of one machine can stop all production.

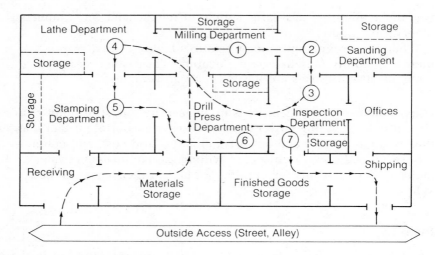

Figure 10–1 Process Layout

Figure 10–2 illustrates a line layout. Notice that the equipment is arranged according to the operations to be performed on the product. This permits work to flow in a straight line. Can you explain why two lathes are required after the milling operation?

Production Equipment

There are two broad categories of production equipment—general purpose and special purpose.

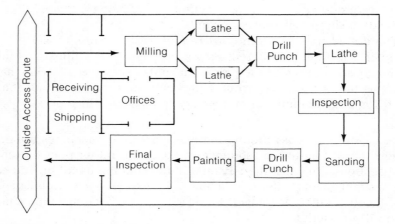

Figure 10–2 Line Layout

1. *General-purpose* machines are capable of performing a variety
of operations. A general-purpose lathe, for example, can shape
many types of materials that come in different sizes. Although general purpose equipment is cheaper to buy, it operates at a relatively
slow speed. Moreover, general-purpose machines normally require
skilled operators who are capable of setting up and adjusting the
equipment for each operation.

2. *Special-purpose* equipment is designed to perform a single
operation at high speed. An example is a special lathe designed to
grind automobile cam shafts to close tolerances. Special-purpose
equipment is expensive, but it can often be operated by unskilled
or semiskilled workers.

As a general rule, special-purpose equipment is used in mass-
production systems, while general-purpose equipment is commonly
found in job shops.

When the production manager selects equipment, he must consider not only the cost of the machines but also the type and volume of production and skills of the factory work force.

Production Planning and Control

The planning and control of production operations aims at the efficient use of resources—men, machines, and materials. The production manager is haunted by a single overriding fact: idle men and
machines cost money. Therefore, he attempts to plan and control
work to avoid delays and downtime.

The production plan is based on a sales forecast or on actual
orders received from customers. After deciding what is to be done,
the production manager must determine how and when the work is
to be accomplished. *Routing* involves deciding how an order will
move from operation to operation as raw materials are converted
into finished goods. In other words, routing means establishing a sequence of operations required to process goods. Figure 10–1 illustrates the routing of one job.

Scheduling is the process of setting up a timetable that shows
when each job is to begin and end. The schedule is both a planning
and control device. It can be used to check how closely actual production is conforming to the production plan.

The complexity of production scheduling is illustrated by the
modern automobile assembly line, where thousands of different
parts must come together at the right time and place. Today, many
large factories use an electronic computer to assist in planning and
controlling production. The computer can schedule complex operations so as to ensure a steady flow of work through the plant and,
in addition, provide up-to-date information on the status of work in
progress.

Make-or-Buy Decisions

A key part of the production plan is the determination of which parts should be purchased from outside suppliers and which should be manufactured by the firm itself. The basis for a make-or-buy decision is a cost analysis of alternative courses of action. In theory the decision is a simple one: the costs of manufacturing the part are compared to the costs of buying from suppliers, and the most economical method is selected. However, make-or-buy decisions can involve large sums of money, and a host of factors must be carefully evaluated. A decision to make a part might require a substantial investment in new tools and equipment. Are there funds available to finance this investment? Does the firm have the expertise and manpower to undertake expanded production? Can quality standards be met? If the firm elects to buy the part, can suppliers be relied on to meet delivery dates? What are the possible effects of inflation on suppliers' prices and manufacturing costs?

A firm may decide to manufacture a part even when the cost analysis shows that it would be less expensive to buy from a supplier. Such a decision could be based on a desire to use idle plant capacity or to retain employees who might otherwise be laid off.

Job Design: Motion-and-Time Study

The production manager is interested in reducing the time and effort required to do a job, thereby boosting worker productivity. Late in the nineteenth century, a pioneer of modern management named Frederick Taylor carefully studied how workers performed their jobs and attempted to develop ways of redesigning jobs to increase efficiency. Taylor called his methods *scientific management;* today they are known as *motion-and-time study.*

Motion study is used to find the most efficient way of performing a job. Without going into detail, motion study begins by breaking a job into parts called *elements* and carefully analyzing the motions used for each element. Then the job is redesigned to eliminate wasteful or unnecessary movements by prepositioning tools, avoiding delays, and emphasizing efficient motions. The basic purpose of motion study is to make a job easy and fast.

Time study is used to determine the time required to perform a job. Each element of a job is timed with a stopwatch. After adding an allowance for fatigue and personal needs, a *time standard* is established for the task.

Time standards are used to evaluate worker performance and to plan and schedule production. For example, suppose the time standard for welding a part is ten minutes. This means that a worker should weld 48 parts in an eight-hour day. If the production schedule calls for 90 parts a day, then two workers will be required to perform this operation.

Quality Control

The control of product quality is a two-step process: (1) the establishment of quality standards, and (2) inspection to determine if the product conforms to these standards.

The production manager recognizes that quality costs money. It is foolish to insist on quality standards that are too high for the intended use of the product. No one expects a two-dollar baseball to last a lifetime. On the other hand, poor quality can antagonize consumers and cause sales to drop.

Inspection is used to reject products that fail to meet established standards of quality. In addition, a good quality-control system attempts to detect and correct the problems which caused the production of below-standard goods.

When quality is of major importance, every unit of output may be carefully examined. However, in most cases inspection is carried out on a sampling basis, where, for example, every fifth or tenth unit is inspected.

PURCHASING AND INVENTORY CONTROL

Purchasing is the acquisition of materials, supplies, and parts required for production. In manufacturing firms, purchases often account for over 50 percent of production costs. Therefore, efficient purchasing can have a significant impact on profits.

Most large firms have purchasing departments headed by a chief purchasing agent, who is assisted by a staff of buyers. The objective of the purchasing department is to get the most for each dollar spent. This does not mean that the purchasing agent always seeks to buy at the lowest price. He must also consider such factors as quality, transportation costs, delivery time, reliability of the supplier, and inventory costs.

Price is dependent on the quantity purchased. Most suppliers offer quantity discounts (a reduction in unit price) for large orders. However, large orders mean increased inventory carrying costs. For this reason, some firms prefer "hand-to-mouth purchasing"; that is, buying in small quantities at frequent intervals.

The purchasing process begins with a *requisition,* which lists the quantity and specifications of the items to be purchased. On receipt of the requisition the purchasing department explores alternative sources of supply. The selection of a supplier may require bidding or simply negotiations on price, delivery date, and quality specifications. After the supplier is selected, a *purchase order* is prepared. When the goods are received, they are checked against the purchase order before payment is made to the supplier. A typical requisition form is shown in Figure 10–3.

FROM:

ALASKAN PLUMBING AND HEATING COMPANY, INC. REQUISITION

ANCHORAGE, ALASKA

DATE_____ P. O. NO._____

SUPPLIER_____ ATTENTION_____

ADDRESS_____

SHIP TO_____

SHIP VIA_____ SIDE MARK_____

ORDERED
BY_____ DELIVERY REQUIRED_____

SPECIAL
ORDER FOR_____ ACCOUNT_____

ITEM NO	QUANTITY	UNIT	DESCRIPTION

SINESS FORMS INC LA

Figure 10–3 A Requisition Form

Inventory control is closely related to purchasing. The objectives of inventory control are twofold: (1) to maintain an adequate supply of inventory on hand, and (2) to minimize inventory costs. The first objective requires that enough materials, parts, and supplies be available to meet production needs. Halting production because of inventory shortages can be disastrous. In addition, enough finished goods must be on hand to meet customer demand.

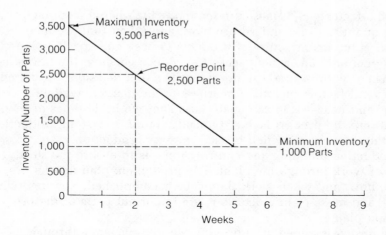

Figure 10–4 Inventory Chart for Part 10A

Inventory costs include the costs of handling and storage, interest on funds tied up in inventory, insurance expense, and the risks of obsolescence and deterioration. Inventory control may be viewed as a sort of balancing act—the risks of running out of inventory must be balanced against the costs of maintaining large supplies on hand.

Inventory-control systems may be highly sophisticated, often involving the use of electronic computers. However, the basic principles can be illustrated with a simple example. Suppose the inventory control manager has determined that Part 10A is used at the rate of 500 per week. It takes three weeks to deliver a minimum order of 2,500 parts. To avoid running out, the manager has decided to keep a two-week's supply on hand at all times. The manager wants to know the answer to two questions: (1) When should an order be placed for additional parts? (2) What will be the maximum inventory on hand?

Figure 10–4 summarizes the inventory levels for Part 10A. The reorder point is 2,500 parts, or two weeks after a shipment is received.

The minimum inventory is 1,000 parts (two weeks × 500 parts per week). The maximum inventory is 3,500 parts—the order size of 2,500 parts plus the minimum inventory.

SUMMARY

Production in the United States is characterized by large-scale operations, mechanization, standardization, specialization, and diversification.

Production may be divided into five processes: extraction, analytic, synthetic, fabrication, and assembly. There are two broad types of manufacturing: (1) mass production, which is the manufacture of large quantities of standard products; and (2) custom production, which is the manufacture of products to customer specifications.

Production management seeks to produce goods at the lowest cost consistent with desired quality. Plant location decisions are based on several factors including nearness to the market, availability of labor, and nearness to raw materials. The two basic types of plant layout are the process layout, typically found in custom production, and the line layout, which is used in mass production.

Production planning and control attempts to ensure the steady flow of work through the plant. The production plan determines what, how, and when work should be accomplished. Routing, scheduling, and make-or-buy decisions are important parts of the production plan.

Job design is aimed at improving worker efficiency through motion and time study. Motion study attempts to find the best way of performing a task. Time study is used to establish time standards for different jobs.

Quality control refers to establishing quality standards and inspecting products to ensure they conform to these standards.

Purchasing is all the activities required to buy materials, supplies, and parts for production. The purchasing agent must consider many factors such as price, quality, delivery time, transportation costs, and the reliability of suppliers.

Inventory control requires balancing inventory costs against the risks of running short of inventory.

Student _____

STUDENT FEEDBACK SYSTEM

Directions: Your questions and ideas are important! Here's a chance to get more information and relate your experiences to the materials in the chapter. Answer the following questions and turn in this page to the instructor. Use the reverse side of the page if you need additional space.

1. What topics, problems, and terms found in this chapter require more explanation by the instructor?

2. Do the concepts presented in this chapter agree with your experience in the business world? Briefly explain why or why not, using examples.

3. Does this chapter suggest any career opportunities to you?

Student _____

BUILDING A BUSINESS VOCABULARY

Directions: Match the terms with their definitions by writing the letter in the appropriate blank.

a. Assembly
b. Standardization
c. Time Study
d. Custom Production
e. Requisition
f. Fabrication
g. General Purpose
   Equipment

h. Process Layout
i. Quality Control
j. Specialization
k. Analytic
l. Scheduling
m. Mechanization
n. Routing
o. Make-or-Buy Decision

p. Extraction
q. Motion Study
r. Synthetic
s. Line Layout
t. Diversification
u. Mass Production
v. Special Purpose
   Equipment

_____ 1. The substitution of machines for manpower.

_____ 2. Manufacturing standard products in large quantities.

_____ 3. A plant design in which similar machines are grouped together.

_____ 4. Machinery designed to perform a single operation at high speed.

_____ 5. Inspecting products to determine if they conform to quality standards.

_____ 6. A form that lists the quantity, size, and description of materials, parts, or supplies to be purchased.

_____ 7. A production process that entails taking material from the earth or water.

_____ 8. Making parts interchangeable.

_____ 9. A production process that involves chemically combining materials into a single product; for example, the production of steel.

_____10. Dividing work into simple jobs or tasks to increase productivity.

_____11. Determining how work will move through the production process.

_____12. A procedure used to establish standard times for jobs.

_____13. A production process in which parts are put together to form finished goods.

_____14. Arrangement of machines according to the sequence of operations.

_____15. A production process that involves changing the form of a material.

_____16. The determination of which parts should be manufactured by a firm and which should be purchased from outside suppliers.

_____17. Manufacturing goods to customer specifications.

_____18. Establishing a timetable for production operations.

_____19. A production process found, for example, in a lumber mill, in which a basic material is broken down into several products.

_____20. A procedure used to find the most efficient way of performing a job.

_____21. Adding new products to increase sales and profits.

_____22. Machinery typically found in job shops, which can perform a variety of operations.

Student _____

REVIEWING MAJOR CONCEPTS

1. Suppose every make and model of automobile came with different size tires. What problems would this create?

2. Does automation cause unemployment? Support your answer.

3. What problems may result from specialization of labor?

4. Which production processes are required to produce automobiles?

5. Is the line layout likely to be found in custom production? Explain why or why not.

6. What are the major *dis*advantages of the process layout?

7. Which type of equipment is typically used in mass production? In custom production? Explain why.

8. "A firm should always strive to achieve the highest quality in its products." Do you agree or disagree? Why?

9. Inventory control has been described as a balancing act. Explain why.

10. What do you consider the most important factors in selecting a location for the following:

    a. A soft-drink bottling plant.

    b. A plant to produce high-quality electric wristwatches.

    c. A lumber mill.

    d. A brewery.

    e. A potato-chip factory.

Student _____

SOLVING PROBLEMS AND CASES

1. *Case:* Stanton Industries, Inc.

   Stanton Industries is a medium-size manufacturer of plumbing fixtures located near Cleveland, Ohio. The company has not been profitable in recent
   years, and two months ago the board of directors hired a new management team to revitalize the firm.

   Keith Goode, the new, young and aggressive production manager, decided
   to use motion and time study to improve worker productivity and to develop
   time standards for more effective production planning. He employed a team
   of industrial engineers to conduct the study.

   Yesterday, the engineers appeared in the plant with clipboards and stop-
   watches. One engineer was assigned to each department. He stood behind
   a worker carefully analyzing and timing his movements.

   Some of the workers became nervous and anxious, and one employee quit
   on the spot. Most of the older workers deliberately slowed their pace.

   At the end of the day, the union lodged a formal grievance charging management with harassment of the workers. The union threatened a strike unless the study was halted immediately.

   a. Why did the workers react as they did?

   b. How could the trouble have been avoided?

2. *Case:* Carter Container Company

The management of the Carter Container Company is considering the purchase of a new machine that costs $300,000 and has an estimated life of five years. The operating costs of the machine are $15,000 a year.

The machine will replace eight workers who are paid $4.50 an hour under the union contract. Each employee works 40 hours a week for an average of 50 weeks a year.

a. What factors should be considered in making the decision?

b. Should the firm purchase the machine? Why or why not?

Student _____

3. *Case:* Norton Foundry Company

The Norton Foundry Company uses 10,000 tons of coal a month. A shipment of 60,000 tons of coal requires three months from the order date for delivery. The inventory control manager wants to keep at least a month's supply on hand at all times to avoid running out of coal.

a. At what level of inventory should the manager place an order for more coal?

b. Draw an inventory chart showing the maximum and minimum inventories and the reorder point.

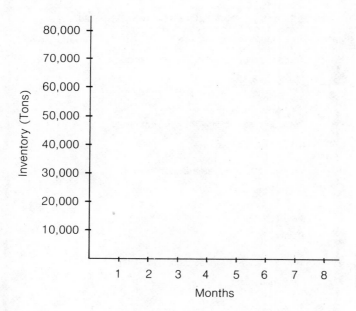

4. *Case:* Barker Manufacturing Company

You have been assigned the job of scheduling in the Production Control Department of the Barker Manufacturing Company, a job shop located in Los Angeles. The head of the department, Rocky Snark, believes in "learning by doing."

At 8:00 A.M. on August 7, you receive an order for 200 Zumpers (Jobs 123 and 124) to be delivered at 8:00 A.M. on August 11. You have a modified flow process chart for Zumpers shown below.

Before leaving for coffee, Rocky says, "Okay, kid, schedule the order on the Gantt chart. Don't forget to work backwards from the delivery date. The inspection after the milling operation takes place in the Milling Department. Get hopping!"

(*Hint:* The flow process chart shows the routing for an order of Zumpers together with time required for each operation. Note the job size is 100 Zumpers. The Gantt chart covers the period from August 7 through August 10. The scale under the dates shows hours. The numbered blocks are jobs already scheduled.)

FLOW PROCESS CHART FOR ZUMPERS—JOB SIZE: 100

Operation	Symbol	Explanation	Time in Hours
1	● ● ■	Transportation to Milling Department Milling Operation Inspection	} 2
2	● ●	Transportation to Drill Punch Department Drill Punch Operation	} 1
3	● ●	Transportation to Lathe Department Lathe Operation	} 3
4	● ●	Transportation to Paint Department Painting	} 6
5	● ■	Transportation to Inspection Department Final Inspection	} 2
6	● ▼	Transportation to Storage Storage	}

●	4 Operation	●	6 Transport	■	2 Inspection	▼	1 Storage

Student _____

GANTT CHART

Departments	August 7	August 8	August 9	August 10
Milling		93	90 | 101	107
Drill Punch	89		93	120 | 93
Lathe	Dept. Picnic ⊠			109
Paint	117			89
Final Inspection	100			90

Index

Absenteeism, 205–206
Accounting, 117–122
  cost, 89
  defined, 118
Accounting equation, 118–119
Accounting statements, 118–122
Advertising, 248–252
  as consumer friend or foe, 253
  institutional, 250
  magazine, 250–251
  media, 250
  newspaper, 250
  product, 250
  radio, 251
  spending on, 251
  television, 251
Advertising agency, 250
Advertising copy, 250
AFL-CIO, 217, 224
Agency shop, 220
Agent middlemen, 246, 248
Air Quality Act, 35
American Federation of Labor (AFL), 215, 217, 224
Amtrak, 34
Amway, 243
Analytic production process, 273
Antitrust laws, 35–37
Application form, 212–213
Aptitude tests, 212
Arbitration, 221
Arithmetic unit, 150
Armour and Company, 272
Array (numerical), 145
Articles of incorporation, 66, 70
Assembly process, 273
Assets, 118–119
Auditing, 145

Authority, 92–94
  delegation of, 93–94
  divided, 63, 96
Automation, 153–154, 270–271
Averages, 145–146
Avon, 243, 254

Balance sheet, 118–121
Banks, 171–172
Bar charts, 148–149
BARUCH, BERNARD, 187
BELL, DANIEL, 72
Bid and ask, 183–184
Blacklist, 222
Board of directors, 66, 177–178
Bond(s), 175–177, 179–180, 189–190
  bearer (coupon), 175
  callable, 176
  debenture, 176
  discounts, 189–190
  mortgage, 176
  premiums, 189–190
  registered, 175
  yields, 189–190
Book value, 119, 189
BOORSTIN, DANIEL J., 248
Boycotts, primary, 221
  secondary, 219, 221–222, 224
Break-even analysis, 129–130
Brokerage firms, 183–184
Brookings Institution, 44–45
Buck passing, 96
Budgeting, 126, 128–130
Bureau of Labor Statistics, 147
BURKE, EDMUND, 45
Business, forms of ownership, 59 ff.
Business arithmetic, 27–30
Business cycles, 13–16
Business giantism, 38

Business unionism, 215
Businessmen, sins of, 17

California Public Utilities Commission, 37
Canada, 4
Capital, 6-7
Capital investment, 6
Capital investment per worker, 6
Capitalism, 8, 31
Cash budget, 128
Catalog showroom, 246
Caveat emptor, 35
Central planning, 12
Central processing unit (CPU), 151
Changing Times, 247
Channels of distribution, 243-244
CHÁVEZ, CÉSAR, 224
China, 12
Clayton Act, 36
Closed-end investment companies, 184
Closed shop, 219-220
COBOL, 151
COHEN, JERRY S., 38
Collective bargaining, 215, 219-221
Colonel Sanders Kentucky Fried Chicken, 247
Commerce, United States Department of, 16, 33
Commissions, brokerage, 184
Committees, 100
Common stock, 15, 120-121, 176, 178-179
Communications, 85, 207-208, 211
Communism, 11-12
Comparative analysis of income statement, 126
Compensation of employees, 214-215, 220
Competition, 9-11, 34
  imperfect, 9-10
  pure or perfect, 9-10
Complaints and grievances, 208, 221
Composite Index of Twelve Leading Indicators, 16
Computer(s), 6, 150-156, 270, 275, 277
  applications of, 157-158
  and automatic control systems, 153-154
  components of, 150-151
  in management decision making, 154
  and privacy, 152
  programming of, 151, 153
  routine applications of, 153
  as thinking machines, 156
Congress of Industrial Organizations (CIO), 217
Consumer Price Index (CPI), 147-148
Consumer spending, 13

Consumers, 9, 10, 11, 239-244
Continental Airlines, 211
Control unit, 151
Controlling, 89, 126
Coordinating, 89
Corporate securities, 175-182
  marketing, 181-182
  selection of, 179-181
Corporation, 34, 43, 66-72
  charter for, 66
  control of, 70
  decline of, 71
  defined, 66
  securities, 69
  structure of, 66-67
COWAN, AILEEN, 253
Credit, line of, 171-172
Credit rating, 62, 174
Credit terms, 171
Current ratio, 124
Custom production, 273-274

D'APRIX, ROGER M., 99
Das Kapital, 11
Data processing, 148, 150-156
Debt, 173
Depreciation, 119, 173
Depression, 13-14
DIMOCK, MARSHALL E., 87, 91
Directing, 88
Discounts, cash, 171
  quantity, 274
Distribution: *See* Marketing
Diversification, 272
Dividends, 43, 69, 176, 178-179
  cash, 176
  stock, 176
Dun & Bradstreet, Inc., 174
DuPont de Nemours, E. I., 67

Economic freedom, 9, 12
Economic indicators (lead, lag, and coincident), 15-16
Economics, 7-8, 14
Education, 7
Eighty-day "cooling-off injunction," 219
EISENHOWER, DWIGHT D., 86
Electronic data processing, 150
Eminent domain, 9
Employee(s), apathy of, 70
  compensation of, 214-215
  evaluation of, 214
  interviewing of, 212
  selection of, 210, 212
  testing of, 212
  theft by, 123
  training of, 212-213

Employment Act of 1946, 14, 37
Entrepreneur, 7–8, 10, 72
Equity, 173
Equity-to-debt ratio, 124, 180
Evaluation of employees, 214
Exclusive contracts, 36
Exodus, 91
Extraction process, 272–273

Fabrication process, 273
Factors (collection agencies), 172
Factors of production, 7, 13, 84
Featherbedding, 219
Federal Reserve Board (FRB), 14, 37
Federal Reserve Bulletin, 144
Federal Trade Commission (FTC), 36–38
Federal Trade Commission Act, 36–37
Finance, 169–187
    with long-term funds, 173, 175–178
    with short-term funds, 170–173
Finance companies, 172–173
Financial analysis, 122, 124–126
Financial management, 170–178
Fiscal policy, 14
Fixed costs, 129–130
FORD, ROBERT, 206
Ford Motor Company, 86, 242, 272
Forecasting, 15–16, 72, 127–128
Foremen, 85, 96
FORTRAN, 151
Four P's, 239–240
France, 4, 10
Franchising, 247
Free enterprise, 34
    See also Capitalism
FRIEDMAN, MILTON, 67
Fringe benefits, 215
Fuller Brush, 243
Functional organization, 96

GALSWORTHY, JOHN, 127
General Electric, 38, 183–184, 272
General Motors, 33
General-purpose equipment, 277
GOMPERS, SAMUEL, 215
Government, 31 ff.
    assistance by, 32–33
    role of, 8, 13–14
    regulation and control by, 35–37, 70, 72
    spending by, 31–32
    taxation by: *See* Taxation
Great Britain, 10
Great Depression, 14, 215
Gross National Product (GNP), 4–5, 13, 15

Hardware, 151
Harvard Business School, 7

Hawthorne Experiments, 204
Health, 7
HERRIOT, ROGER, 45
Hiring, 210–211
Hiring hall, 224
HOF, ROBERT T., 91
HOFFA, JIMMY, 17
Hoover Dam, 37
Human relations, 204–210

Income statement, 121–122
Index of industrial production, 15, 147
Index numbers, 146–147
India, 4, 12
Inflation, 14–15
Information feedback principle, 153–154
Injunction, 219, 222
Input device, 150
Installment contracts, 173
Insurance, 132
Interest, 28, 171–172, 175, 180
Interlocking directorates, 36
Internal Revenue Service, 43
Internally generated funds, 173
International Brotherhood of Teamsters
    (IBT), 17, 217, 224
International Business Machines (IBM),
    23, 38, 88, 254
Interstate Commerce Commission (ICC),
    37
Inventory, 119
    control of, 153, 279–281
    turnover of, 124
Investment, 6
    frozen, 63
Investment banker, 181–182
Investment companies, 184–185
Investors, 185, 187
Invoice, 170–171

JACKSON, ANDREW, 37
Japan, 4, 254
JAY, ANTONY, 91
Job, importance of, 207
Job design, 278
Job enrichment, 206, 272
Job psychology, 216
Job shops, 273–274
Job specifications, 210

KENNEDY, JOHN F., 86
KENNEDY, ROBERT, 224
KENNEDY, TED, 224
KEYNES, JOHN MAYNARD, 14

Labor, 7, 274–275
Labor contract, 220
Labor laws, 219–220

Labor–management conflict, 221–222
Labor relations, 215–224
Labor unions: See Unions
Land, 7
Landrum–Griffin Act, 220
LAO-TZU, 210
Leadership, 91, 208–210
Legal entity, 66
Leverage, 180
Liabilities, 118–121
Limit order, 184
Limited liability, 68
Limited partnership, 64–65
Line charts, 147–148
Line layout, 275–276
Line organization, 95–96
Line-and-staff organization, 97
Load, 185
Loans: See Credit; Finance
Lockheed Corporation, 33
Lockout, 222

McDonald's, 247
McGREGOR, DOUGLAS, 208–210
McNAMARA, ROBERT, 86
Make-or-buy decisions, 278
Management, 7, 83–100
    defined, 84
    functions of, 86–89
    importance of, 84–85
    levels of, 85–86
    by objectives (MBO), 90–92
    perspectives on, 91
    principles of, 92–95
    specialization of, 62–63, 69
    universality of, 86
Manufacturers' agent, 244
Manufacturing systems, 273–274
Margin, 183
Market(s), 239–242
    final consumer, 241–242
    industrial user, 241–242, 244
    nearness to, 274
Market order, 184
Market research, 145, 241–242
Marketing, 237–255
    concept of, 238
    defined, 238
    management of, 238–239, 249
Marketing mix, 239–240, 252, 254–255
Marketing strategy, 239–240
Murphy's Laws, 88
Mutual funds, 184–185

NADER, RALPH, 34, 67, 253
NAPOLEON, 204

National Bureau of Economic Research,
    15
National Labor Relations Board (NLRB),
    219, 224
Natural monopolies, 35
Needs, hierarchy of, 204–205
Net profit: See Profit
Net profit as a percent of sales, 124
New economics, 14
New York Stock Exchange (NYSE),
    182–183, 185–186
NIXON, RICHARD, 14, 34

Objectives, 86–87, 90, 92
Odd lot, 184
Open-book accounts, 170
Open-end investment companies, 184–185
Open shop, 220
Organization, internal, 95–100
Organization man, 99
Organizational change, 94–95
Organizational stability, 93–94
Organizing, 88
Orientation, 212
ORWELL, GEORGE, 152
Output per capita, 4
Output unit, 151
Over-the-counter market, 182–183
Owners' equity, 118–121
Ownership, forms of, 59–70

Pacific Gas and Electric Company, 177
Pacific Stock Exchange, 182
PAPPAS, ALEX, 132
Par value, 176, 189
Partnership, 43, 62–66
    division of profits and losses in, 65–66
Partnership agreement, 63
Penn Central Transportation Company,
    170
Performance tests, 212
Personal selling, 249
Personality tests, 212
Personnel management, 210–215
Picketing, 221
Pie diagrams, 147, 149
Piece rate, 214
Place, 239, 243–248
Planning, 87–88
Plant layout, 275–276
Plant location, 274–275
Policies, 87
Population, 4
Population (statistical), 145
Preferred stock, 178–179, 181
    cumulative, 178

noncumulative, 178
participating, 178
Premium, 132
Price discrimination, 36
Pricing, 240, 252, 254–255
   penetration, 254
   skim-the-cream, 254
Printer's Ink, 253
Private property, right of, 8–10, 12
Privileged subscription, 182
Process layout, 275–276
Product, 239, 242–243
Production, 269–281
   equipment for, 276–277
   large-scale, 270
   management of, 274
   planning and control of, 277
   processes in, 272–273
   scheduling of, 153
Productivity, 4–7, 205–206
Profit, 10, 180
   gross, 121, 252
   net, 122
   per share, 125
Profit motive, 10
Profit sharing, 214
Programming, 151, 153
Progressive tax, 39–40, 44
Projected income statement, 128–129
Promissory notes, 172
Promotion, 239–240, 248–252
Promotional mix, 248–249
Proportional tax, 39–40, 45
Proprietorship, 43, 60–62
Prospectus, 181
Public ownership, 10–12, 36–37
Purchase order, 279
Purchasing, 279–281
Pure capitalism, 8–9
Pure Food and Drug Act, 35

Quality control, 145, 279

Random sampling, 145
Rate of return on investment, 125
Ratio analysis, 124–125
Ratios, 124–125
Recession, 10, 13–14
Recognition, 207
Recruiting, 210–211
Regressive tax, 39–40
Requisition, 279–280
Responsibility, 92–93
Retailers, 244
Retailing, 244–246
   decentralization of, 245
   large-scale, 245

self-service, 245
small-scale, 245
Retained earnings, 122
Revlon, 254
Rexall Drug Stores, 247
Right-to-work laws, 219
Risk, 132, 187, 189
Risk management, 132
ROCKEFELLER, JOHN D., 34
ROOSEVELT, FRANKLIN, 215
ROOSEVELT, THEODORE, 35
Round lot, 184
Routing, 277
Rule of seven, 93

Saab, 206
Safeway, 23, 38, 244–245
Sales force, 244–245
Savings and loan associations, 173
Scheduling, 88, 277
Scientific management, 278
Scrambled merchandising, 245–246
Sears, 244
Securities, corporate, 175–178
   dealers in, 183
   marketing of, 178–179, 181–182
   markets for, 182–187
   selection of, 179–181
   unlisted, 183
Securities and Exchange Commission
   (SEC), 37, 181
See's Candies, 244
Self-respect, 207
SHAKESPEARE, WILLIAM, 127, 156
Sherman Act, 36
Shop agreements, 220
Simplification, 272
Simulation, 154
SINCLAIR, UPTON, 35
SIX, ROBERT F., 211
Small Business Administration, 33, 173
SMITH, ADAM, 33
Social Security, 42, 132
Social responsibility, 67
Socialism, 8–10, 12, 34
Software, 151
Soviet Union, 4, 7, 12
Span of control, 93–94
Special-purpose equipment, 277
Specialization, 206, 272
Speculators, 185, 187
Spread, 181–182
Staff, 96–98
Staffing, 88
Standard of living, 4, 7
Standard Oil Company, 34
Standard & Poor's, 189
Standardization, 270
Stanford Business School, 7
*Statistical Abstract of the United
   States,* 144
Statistics, 143–148

Statistics *(cont.)*
　external sources of, 144
　internal sources of, 144
　interpretation of, 148
　presentation of, 147–148
Stock, 176, 178–179
Stock exchanges, 182
Stock quotations, 185–186
Stockholders, 66
Strikes, 205, 221
Subsidies, 33
Survey of Current Business, 144
Sweden, 10, 12, 206
Synthetic production process, 273

Taft–Hartley Act, 219
Target market, 239–242, 249
Tariffs, 32–33
Taxation, 10, 37, 39–45, 179–180
　ability-to-pay principle of, 39
　benefits principle of, 39
　and business decisions, 42–43
　double, 69
　exemptions and deductions in, 40–41
　rates of, 39–40
Taxes, corporation income, 41–42, 69
　death, 42
　excise, 41–42
　individual income, 40–41, 44, 69
　property, 41–42
　sales, 41–42
　Social Security, 41–42, 132
TAYLOR, FREDERICK, 96, 278
Teamsters Union (IBT), 17, 217, 224
Technology, 6
Tennessee Valley Authority (TVA), 12
Theory X and Theory Y, 209–210
Time rate, 214
Time standard, 278
Total cost, 130
Total revenue, 130
TOWNSEND, ROBERT, 87, 91
Toy Safety Act, 35
Trade creditors, 170–171
Trading on equity, 180
Training, 7, 212–214
　classroom, 214
　on-the-job, 213
　vestibule, 213
Tying contracts, 36

Underwriter, 181–182
Unemployment, 10, 15
Unfair labor practices, 219

Unions, 9, 215–224
　craft, 215, 217–218
　industrial, 217
　membership in, 217–218
　problems and prospects of, 217–218
Union shop, 220
United Auto Workers (UAW), 217
United Farm Workers (UFW), 224
United Kingdom, 12
　See also Great Britain
United Mine Workers, 217
United Rubber Workers, 217
United States, 4, 12
United States Constitution, 8
United States Department of Commerce,
　16, 33
United States Government Printing
　Office, 37
United States Postal Service, 37
United States Steel Corporation, 34
United Steel Workers, 217
Unity of command, 92, 96, 97
Universe (statistical), 145
Unlimited liability, 61, 63
Utilities, 35

Variable costs, 129–130
Volvo, 206
VON NEUMANN, JOHN, 271
Voting (for board of directors), 66,
　68, 178, 180

Wages: *See* Compensation of employees
Wagner Act, 219, 222
Water Quality Act, 35
WEST, RON, 157
Western Electric Company, 204
Wholesalers, 244
　types of, 246, 248
Wholesaling, 246, 248
　functions of, 246
WHYTE, WILLIAM H., JR., 99
WILCOX, CLAIR, 11
Woolworth, 244
Work force, 7, 217
Worker(s), alienation of, 206
　blue-collar, 217
　white-collar, 217
　See also Employee(s)

Yellow-dog contract, 222
Yield, 29, 189–190

ZEITLIN, LAWRENCE R., 123